Contents

Vaulted ceilings in the living room and dining room and a covered front porch lend a feeling of spaciousness to this compact country home. See plan J-86119 on page 39.

Attainable Dreams

From starter homes for young couples to scaled-down versions for empty-nesters, one of the most powerful forces shaping today's home-building industry is affordability. One way to maximize your dollars is to build a home that's designed to be attainable—a home with all the modern amenities but scaled down in size and planned for affordable construction. Every house plan in this book will help you do just that.

By building your own home, you can create a house that's just right for you, one that's sized and tailored to your family's needs. You can include the special features you want and eliminate unneeded space and unnecessary frills.

The two keys to success in building an affordable home are capable project management and good design. The next few pages will walk you through some of the most important aspects of project management: you'll find an overview of the building process, directions for selecting the right plan and getting the most from it, and methods for successfully working with a builder and other professionals.

The balance of the book presents professionally designed stock plans for affordable houses in a wide range of styles and configurations. Even if you're just dreaming about building a home, you'll enjoy browsing through the hundreds of wonderful choices. Once you find a plan that will work for you—perhaps with a few modifications made later to personalize it for your family—you can order construction blueprints for a fraction of the cost of a custom design, a savings of many thousands of dollars (see pages 12–15 for information on how to order).

Featuring a distinctive exterior of brick and wood, this budget-minded single-story home uses shared interior areas to maximize space. See plan R-1063 on page 88.

A classic front porch and a façade punctuated with Palladian windows distinguishes this 1,724-square-foot home, designed for easy construction. See plan B-129-8510 on page 217.

Savings come year-round in this home, thanks to its energy-efficient design, which includes a passive solar room. See plans H-855-3A and -3B on page 209.

In a scant 1,305 square feet, this compact home offers such features as a sunny breakfast nook, double-door entry to the master bedroom, and a walk-in closet. See plan R-1028 on page 16.

The Art of Building

As you embark on your home-building project, think of it as a trip—clearly not a vacation but rather an interesting, adventurous, at times difficult expedition. Meticulous planning will make your journey not only far more enjoyable but also much more successful. By careful planning, you can avoid—or at least minimize—some of the pitfalls along the way.

Start with realistic expectations of the road ahead. To do this, you'll want to gain an understanding of the basic house-building process, settle on a design that will work for you and your family, and make sure your project is actually doable. By taking those initial steps, you can gain a clear idea of how much time, money, and energy you'll need to invest to make your dream come true.

The Building Process

Your role in planning and managing a house-building project can be divided into two parts: prebuilding preparation and construction management.

■ **Prebuilding preparation.** This is where you should focus most of your attention. In the hands of a qualified contractor whose expertise you can rely on, the actual building process should go fairly smoothly. But during most of the prebuilding stage, you're generally on your own. Your job will be to launch the project and develop a talented team that can help you bring your new home to fruition.

When you work with stock plans, the prebuilding process usually goes as follows:

First, you research the general area where you want to live, selecting one or more possible home sites (unless you already own a suitable lot). Then you choose a basic house design, with the idea that it may require some modification. Finally, you analyze the site, the design, and your budget to determine if the project is actually attainable.

If you decide that it is, you purchase the land and order blueprints. If you want to modify them, you consult an architect, designer, or contractor. Once the plans are finalized, you request bids from contractors and arrange any necessary construction financing.

After selecting a builder and signing a contract, you (or your contractor) then file the plans with the building department. When the plans are approved, often several weeks—or even months—later, you're ready to begin construction.

■ **Construction management.** Unless you intend to act as your own contractor, your role during the building process is mostly one of quality control and time management. Even so, it's important to know the sequence of events and something about construction methods so you can discuss progress with your builder and prepare for any important decisions you may need to make along the way.

Decision-making is critical. Once construction begins, the builder must usually plunge ahead, keeping his carpenters and subcontractors progressing steadily. If you haven't made a key decision—which model bathtub or sink to install, for example—it can bring construction to a frustrating and expensive halt.

Usually, you'll make such decisions before the onset of building, but, inevitably, some issue or another will arise during construction. Being knowledgeable about the building process will help you anticipate and circumvent potential logjams.

Selecting a House Plan

Searching for the right plan can be a fun, interactive family experience—one of the most exciting parts of a house-building project. Gather the family around as you peruse the home plans in this book. Study the size, location, and configuration of each room; traffic patterns both inside the house and to the outdoors; exterior style; and how you'll use the available space. Discuss the pros and cons of the various plans.

Browse through pictures of homes in magazines to stimulate ideas. Clip the photos you like so you can think about your favorite options. When you visit the homes of friends, note special features that appeal to you. Also, look carefully at the homes in your neighborhood, noting their style and how they fit the site.

Mark those plans that most closely suit your ideals. Then, to narrow down your choices, critique each plan, using the following information as a guide.

■ **Overall size and budget.** How large a house do you want? Will the house you're considering fit your family's requirements? Look at the overall square footage and room sizes. If you have a hard time visualizing room sizes, measure some of the rooms in your present home and compare.

It's often better for the house to be a little too big than a little too small, but remember that every extra square foot will cost more money to build and maintain.

■ **Number and type of rooms.** Beyond thinking about the number of bedrooms and baths you want, consider your family's life-style and how you use space. Do you want both a family room and a living room? Do you need a formal dining space? Will you require some extra rooms, or "swing spaces," that can serve multiple purposes, such as a home office–guest room combination?

■ **Room placement and traffic patterns.** What are your preferences for locations of formal living areas, master bedroom, and children's rooms? Do you prefer a kitchen that's open to family areas or one that's private and out of the way? How much do you use exterior spaces and how should they relate to the interior?

Once you make those determinations, look carefully at the floor plan of the house you're considering to see if it meets your needs and if the traffic flow will be convenient for your family.

■ **Architectural style.** Have you always wanted to live in a Victorian farmhouse? Now is your chance to create a house that matches your idea of "home" (taking into account, of course, styles in your neighborhood). But don't let your preference for one particular architectural style dictate your home's floor plan. If the floor plan doesn't work for your family, keep looking.

■ **Site considerations.** Most people choose a site before selecting a plan—or at least they've zeroed in on the basic type of land where they'll situate their house. It sounds elementary, but choose a house that will fit the site.

When figuring the "footprint" of a house, you must know about any restrictions that will affect your home's height or proximity to the property lines. Call the local building department (look under city or county listings in the phone book) and get a very clear description of any restrictions, such as setbacks, height limits, and lot coverage, that will affect what you can build on the site (see "Working with City Hall," at right).

When you visit potential sites, note trees, rock outcroppings, slopes, views, winds, sun, neighboring homes, and other factors. All will impact on how your house works on a particular site.

Once you've narrowed down the choice of sites, consult an architect or building designer (see page 8) to help you evaluate how some potential houses will work on the sites you have in mind.

Is Your Project Doable?

Before you purchase land, make sure your project is doable. Although it's too early at this stage to pinpoint costs, making a few phone calls will help you determine whether your project is realistic. You'll be able to learn if you can afford to build the house, how long it will take, and what obstacles may stand in your way.

To get a ballpark estimate of cost, multiply a house's total square footage (of livable space) by the local average cost per square foot for new construction. (To obtain local averages, call a contractor, an architect, a realtor, or the local chapter of the National Association of Home Builders.) Some contractors may even be willing to give you a preliminary bid. Once you know approximate costs, speak to your lender to explore financing.

Working with City Hall

For any building project, even a minor one, it's essential to be familiar with building codes and other restrictions that can affect your project.

■ **Building codes,** generally implemented by the city or county building department, set the standards for safe, lasting construction. Codes specify minimum construction techniques and materials for foundations, framing, electrical wiring, plumbing, insulation, and all other aspects of a building. Although codes are adopted and enforced locally, most regional codes conform to the standards set by the national Uniform Building Code, Standard Building Code, or Basic Building Code. In some cases, local codes set more restrictive standards than national ones.

■ **Building permits** are required for home-building projects nearly everywhere. If you work with a contractor, the builder's firm should handle all necessary permits.

More than one permit may be needed; for example, one will cover the foundation, another the electrical wiring, and still another the heating equipment installation. Each will probably involve a fee and require inspections by building officials before work can proceed. (Inspections benefit *you*, as they ensure that the job is being done satisfactorily.) Permit fees are generally a percentage (1 to 1.5 percent) of the project's estimated value, often calculated on square footage.

It's important to file for the necessary permits. Failure to do so can result in fines or legal action against you. You can even be forced to undo the work performed. At the very least, your negligence may come back to haunt you later when you're ready to sell your house.

■ **Zoning ordinances,** particular to your community, restrict setbacks (how near to property lines you may build), your house's allowable height, lot coverage factors (how much of your property you can cover with structures), and other factors that impact design and building. If your plans don't conform to zoning ordinances, you can try to obtain a variance, an exception to the rules. But this legal work can be expensive and time-consuming. Even if you prove that your project won't negatively affect your neighbors, the building department can still refuse to grant the variance.

■ **Deeds and covenants** attach to the lot. Deeds set out property lines and easements; covenants may establish architectural standards in a neighborhood. Since both can seriously impact your project, make sure you have complete information on any deeds or covenants before you turn over a spadeful of soil.

It's a good idea to discuss your project with several contractors (see page 8). They may be aware of problems in your area that could limit your options—bedrock that makes digging basements difficult, for example. These conversations are actually the first step in developing a list of contractors from which you'll choose the one who will build your home.

Recruiting Your Home Team

A home-building project will inject you and your family into the building business, an area that may be unfamiliar territory. Among the people you'll be working with are architects, designers, landscapers, contractors, and subcontractors.

Design Help

A qualified architect or designer can help you modify and personalize your home plan, taking into account your family's needs and budget and the house's style. In fact, you may want to consider consulting such a person while you're selecting a plan to help you articulate your needs.

Design professionals are capable of handling any or all aspects of the design process. For example, they can review your house plans, suggest options, and then provide rough sketches of the options on tracing paper. Many architects will even secure needed permits and negotiate with contractors or subcontractors, as well as oversee the quality of the work.

Of course, you don't necessarily need an architect or designer to implement minor changes in a plan; although most contractors aren't trained in design, some can help you with modifications.

An open-ended, hourly-fee arrangement that you work out with your architect or designer allows for flexibility, but it often turns out to be more costly than working on a flat-fee basis. On a flat fee, you agree to pay a specific amount of money for a certain amount of work.

To find architects and designers, contact such trade associations as the American Institute of Architects (AIA), American Institute of Building Designers (AIBD), American Society of Landscape Architects (ASLA), and American Society of Interior Designers (ASID). Although many professionals choose not to belong to trade associations, those who do have met the standards of their respective associations. For phone numbers of local branches, check the Yellow Pages.

■ **Architects** are licensed by the state and have degrees. They're trained in all facets of building design and construction. Although some can handle interior design and structural engineering, others hire specialists for those tasks.

■ **Building designers** are generally unlicensed but may be accredited by the American Institute of Building Designers. Their backgrounds are varied: some may be unlicensed architects in apprenticeship; others are interior designers or contractors with design skills.

■ **Draftspersons** offer an economical route to making simple changes on your drawings. Like building designers, these people may be unlicensed architect apprentices, engineers, or members of related trades. Most are accomplished at drawing up plans.

■ **Interior designers,** as their job title suggests, design interiors. They work with you to choose room finishes, furnishings, appliances, and decorative elements. Part of their expertise is in arranging furnishings to create a workable space plan. Some interior designers are employed by architectural firms; others work independently. Financial arrangements vary, depending on the designer's preference.

Related professionals are kitchen and bathroom designers, who concentrate on fixtures, cabinetry, appliances, materials, and space planning for the kitchen and bath.

■ **Landscape architects, designers, and contractors** design outdoor areas. Landscape architects are state-licensed to practice landscape design. A landscape designer usually has a landscape architect's education and training but does not have a state license. Licensed landscape contractors specialize in garden construction, though some also have design skills and experience.

■ **Soils specialists and structural engineers** may be needed for projects where unstable soils or uncommon wind loads or seismic forces must be taken into account. Any structural changes to a house require the expertise of a structural engineer to verify that the house won't fall down.

Services of these specialists can be expensive, but they're imperative in certain conditions to ensure a safe, sturdy structure. Your building department will probably let you know if their services are required.

General Contractors

To build your house, hire a licensed general contractor. Most states require a contractor to be licensed and insured for worker's compensation in order to contract a building project and hire other subcontractors. State licensing ensures that contractors have met minimum training standards and have a specified level of experience. Licensing does not guarantee, however, that they're good at what they do.

When contractors hire subcontractors, they're responsible for overseeing the quality of work and materials of the subcontractors and for paying them.

■ **Finding a contractor.** How do you find a good contractor? Start by getting referrals from people you know who have built or remodeled their home. Nothing beats a personal recommendation. The best contractors are usually busily moving from one satisfied client to another prospect, advertised only by word of mouth.

You can also ask local real estate brokers and lenders or even your building inspector for names of qualified builders. Experienced lumber dealers are another good source of names.

In the Yellow Pages, look under "Contractors–Building, General"; or call the local chapter of the National Association of Home Builders.

■ **Choosing a contractor.** Once you have a list of names of prospective builders, call several of them. On the telephone, ask first whether they handle your type of job and can work within your schedule. If they can, arrange a meeting with each one and ask them to be prepared with references of former clients and photos of previous jobs. Better still, meet them at one of their current work sites so you can get a glimpse of the quality of their work and how organized and thorough they are.

Take your plan to the meeting and discuss it enough to request a rough estimate (some builders will comply, while others will be reluctant to offer a ballpark estimate, preferring to give you a hard bid based on complete drawings). Don't hesitate to probe for advice or suggestions that might make building your house less expensive.

Be especially aware of each contractor's personality and how well you communicate. Good chemistry between you and your builder is a key ingredient for success.

Narrow down the candidates to three or four. Ask each for a firm bid, based on the exact same set of plans and specifications. For the bids to be accurate, your plans need to be complete and the specifications as precise as possible, calling out particular appliances, fixtures, floorings, roofing material, and so forth. (Some of these are specified in a stock-plan set; others are not.)

Call the contractors' references and ask about the quality of their work, their relationship with their clients, their promptness, and their readiness to follow up on problems. Visit former clients to check the contractor's work firsthand.

Be sure your final candidates are licensed, bonded, and insured for worker's compensation, public liability, and property damage. Also, try to determine how financially solvent they are (you can call their bank and credit references). Avoid contractors who are operating hand-to-mouth.

Don't automatically hire the contractor with the lowest bid if you don't think you'll get along well or if you have any doubts about the quality of the person's work. Instead, look for both the most reasonable bid and the contractor with the best credentials, references, terms, and compatibility with your family.

A word about bonds: You can request a performance bond that guarantees that your job will be finished by your contractor. If the job isn't completed, the bonding company will cover the cost of hiring another contractor to finish it. Bonds cost from 2 to 6 percent of the value of the project.

Your Building Contract

A building contract (see below) binds and protects both you and your contractor. It isn't just a legal document. It's also a list of the expectations of both parties. The best way to minimize the possibility of misunderstandings and costly changes later on is to write down every possible detail. Whether the contract is a standard form or one composed by you, have an attorney look it over before both you and the contractor sign it.

The contract should clearly specify all the work that needs to be done, including particular materials and work descriptions, the time schedule, and method of payment. It should be keyed to the working drawings.

A Sample Building Contract

Project and participants. Give a general description of the project, its address, and the names and addresses of both you and the builder.

Construction materials. Identify all construction materials by brand name, quality markings (species, grades, etc.), and model numbers where applicable. Avoid the clause "or equal," which allows the builder to substitute other materials for your choices. For materials you can't specify now, set down a budget figure.

Time schedule. Include both start and completion dates and specify that work will be "continuous." Although a contractor cannot be responsible for delays caused by strikes and material shortages, your builder should assume responsibility for completing the project within a reasonable period of time.

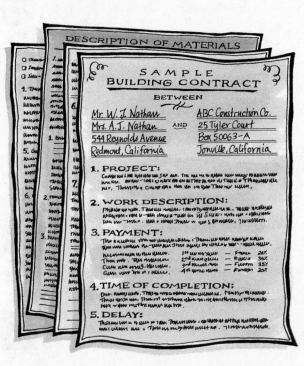

Work to be performed. State all work you expect the contractor to perform, from initial grading to finished painting.

Method and schedule of payment. Specify how and when payments are to be made. Typical agreements specify installment payments as particular phases of work are completed. Final payment is withheld until the job receives its final inspection and is cleared of all liens.

Waiver of liens. Protect yourself with a waiver of liens signed by the general contractor, the subcontractors, and all major suppliers. That way, subcontractors who are not paid for materials or services cannot place a lien on your property.

Personalizing Stock Plans

The beauty of buying stock plans for your new home is that they offer tested, well-conceived design at an affordable price. And stock plans dramatically reduce the time it takes to design a house, since the plans are ready when you are.

Because they were not created specifically for your family, stock plans may not reflect your personal taste. But it's not difficult to make revisions in stock plans that will turn your home into an expression of your family's personality. You'll surely want to add personal touches and choose your own finishes.

Ideally, the modifications you implement will be fairly minor. The more extensive the changes, the more expensive the plans. Major changes take valuable design time, and those that affect a house's structure may require a structural engineer's approval.

If you anticipate wholesale changes, such as moving a number of bearing walls or changing the roofline significantly, you may be better off selecting another plan. On the other hand, reconfiguring or changing the sizes of some rooms can probably be handled fairly easily.

Some structural changes may even be necessary to comply with local codes. Your area may have specific requirements for snow loads, energy codes, seismic or wind resistance, and so forth. Those types of modifications are likely to require the services of an architect or structural engineer.

Plan Modifications

Before you pencil in any changes, live with your plans for a while. Study them carefully—at your building site, if possible. Try to picture the finished house: how rooms will interrelate, where the sun will enter and at what angle, what the view will be from each window. Think about traffic patterns, access to rooms, room sizes, window and door locations, natural light, and kitchen and bathroom layouts.

Typical changes might involve adding windows or skylights to bring in natural light or capture a view. Or you may want to widen a hallway or doorway for roomier access, extend a room, eliminate doors, or change window and door sizes. Perhaps you'd like to shorten a room, stealing the gained space for a large closet. Look closely at the kitchen; it's not difficult to reconfigure the layout if it makes the space more convenient for you.

Above all, take your time—this is your home and it should reflect your taste and needs. Make your changes now, during the planning stage. Once construction begins, it will take crowbars, hammers, saws, new materials, and, most significantly, time to alter the plans. Because changes are not part of your building contract, you can count on them being expensive extras once construction begins.

Specifying Finishes

One way to personalize a house without changing its structure is to substitute your favorite finishes for those specified on the plan.

Would you prefer a stuccoed exterior rather than the wood siding shown on the plan? In most cases, this is a relatively easy change. Do you like the look of a wood shingle roof rather than the composition shingles shown on the plan? This, too, is easy. Perhaps you would like to change the windows from sliders to casements, or upgrade to high-efficiency glazing. No problem. Many of those kinds of changes can be worked out with your contractor.

Inside, you may want hardwood where vinyl flooring is shown. In fact, you can—and should—choose types, colors, and styles of floorings, wall coverings, tile, plumbing fixtures, door hardware, cabinetry, appliances, lighting fixtures, and other interior details, for it's these materials that will personalize your home. For help in making selections, consult an architect or interior designer (see page 8).

Each material you select should be spelled out clearly and precisely in your building contract.

Finishing touches can transform a house built from stock plans into an expression of your family's taste and style. Clockwise, from far left: Colorful tilework and custom cabinetry enliven a bathroom (Design: Osburn Design); highly organized closet system maximizes storage space (Architect: David Jeremiah Hurley); low-level deck expands living space to outdoor areas (Landscape architects: The Runa Group, Inc.); built-ins convert the corner of a guest room into a home office (Design: Lynn Williams of The French Connection); French country cabinetry lends style and old-world charm to a kitchen (Design: Garry Bishop/Showcase Kitchens).

What the Plans Include

Complete construction blueprints are available for every house shown in this book. Clear and concise, these detailed blueprints are designed by licensed architects or members of the American Institute of Building Designers (AIBD). Each plan is designed to meet standards set down by nationally recognized building codes (the Uniform Building Code, Standard Building Code, or Basic Building Code) at the time and for the area where they were drawn.

Remember, however, that every state, county, and municipality has its own codes, zoning requirements, ordinances, and building regulations. Modifications may be necessary to comply with such local requirements as snow loads, energy codes, seismic zones, and flood areas.

Although blueprint sets vary depending on the size and complexity of the house and on the individual designer's style, each set may include the elements described below and shown at right.

■ **Exterior elevations** show the front, rear, and sides of the house, including exterior materials, details, and measurements.

■ **Foundation plans** include drawings for a full, partial, or daylight basement, crawlspace, pole, pier, or slab foundation. All necessary notations and dimensions are included. (Foundation options will vary for each plan. If the plan you choose doesn't have the type of foundation you desire, a generic conversion diagram is available.)

■ **Detailed floor plans** show the placement of interior walls and the dimensions of rooms, doors, windows, stairways, and similar elements for each level of the house.

■ **Cross sections** show details of the house as though it were cut in slices from the roof to the foundation. The cross sections give the home's construction, insulation, flooring, and roofing details.

■ **Interior elevations** show the specific details of cabinets (kitchen, bathroom, and utility room), fireplaces, built-in units, and other special interior features.

■ **Roof details** give the layout of rafters, dormers, gables, and other roof elements, including clerestory windows and skylights. These details may be shown on the elevation sheet or on a separate diagram.

■ **Schematic electrical layouts** show the suggested locations for switches, fixtures, and outlets. These details may be shown on the floor plan or on a separate diagram.

■ **General specifications** provide instructions and information regarding excavation and grading, masonry and concrete work, carpentry and woodwork, thermal and moisture protection, drywall, tile, flooring, glazing, and caulking and sealants.

Other Helpful Building Aids

In addition to the construction information on every set of plans, you can buy the following guides.

■ **Reproducible blueprints** are helpful if you'll be making changes to the stock plan you've chosen. These blueprints are original line drawings produced on erasable, reproducible paper for the purpose of modification. When alterations are complete, working copies can be made.

■ **Itemized materials list** details the quantity, type, and size of materials needed to build your home. (This list is extremely helpful in obtaining an accurate construction bid. It's not intended for use to order materials.)

■ **Mirror-reverse plans** are useful if you want to build your home in the reverse of the plan that's shown. Because the lettering and dimensions read backwards, be sure to buy at least one regular-reading set of blueprints.

■ **Description of materials** gives the type and quality of materials suggested for the home. This form may be required for obtaining FHA or VA financing.

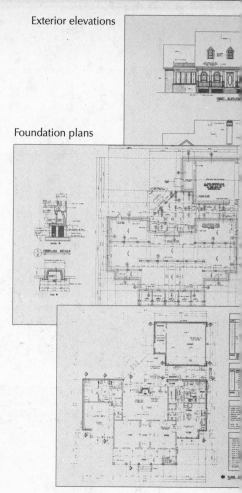

Exterior elevations

Foundation plans

Detailed floor plans

■ **How-to diagrams** for plumbing, wiring, solar heating, framing and foundation conversions show how to plumb, wire, install a solar heating system, convert plans with 2 by 4 exterior walls to 2 by 6 construction (or vice versa), and adapt a plan for a basement, crawlspace, or slab foundation. These diagrams are not specific to any one plan.

NOTE: Due to regional variations, local availability of materials, local codes, methods of installation, and individual preferences, detailed heating, plumbing, and electrical specifications are not included on plans. The duct work, venting, and other details will vary, depending on the heating and cooling system you use and the type of energy that operates it. These details and specifications are easily obtained from your builder or local supplier.

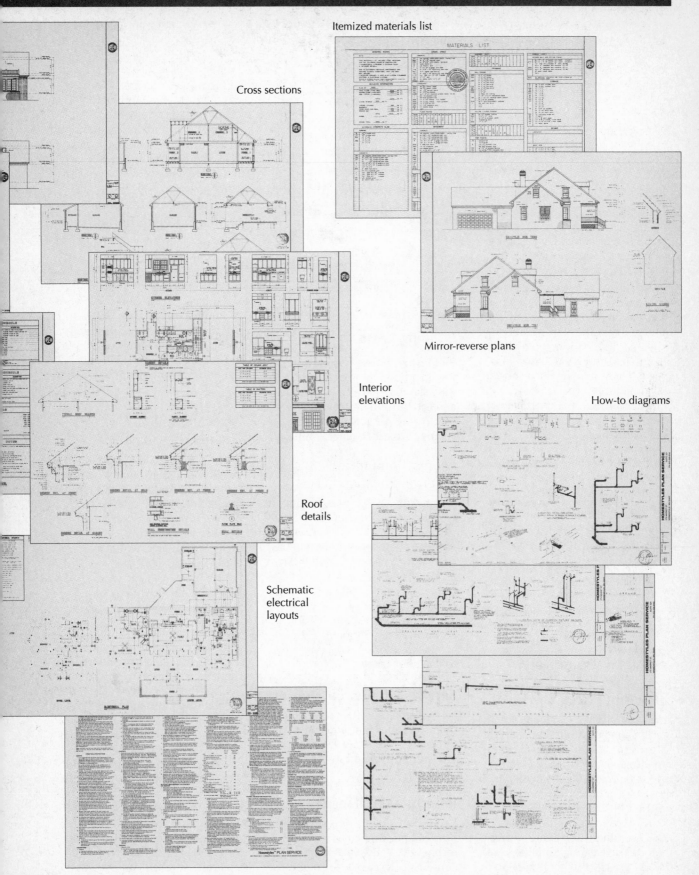

Itemized materials list

Cross sections

Mirror-reverse plans

Interior
elevations

How-to diagrams

Roof
details

Schematic
electrical
layouts

General specifications

Before You Order

Once you've chosen the one or two house plans that work best for you, you're ready to order blueprints. Before filling in the form on the facing page, note the information that follows.

How Many Blueprints Will You Need?

A single set of blueprints will allow you to study a home design in detail. You'll need more for obtaining bids and permits, as well as some to use as reference at the building site. If you'll be modifying your home plan, order a reproducible set (see page 12).

Figure you'll need at least one set each for yourself, your builder, the building department, and your lender. In addition, some subcontractors—foundation, plumber, electrician, and HVAC—may also need at least partial sets. If they do, ask them to return the sets when they're finished. The chart below can help you calculate how many sets you're likely to need.

Blueprint Checklist

____ Owner's set(s)

____ Builder usually requires at least three sets: one for legal documentation, one for inspections, and a minimum of one set for subcontractors.

____ Building department requires at least one set. Check with your local department before ordering.

____ Lending institution usually needs one set for a conventional mortgage, three sets for FHA or VA loans.

____ TOTAL SETS NEEDED

Blueprint Prices

The cost of having an architect design a new custom home typically runs from 5 to 15 percent of the building cost, or from $5,000 to $15,000 for a $100,000 home. A single set of blueprints for the plans in this book ranges from $295 to $505, depending on the house's size. Working with these drawings, you can save enough on design fees to add a deck, a swimming pool, or a luxurious kitchen.

Pricing is based on "total finished living space." Garages, porches, decks, and unfinished basements are not included.

Price Code (Size)	1 Set	4 Sets	7 Sets	Reproducible Set
A (under 1,500 sq. ft.)	$295	$345	$380	$455
B (1,500-1,999 sq. ft.)	$330	$380	$415	$490
C (2,000-2,499 sq. ft.)	$365	$415	$450	$525
D (2,500-2,999 sq. ft.)	$400	$450	$485	$560
E (3,000-3,499 sq. ft.)	$435	$485	$520	$595
F (3,500-3,999 sq. ft.)	$470	$520	$555	$630
G (4,000 sq. ft. and up)	$505	$555	$590	$665

Building Costs

Building costs vary widely, depending on a number of factors, including local material and labor costs and the finishing materials you select. For help estimating costs, see "Is Your Project Doable?" on page 7.

Foundation Options & Exterior Construction

Depending on your site and climate, your home will be built with a slab, pier, pole, crawlspace, or basement foundation. Exterior walls will be framed with either 2 by 4s or 2 by 6s, determined by structural and insulation standards in your area. Most contractors can easily adapt a home to meet the foundation and/or wall requirements for your area. Or ask for a conversion how-to diagram (see page 12).

Service & Blueprint Delivery

Service representatives are available to answer questions and assist you in placing your order. Every effort is made to process and ship orders within 48 hours.

Returns & Exchanges

Each set of blueprints is specially printed and shipped to you in response to your specific order; consequently, requests for refunds cannot be honored. However, if the prints you order cannot be used, you may exchange them for another plan from any Sunset home plan book. For an exchange, you must return all sets of plans within 30 days. A nonrefundable service charge will be assessed for all exchanges; for more information, call the toll-free number on the facing page. Note: Reproducible sets cannot be exchanged.

Compliance with Local Codes & Regulations

Because of climatic, geographic, and political variations, building codes and regulations vary from one area to another. These plans are authorized for your use expressly conditioned on your obligation and agreement to comply strictly with all local building codes, ordinances, regulations, and requirements, including permits and inspections at time of construction.

Architectural & Engineering Seals

With increased concern about energy costs and safety, many cities and states now require that an architect or engineer review and "seal" a blueprint prior to construction. To find out whether this is a requirement in your area, contact your local building department.

License Agreement, Copy Restrictions & Copyright

When you purchase your blueprints, you are granted the right to use those documents to construct a single unit. All the plans in this publication are protected under the Federal Copyright Act, Title XVII of the United States Code and Chapter 37 of the Code of Federal Regulations. Each designer retains title and ownership of the original documents. The blueprints licensed to you cannot be used by or resold to any other person, copied, or reproduced by any means. The copying restrictions do not apply to reproducible blueprints. When you buy a reproducible set, you may modify and reproduce it for your own use.

Blueprint Order Form

Complete this order form in just three easy steps. Then mail in your order or, for faster service, call toll-free.

1. Blueprints & Accessories

BLUEPRINT CHART

Price Code	1 Set	4 Sets	7 Sets	Reproducible Set*
A	$295	$345	$380	$455
B	$330	$380	$415	$490
C	$365	$415	$450	$525
D	$400	$450	$485	$560
E	$435	$485	$520	$595
F	$470	$520	$555	$630
G	$505	$555	$590	$665

Prices subject to change

*A reproducible set is produced on erasable paper for the purpose of modification. It is only available for plans with prefixes A, AG, AGH, AH, AHP, APS, AX, B, C, CC, CPS, DCL, DD, DW, E, EOF, FB, GL, GMA, GML, GSA, H, HDS, HFL, J, K, KD, KLF, LMB, LRD, M, NW, OH, PH, PI, RD, S, SDG, THD, U, UDG, V.

Mirror-Reverse Sets: $40 surcharge. From the total number of sets you ordered above, choose the number you want to be reversed. *Note: All writing on mirror-reverse plans is backwards. Order at least one regular-reading set.*

Itemized Materials List: One set $40; each additional set $10. Details the quantity, type, and size of materials needed to build your home.

Description of Materials: Sold in a set of two for $40 (for use in obtaining FHA or VA financing).

Typical How-To Diagrams: One set $15; two sets $25; three sets $35; four sets $40. General guides on plumbing, wiring, and solar heating, plus information on how to convert from one foundation or exterior framing to another. *Note: These diagrams are not specific to any one plan.*

2. Sales Tax & Shipping

Determine your subtotal and add appropriate local state sales tax, plus shipping and handling (see chart below).

SHIPPING & HANDLING

	1–3 Sets	4–6 Sets	7 or More Sets	Reproducible Set
U.S. Regular (4–6 working days)	$15.00	$17.50	$20.00	$15.00
U.S. Express (2–3 working days)	$27.50	$30.00	$32.50	$27.50
Canada Regular (2–3 weeks)	$15.00	$17.50	$20.00	$15.00
Canada Express (4–6 working days)	$27.50	$32.50	$37.50	$27.50
Overseas/Airmail (7–10 working days)	$52.50	$62.50	$72.50	$52.50

3. Customer Information

Choose the method of payment you prefer. Include check, money order, or credit card information, complete name and address portion, and mail to:

Sunset/HomeStyles Plan Service
P.O. Box 50670
Minneapolis, MN 55405

FOR FASTER SERVICE CALL 1-800-547-5570

SS14

COMPLETE THIS FORM

Plan Number _____ Price Code _____

Foundation_____
(Review your plan carefully for foundation options—basement, pole, pier, crawlspace, or slab. Many plans offer several options; others offer only one.)

Number of Sets: $_____
(See chart at left)
☐ One Set
☐ Four Sets
☐ Seven Sets
☐ One Reproducible Set

Additional Sets _____ $_____
($40 each)

Mirror-Reverse Sets _____ $_____
($40 surcharge)

Itemized Materials List $_____
Only available for plans with prefixes AH, AHP, APS*, AX*, B*, C, CAR, CC, CDG*, CPS, DD*, DW, E, GSA, H, HFL, I*, J, K, LMB*, LRD, NW*, P, PH, R, S, THD, U, UDG, VL. *Not available on all plans. Please call before ordering.

Description of Materials $_____
Only available for plans with prefixes AHP, C, DW, H, HFL, J, K, LMB, P, PH, VL.

Typical How-To Diagrams $_____
☐ Plumbing ☐ Wiring ☐ Solar Heating ☐ Foundation & Framing Conversion

SUBTOTAL $_____

SALES TAX $_____

SHIPPING & HANDLING $_____

GRAND TOTAL $_____

☐ Check/money order enclosed (in U.S. funds)
☐ VISA ☐ MasterCard ☐ AmEx ☐ Discover

Credit Card # _____ Exp. Date _____

Signature _____

Name _____

Address _____

City _____ State ____ Country _____

Zip_____ Daytime Phone (_____)_____
☐ Please check if you are a contractor.

Mail form to: Sunset/HomeStyles Plan Service
P.O. Box 50670
Minneapolis, MN 55405

Or fax to: (612) 338-1626

FOR FASTER SERVICE CALL 1-800-547-5570

SS14

Photo courtesy of Barclay Home Designs

Light-Filled, Flowing Spaces

**NOTE: The above photographed home may have been modified by the homeowner. Please refer to floor plan and/or drawn elevation shown for actual blueprint details.

- A beautiful bay window in the living room and an open, light-filled floor plan distinguish this stylish home.
- The large combined living and dining area—equally suitable for family gatherings or for more formal entertaining—features a fireplace and a view of a covered patio.
- The sunny, bayed breakfast nook accesses the patio, while the efficient kitchen includes a sizable pantry.
- Double doors open to the spacious master suite, which features a private bath and a walk-in closet.
- The two remaining bedrooms have large windows overlooking the backyard and share a full bath. One of the bedrooms is conveniently located off the breakfast nook, and could be used as a TV room, study or guest bedroom.
- Nice laundry facilities are located near the entrance to the two-car garage.

Plan R-1028

Bedrooms: 2+	**Baths:** 2

Living Area:

Main floor	1,305 sq. ft.
Total Living Area:	**1,305 sq. ft.**
Garage	429 sq. ft.
Exterior Wall Framing:	2x6

Foundation Options:

Crawlspace
(All plans can be built with your choice of foundation and framing. A generic conversion diagram is available. See order form.)

BLUEPRINT PRICE CODE:	**A**

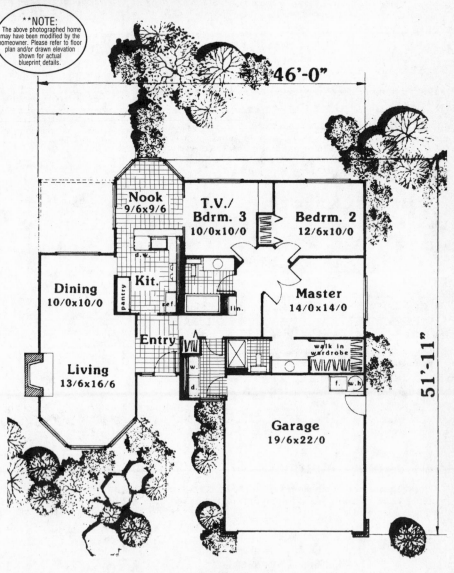

46'-0"

51'-11"

Nook 9/6x9/6

T.V./ Bdrm. 3 10/0x10/0

Bedrm. 2 12/6x10/0

Dining 10/0x10/0

Kit.

pantry

Master 14/0x14/0

Entry

walk in wardrobe

Living 13/6x16/6

Garage 19/6x22/0

MAIN FLOOR

Weekend Retreat

For those whose goal is a small, affordable retreat at the shore or in the mountains, this plan may be the answer. Although it measures less than 400 sq. ft. of living space on the main floor, it lacks nothing in comfort and convenience. A sizeable living room boasts a masonry hearth on which to mount your choice of a wood stove or a pre-fab fireplace. There is plenty of room for furniture, including a dining table.

The galley-type kitchen is a small marvel of compact convenience and utility, even boasting a dishwasher and space for a stackable washer and dryer. The wide open nature of the first floor guarantees that even the person working in the kitchen area will still be included in the party. On the floor plan, a dashed line across the living room indicates the limits of the balcony bedroom above. In front of this line, the A-frame shape of the living room soars from the floor boards to the ridge beam high above. Clerestory windows lend a further note of spaciousness and unity with nature's outdoors. A huge planked deck adds to the indoor-outdoor relationship.

A modest-sized bedroom on the second floor is approached by a standard stairway, not an awkward ladder or heavy pull-down stairway as is often the case in small A-frames. The view over the balcony rail to the living room below adds a note of distinction. The unique framing pattern allows a window at either end of the bedroom, improving both outlook and ventilation.

A compact bathroom serves both levels and enjoys natural daylight through a skylight window.

First floor:	391 sq. ft.
Upper level:	144 sq. ft.
Total living area:	535 sq. ft.

FRONT VIEW

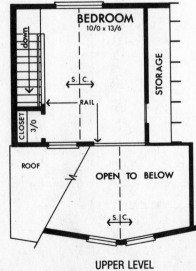

UPPER LEVEL
144 SQUARE FEET

(Exterior walls are 2x6 construction)

PLAN H-968-1A
WITHOUT BASEMENT
(CRAWLSPACE FOUNDATION)

Blueprint Price Code A

FIRST FLOOR
391 SQUARE FEET

Cozy, Cost-Saving Retreat

- This cozy cabin is the perfect vacation retreat for that special mountain, lake or river location.
- The design is large enough to provide comfortable living quarters and small enough to fit a modest building budget.
- An 18½-ft. vaulted ceiling and expanses of glass add volume to the living and dining area. Double doors provide access to an inviting deck or patio.
- The U-shaped kitchen offers a bright sink and a convenient pass-through to the dining area.
- A quiet bedroom and a hall bath complete the main floor.
- The upper floor consists of a railed loft that provides sweeping views of the living areas below and the scenery outside. The loft could serve as an extra sleeping area or a quiet haven for reading, relaxing and other activities.

Plan I-880-A

Bedrooms: 1+	Baths: 1
Living Area:	
Upper floor	308 sq. ft.
Main floor	572 sq. ft.
Total Living Area:	**880 sq. ft.**
Exterior Wall Framing:	2x6

Foundation Options:

Crawlspace

(All plans can be built with your choice of foundation and framing. A generic conversion diagram is available. See order form.)

BLUEPRINT PRICE CODE: **A**

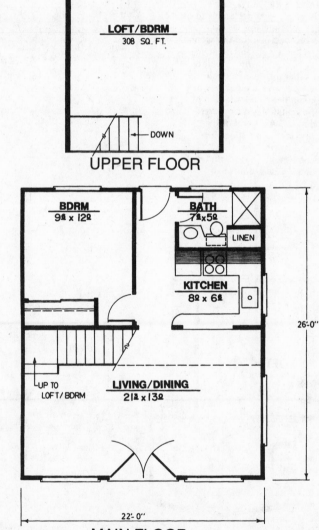

UPPER FLOOR

LOFT/BDRM
308 SQ. FT.

DOWN

MAIN FLOOR

BDRM
9⁸ x 12⁰

BATH
7⁴ x 5⁰

LINEN

KITCHEN
8⁰ x 6⁴

UP TO LOFT/BDRM

LIVING/DINING
21⁴ x 13⁰

26'-0"

22'-0"

Versatile A-Frame

Perfect as a weekend retreat or outdoor-sports headquarters, this 882 sq. ft. A-Frame is completely equipped to serve as either a full time or retirement home, especially if built with the daylight basement that includes a large bedroom, bath, shop and garage.

Sliding glass doors open from the wide wood entry deck into the great room and dining area, brightened with six skylights and warmed with a wood-burning stove. Another skylight is located over the work area of the corridor kitchen. The adjacent utility room has a door opening onto a rear-entry porch.

The master bedroom has a large wardrobe closet and a bump-out window seat. Stairs next to the bathroom lead up to a loft which can be used as a study, craft room or additional sleeping space. From the loft, an open railing overlooks the great room.

This multi-level A-Frame has diagonal board siding on the end walls and a boxed chimney to add a custom touch and accent the roof lines. Only 26' wide, the house can be built on a small lot.

Main floor:	720 sq. ft.
Loft:	162 sq. ft.
Total living area:	882 sq. ft.

(Not counting basement or garage)

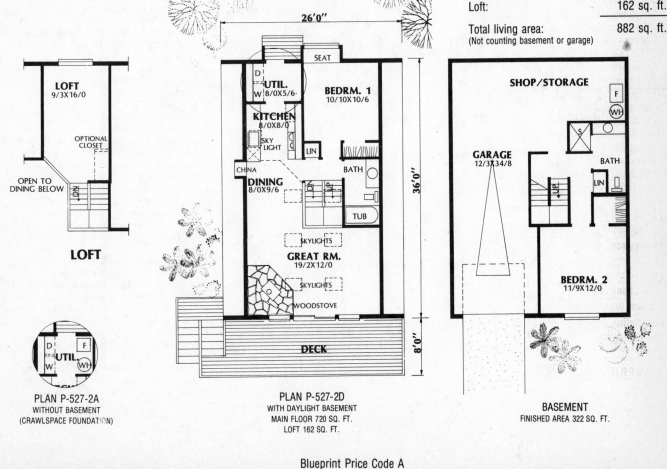

LOFT 9/3X16/0

OPTIONAL CLOSET

OPEN TO DINING BELOW

LOFT

PLAN P-527-2A
WITHOUT BASEMENT
(CRAWLSPACE FOUNDATION)

26'0"

SEAT

UTIL. 8/0X5/6

BEDRM. 1 10/10X10/6

KITCHEN 8/0X8/0

SKY LIGHT

LIN

CHINA

DINING 8/0X9/6

BATH

TUB

SKYLIGHTS

GREAT RM. 19/2X12/0

SKYLIGHTS

WOODSTOVE

36'0"

8'0"

DECK

PLAN P-527-2D
WITH DAYLIGHT BASEMENT
MAIN FLOOR 720 SQ. FT.
LOFT 162 SQ. FT.

SHOP/STORAGE

F

WH

GARAGE 12/3X34/8

BATH

LIN

UP

BEDRM. 2 11/9X12/0

BASEMENT
FINISHED AREA 322 SQ. FT.

Blueprint Price Code A

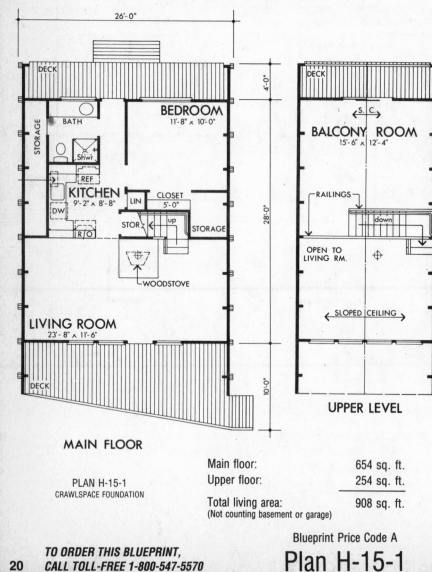

Carefree Vacation Home

Scoffers and non-believers had a field day when the A-Frame first began to appear. Impractical, some said; uncomfortable, declared others; too expensive, ugly and more. And yet people built them and enjoyed them — and like the Volkswagen Bug, found them to be economical and practical, and yes, even beautiful to many beholders. Through the years, there has been a steady demand for these ubiquitous structures, and Plan H-15-1 is one of our more popular models. With this design, you will not be experimenting or pioneering because it has been built sucessfully many times.

Though it covers only 654 sq. ft. of main floor living space, it boasts an oversized living/dining room, a U-shaped kitchen, large bedroom and closet spaces, fully equipped bath plus a standard stairway (not a ladder) to the large second floor balcony dormitory. An old fashioned wood stove or a modern pre-fabricated fireplace adds warmth and cheer to the main living room.

The huge glass wall that dominates the front facade enhances the romantic atmosphere of the vaulted interior. And in ideal locations, where this wall can face south, a surprising amount of solar energy can help minimize heating costs.

One particular advantage of the A-Frame as a part-time or holiday home is easy maintenance. Use of penetrating stains that resist flaking and powdering on the small areas of siding and trim at the front and rear of the building is all that is required. The rest is roofing which resists weather without painting or other treatment.

MAIN FLOOR

PLAN H-15-1
CRAWLSPACE FOUNDATION

Main floor:	654 sq. ft.
Upper floor:	254 sq. ft.
Total living area:	908 sq. ft.

(Not counting basement or garage)

Blueprint Price Code A

Plan H-15-1

Build It Yourself

- Everything you need for a leisure or retirement retreat is neatly packaged in this affordable, easy-to-build design.
- The basic rectangular shape features a unique wraparound deck, entirely covered by a projecting roofline.
- A central fireplace and a vaulted ceiling that rises to 10 ft. visually enhance the cozy living and dining rooms.
- The efficient kitchen offers convenient service to the adjoining dining room. In the crawlspace version, the kitchen also includes a snack bar.
- Two main-floor bedrooms share a large full bath.
- The daylight-basement option is suitable for building on a sloping lot and consists of an extra bedroom, a general-purpose area and a garage.

Plans H-833-7 & -7A

Bedrooms: 2+	Baths: 1
Living Area:	
Main floor	952 sq. ft.
Daylight basement	676 sq. ft.
Total Living Area:	**952/1,628 sq. ft.**
Tuck-under garage	276 sq. ft.
Exterior Wall Framing:	2x6
Foundation Options:	**Plan #**
Daylight basement	H-833-7
Crawlspace	H-833-7A

(All plans can be built with your choice of foundation and framing. A generic conversion diagram is available. See order form.)

BLUEPRINT PRICE CODE:	**A/B**

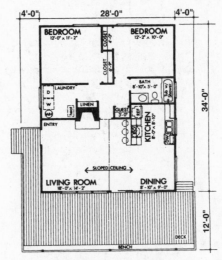

MAIN FLOOR
Crawlspace version

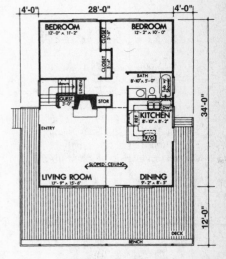

MAIN FLOOR
Basement version

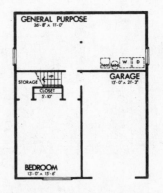

DAYLIGHT BASEMENT

Sunny Chalet

- This captivating home is designed to maximize indoor and outdoor living. It features expansive windows, an open main floor and a large deck.
- The lower-level entry leads up a staircase to the spacious living room, which features a 12-ft. cathedral ceiling, an energy-efficient fireplace, a

railed balcony overlooking the foyer and sliding glass doors to the deck.
- The adjacent bayed dining room merges with the skylighted kitchen, which also boasts a handy serving bar.
- The lower floor features two spacious bedrooms that share a full bath, complete with a whirlpool tub.
- The quiet den could serve as a third bedroom or a guest room.

Plan K-532-L	
Bedrooms: 2+	**Baths:** 1½
Living Area:	
Main floor	492 sq. ft.
Lower floor	488 sq. ft.
Total Living Area:	**980 sq. ft.**
Exterior Wall Framing:	2x4 or 2x6
Foundation Options:	

Crawlspace
(All plans can be built with your choice of foundation and framing. A generic conversion diagram is available. See order form.)

BLUEPRINT PRICE CODE:	**A**

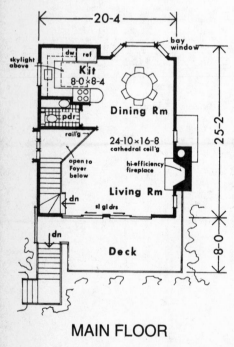

MAIN FLOOR

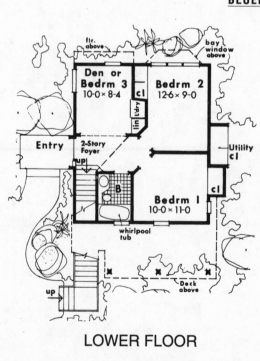

LOWER FLOOR

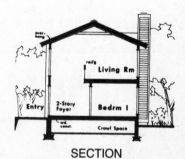

SECTION

VIEW INTO LIVING ROOM AND DINING ROOM

Make It a Double!

- This compact design can be built as a single-family home or as a duplex. The second unit may be added later.
- The main floor's open layout is designed for informal family living. The living and dining areas share a cozy fireplace and views of the backyard.
- The efficient, U-shaped kitchen nicely services the dining room, which opens to a patio through sliding glass doors.
- Laundry facilities are located in the convenient powder room off the entry.
- A large clerestory window brightens the open stairway, which leads from the two-story entry to the upper floor. A railed overlook offers views of the living room and the entry below.
- The upper floor hosts three bedrooms and a full bath. A balcony railing at the top of the stairs overlooks the vaulted entry below.

Plan SD-8231

Bedrooms: 3	**Baths:** 1½
Living Area:	
Upper floor	536 sq. ft.
Main floor	448 sq. ft.
Total Living Area:	**984 sq. ft.**
Garage	203 sq. ft.
Exterior Wall Framing:	2x4 or 2x6
Foundation Options:	
Crawlspace	
BLUEPRINT PRICE CODE:	**A**

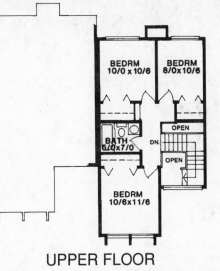

UPPER FLOOR

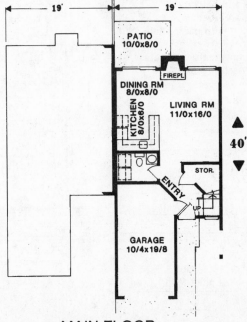

MAIN FLOOR

REAR

Small Home Generous with Living Comforts

- Open, space-saving Great Room with vaulted ceilings and stone fireplace; expansive front adjoining deck.
- Open staircase and balcony overlook living area below.
- U-shaped kitchen with pantry and snack bar.
- All three bedrooms feature private access to rear decks.

Plan H-5

Bedrooms: 3	Baths: 1

Space:

Upper floor:	332 sq. ft.
Main floor:	660 sq. ft.
Total living area:	**992 sq. ft.**
Exterior Wall Framing:	2x4

Foundation options:
Crawlspace only.
(Foundation & framing conversion diagram available — see order form.)

Blueprint Price Code:	A

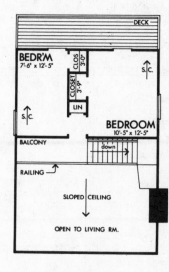

FRONT

FRONT OF HOME

MAIN FLOOR

DECK

BEDROOM
10'-5" x 10'-0"

Shwr
BATH
WH
REF.
KITCHEN
10'-6" x 9'-6"
STOR
CLOSET
5'-1"
CLOS
3'-0"
up
SHELVES

LIVING ROOM
21'-2" x 16'-5"

DECK

3'-4"   22'-0"

4'-0"

30'-0"

8'-0"

UPPER FLOOR

DECK

BEDR'M
7'-6" x 12'-5"
CLOSET 3'-9"
CLOS
3'-0"
LIN
S.C.
S.C.
BEDROOM
10'-5" x 12'-5"
BALCONY
down
RAILING
SLOPED CEILING
OPEN TO LIVING RM.

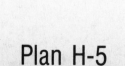

Plan H-5

PRICES AND DETAILS ON PAGES 12-15

UPPER FLOOR

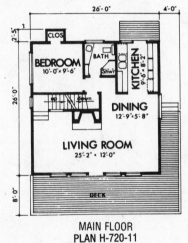

26'-0"   4'-0"

CLOS

BATH

BEDROOM
10'-0" x 9'-6"

KITCHEN
9'-6" x 8'-2"

Shwr

DINING
12'-9" x 5'-8"

LIVING ROOM
25'-2" x 12'-0"

DECK

**MAIN FLOOR
PLAN H-720-11**

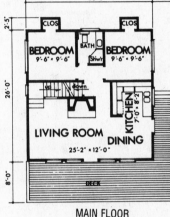

26'-0"   4'-0"

CLOS   CLOS

BEDROOM
9'-6" x 9'-6"

BATH

BEDROOM
9'-6" x 9'-6"

Shwr

KITCHEN
7'-0" x 8'-2"

LIVING ROOM
25'-2" x 12'-0"

DINING

DECK

**MAIN FLOOR
PLAN H-720-10**

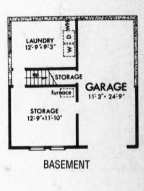

LAUNDRY
12'-9" x 9'-3"

W D

STORAGE

furnace

GARAGE
11'-3" x 24'-9"

STORAGE
12'-9" x 11'-10"

BASEMENT

Chalet with Variations

- Attractive chalet offers several main level variations, with second floor and basement layouts identical.
- All versions feature well-arranged kitchen, attached dining area, and large living room.
- Second-floor amenities include private decks off each bedroom and storage space in every corner!

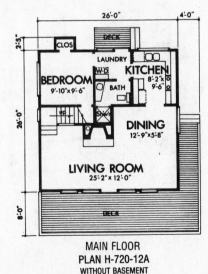

26'-0"   4'-0"

DECK

CLOS

LAUNDRY

W D

KITCHEN
8'-2" x 9'-6"

BEDROOM
9'-10" x 9'-6"

BATH

SHWR

DINING
12'-9" x 5'-8"

LIVING ROOM
25'-2" x 12'-0"

DECK

**MAIN FLOOR
PLAN H-720-12A
WITHOUT BASEMENT**

Plans H-720-10, -11 & -12A

Bedrooms: 3-4	Baths: 2

Space:

Upper floor:	328 sq. ft.
Main floor:	686 sq. ft.
Total living area:	**1,014 sq. ft.**
Basement:	approx. 686 sq. ft.
Garage: (incl. in basement)	278 sq. ft.

Exterior Wall Framing: 2x4

Foundation options:
Daylight basement
(Plans H-720-10 or -11).
Crawlspace (Plan H-720-12A)
(Foundation & framing conversion
diagram available — see order form.)

Blueprint Price Code:

Without basement:	A
With basement:	B

**TO ORDER THIS BLUEPRINT,
CALL TOLL-FREE 1-800-547-5570**   **Plans H-720-10, -11 & -12A**   **PRICES AND DETAILS
ON PAGES 12-15**

25

Designed for Today's Family

- Compact and affordable, this home is designed for today's young families.
- The Great Room features corner windows, an impressive fireplace and a 12-ft.-high vaulted ceiling.
- The kitchen/dining room combination offers space for two people to share food preparation and clean-up chores.
- The master suite is impressive for a home of this size, and includes a cozy window seat, a large walk-in closet and a private bath.
- Another full bath serves the remainder of the main floor. The optional third bedroom could be used as a den or as an expanded dining area.

Plan B-8317

Bedrooms: 2+	Baths: 2
Living Area:	
Main floor	1,016 sq. ft.
Total Living Area:	**1,016 sq. ft.**
Exterior Wall Framing:	2x4

Foundation Options:

Slab

(All plans can be built with your choice of foundation and framing. A generic conversion diagram is available. See order form.)

BLUEPRINT PRICE CODE: A

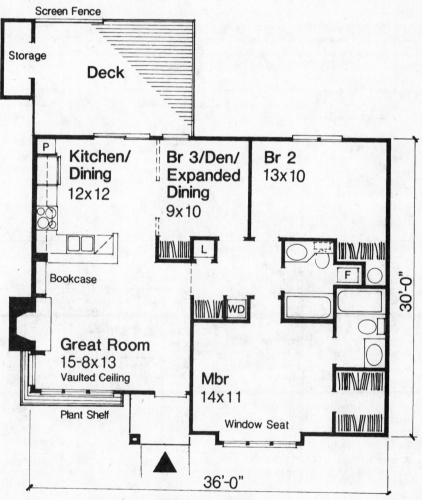

MAIN FLOOR

Casual Flexibility

- This beautifully designed vacation or year-round home is spacious and flexible.
- The interior is brightened by an abundance of windows.
- The open, vaulted living room boasts a central fireplace that makes a great conversation place or a cozy spot for spending cold winter evenings.
- The kitchen opens to the dining room and the scenery beyond through the dramatic window wall with half-round transom.
- The sleeping room and loft upstairs can easily accommodate several guests or could be used as multi-purpose space.

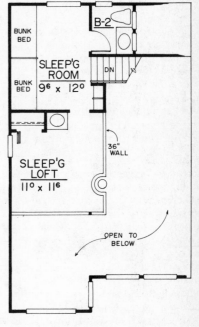

UPPER FLOOR

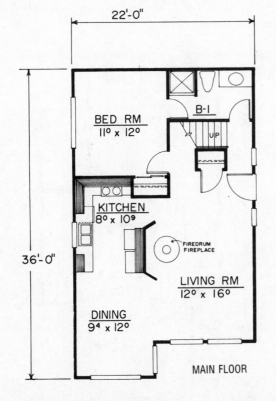

MAIN FLOOR

Plan I-1032-A

Bedrooms: 2-3	Baths: 1½
Living Area:	
Upper floor	288 sq. ft.
Main floor	744 sq. ft.
Total Living Area:	**1,032 sq. ft.**
Exterior Wall Framing:	2x6

Foundation Options:

Crawlspace
(Typical foundation & framing conversion diagram available—see order form.)

BLUEPRINT PRICE CODE: **A**

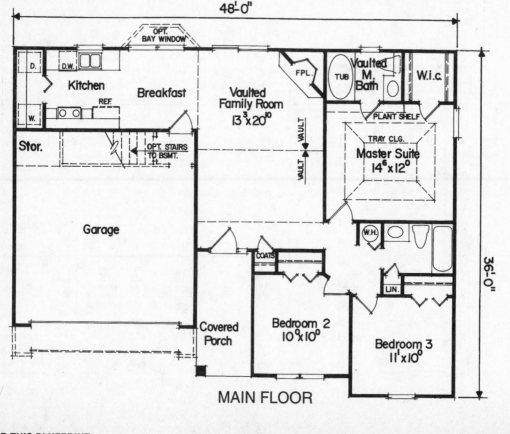

High Ceilings, Large Spaces!

- This affordable home is filled with large spaces that are further enhanced by high ceilings and lots of windows.
- The charming exterior is complemented by a combination of lap siding and brick, along with a columned front porch and a sidelighted entry door.
- Inside, the first area to come into view is the huge family room, which features a 15½-ft. vaulted ceiling and an efficient corner fireplace. Sliding glass doors open up the room to the backyard.

- The family room flows into the spacious breakfast room and kitchen. A picture window or an optional bay window brightens the breakfast room, while the kitchen offers a window above the sink and a convenient laundry closet that hides the clutter.
- The master suite leaves out nothing. An 11-ft. tray ceiling in the sleeping area gives way to the vaulted master bath, which is accented with a plant shelf above the entrance. A roomy walk-in closet is also included. The two smaller bedrooms share a hall bath.
- The optional basement doubles the home's size, providing ample expansion space.

Plan FB-1070	
Bedrooms: 3	**Baths:** 2
Living Area:	
Main floor	1,070 sq. ft.
Total Living Area:	**1,070 sq. ft.**
Daylight basement	1,070 sq. ft.
Garage	484 sq. ft.
Exterior Wall Framing:	2x4

Foundation Options:
Daylight basement
Crawlspace
Slab
(All plans can be built with your choice of foundation and framing. A generic conversion diagram is available. See order form.)

BLUEPRINT PRICE CODE:	A

MAIN FLOOR

Plan FB-1070

PRICES AND DETAILS ON PAGES 12-15

Living With Sunpower

Angled wood siding accentuates the architectural geometry of this flexible leisure home. The house is designed to exploit sun power and conserve energy. Focal point of the plan is an outsized living lounge that has pitched ceiling and overall dimensions of 18'-8" by 26'-0". Note the glass wall that leads to the spacious sun deck. A roomy kitchen is accessible from another sun deck and serves two eating bars as well as the dining room. The three bedrooms are well isolated from noise and traffic. Adjacent to the kitchen is the utility-storage room that can accommodate laundry facilities.

As an option, two solar collectors can be installed on the roof, either over the living lounge, or on the opposite roof, depending on the southern exposure. Solar equipment may be installed now or in the future.

Total living area: 1,077 sq. ft.

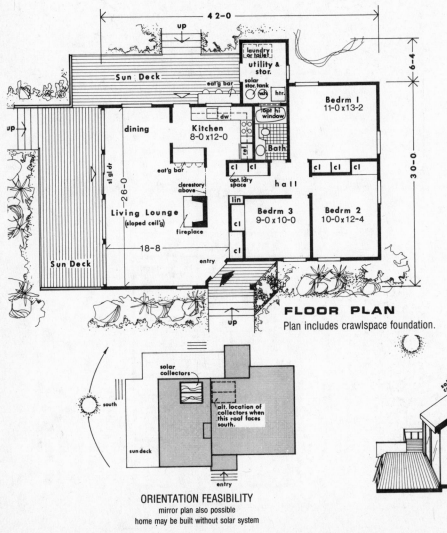

FLOOR PLAN
Plan includes crawlspace foundation.

ORIENTATION FEASIBILITY
mirror plan also possible
home may be built without solar system

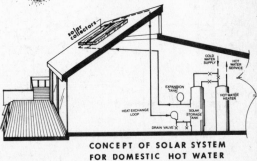

CONCEPT OF SOLAR SYSTEM FOR DOMESTIC HOT WATER

Blueprint Price Code A
Plan K-166-T

Lofty Cottage Retreat

- This generous cottage home offers wide-open living areas and a delightful balcony space.
- Off the recessed entry, the living room merges into the dining room for a spacious effect. A woodstove or fireplace adds an inviting ambience.
- The adjacent kitchen has a convenient raised service counter over the sink area and handy access to both the laundry closet and the back porch.
- The master suite offers a huge walk-in closet, a bayed sitting alcove and private access to the main bath, which features a soaking tub and a sit-down angled vanity.
- Upstairs, a large balcony bedroom overlooks the living areas below. This lofty space boasts a built-in desk and a bath with a shower.

Plan E-1002

Bedrooms: 1+	Baths: 2
Living Area:	
Upper floor	267 sq. ft.
Main floor	814 sq. ft.
Total Living Area:	**1,081 sq. ft.**
Standard basement	814 sq. ft.
Exterior Wall Framing:	2x4

Foundation Options:

Standard basement

Crawlspace

Slab

(All plans can be built with your choice of foundation and framing. A generic conversion diagram is available. See order form.)

BLUEPRINT PRICE CODE: A

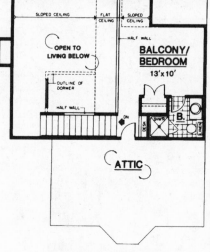

UPPER FLOOR

MAIN FLOOR

Extra-Special Ranch-Style

- Repeating gables, wood siding and brick adorn this ranch-style home, which offers numerous amenities in its compact interior.
- The entry leads directly into a spectacular 21-ft.-high vaulted family room, an ideal entertainment area accented by a corner fireplace and a French door to the backyard.
- A serving bar connects the family room with the efficient kitchen, which has a handy pantry, ample counter space and a sunny breakfast room.
- The luxurious master suite boasts a 10½-ft. tray ceiling, a large bank of windows and a walk-in closet. The master bath features a garden tub.
- Two more bedrooms, one with a 14½-ft. vaulted ceiling, share another full bath.
- The two-car garage provides convenient access to the kitchen and laundry area.

Plan FB-1104

Bedrooms: 3	Baths: 2
Living Area:	
Main floor	1,104 sq. ft.
Total Living Area:	**1,104 sq. ft.**
Daylight basement	1,104 sq. ft.
Garage	400 sq. ft.
Exterior Wall Framing:	2x4

Foundation Options:

Daylight basement

Crawlspace

(All plans can be built with your choice of foundation and framing. A generic conversion diagram is available. See order form.)

BLUEPRINT PRICE CODE: A

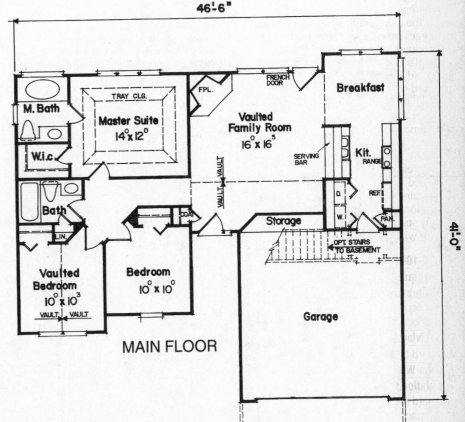

MAIN FLOOR

46'-6"

41'-0"

M. Bath

Master Suite
14⁰ x 12⁰
TRAY CLG.

FPL.

FRENCH DOOR

Breakfast

Vaulted Family Room
16⁰ x 16⁵

W.i.c.

SERVING BAR

Kit.
RANGE

Bath

VAULT VAULT

COAT

REF.

Storage

W.

PAN.

LIN.

Vaulted Bedroom
10⁰ x 10³

Bedroom
10⁰ x 10⁰

OPT STAIRS TO BASEMENT

VAULT   VAULT

Garage

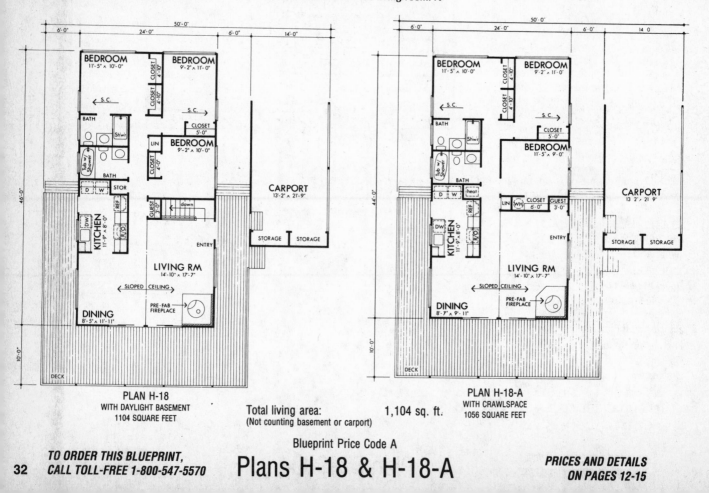

Compact, Easy to Build

This compact vacation or retirement home is economical and easy to construct. Only 24' x 46' for the daylight basement version, it nonetheless contains all the necessities and some of the luxuries one desires in a three-bedroom home. The non-basement version measures 24' x 44'.

Overall width for both versions including deck and carport is 50'.

One luxury is the separate, private bath adjoining the master bedroom; another is the double "His & Hers" wardrobe closets for the same room. The other two bedrooms are equipped with good-sized closets and share a second bathroom. Even if you choose the basement version, the convenience of first floor laundry facilities is yours.

The open stairway to the basement adds 3' to the visual size of the living room. A

pre-fab fireplace is located to allow enjoyment of a cozy hearth and a beautiful view from the same chair.

The plans are so completely detailed that a handyman amateur might frame this building (with the help of a few friends). Why not try it? (Be sure to order a materials list, too!).

PLAN H-18
WITH DAYLIGHT BASEMENT
1104 SQUARE FEET

PLAN H-18-A
WITH CRAWLSPACE
1056 SQUARE FEET

Total living area:
(Not counting basement or carport)   1,104 sq. ft.

Blueprint Price Code A

Plans H-18 & H-18-A

TO ORDER THIS BLUEPRINT,
CALL TOLL-FREE 1-800-547-5570

PRICES AND DETAILS
ON PAGES 12-15

Wonderfully Space-Efficient

- With multiple gables, big windows and a modern, free-flowing floor plan, this wonderfully space-efficient one-story home offers plenty of excitement.
- Past the inviting columned entrance, the living room is highlighted by tall front windows and a vaulted ceiling that rises to a height of more than 13 feet.
- The adjoining dining room offers sliding glass doors to a backyard deck. The nearby U-shaped kitchen includes a pantry and a convenient laundry closet.
- The master bedroom boasts a 10-ft. vaulted ceiling, plenty of windows and a private bath.
- Rounding out the sleeping wing are two additional bedrooms with easy access to a hallway linen closet and a full bath.

Plan B-89054

Bedrooms: 3	Baths: 2
Living Area:	
Main floor	1,135 sq. ft.
Total Living Area:	**1,135 sq. ft.**
Standard basement	1,135 sq. ft.
Garage	271 sq. ft.
Exterior Wall Framing:	2x4

Foundation Options:

Standard basement

(All plans can be built with your choice of foundation and framing. A generic conversion diagram is available. See order form.)

BLUEPRINT PRICE CODE:	**A**

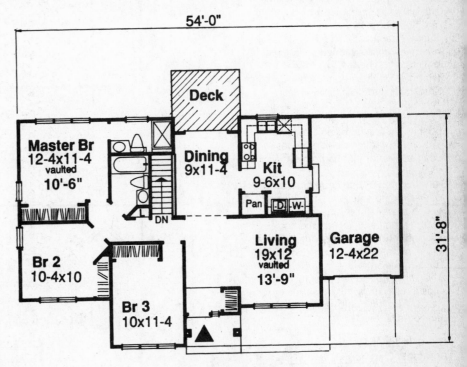

MAIN FLOOR

Cottage with Open Interior

- The exterior of this contemporary cottage features a delightful covered porch and a pair of matching dormers.
- The entry has a dramatic 13-ft. ceiling and flows into an expansive Great Room. The Great Room is also highlighted by a vaulted ceiling that rises to a height of 17 feet. Tall windows brighten both corners, while a fireplace serves as a handsome centerpiece. Sliding doors between the Great Room and the breakfast nook open to an angled backyard deck.
- The sunny vaulted nook provides a cozy setting for family dining with a view of the backyard.
- Ample cabinets and counter space are offered in the efficient galley kitchen, which also features a handy snack counter that extends into the nook.
- The main-floor master bedroom has a walk-in closet and easy access to the full bath beyond.
- The upper floor offers another bedroom, plus a full bath with space for a laundry closet. The loft could serve as an extra bedroom.

Plan JWB-9307

Bedrooms: 2+	Baths: 2
Living Area:	
Upper floor	349 sq. ft.
Main floor	795 sq. ft.
Total Living Area:	**1,144 sq. ft.**
Standard basement	712 sq. ft.
Exterior Wall Framing:	2x4 or 2x6

Foundation Options:

Standard basement

(Typical foundation & framing conversion diagram available—see order form.)

BLUEPRINT PRICE CODE: A

UPPER FLOOR

Bedroom 2
10'8 x 12'

Loft
7'2 x 8'10

Open To Below

dn

MAIN FLOOR

33'4

26'0

Deck

Nook
7'8 x 7'
Vault

Master Bedroom
10'8 x 13'8

Great Room
13'4 x 19'2
Vault

Kitchen
7'4 x 9'4

up

dn

Entry

Porch

Plan JWB-9307

PRICES AND DETAILS ON PAGES 12-15

Economical Starter Home

- This economical one-story is ideal for a first home or small family.
- Two or three bedrooms can be finished, as needed.
- A generous sized vaulted living room with large fireplace and corner windows and dining room overlook the rear patio.
- The kitchen offers convenient laundry facilities.

Plan B-88003

Bedrooms: 2-3	Baths: 2
Space:	
Main floor:	1,159 sq. ft.
Total living area:	1,159 sq. ft.
Garage:	425 sq. ft.
Exterior Wall Framing:	2x4

Foundation options:
Slab.
(Foundation & framing conversion diagram available — see order form.)

Blueprint Price Code: A

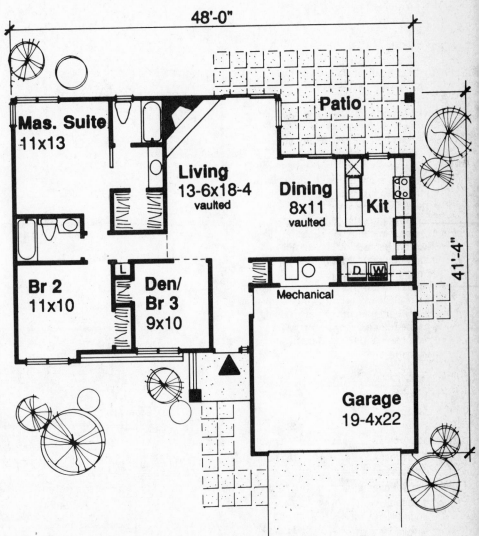

48'-0"

41'-4"

Mas. Suite
11x13

Living
13-6x18-4
vaulted

Patio

Dining
8x11
vaulted

Kit

Br 2
11x10

Den/
Br 3
9x10

Mechanical

D W

Garage
19-4x22

Space-Saving Tri-Level

- This clever tri-level design offers an open, airy interior while taking up a minimum of land space.
- The Great Room features a spectacular 15-ft. vaulted and skylighted ceiling, an inviting woodstove and sliding glass doors to a full-width deck.
- The Great Room also incorporates a dining area, which is easily serviced from the efficient, space-saving kitchen.
- The main-floor bedroom boasts two closets. A compact laundry closet, a guest closet and a storage area line the hallway to the spacious main bath.
- The large loft offers infinite possibilities, such as extra sleeping quarters, a home office, an art studio or a recreation room. Clerestory windows and a sloped ceiling enhance the bright, airy feeling.
- The tuck-under garage saves on building costs and lets you make the most of your lot.

Plan H-963-2A

Bedrooms: 1+	Baths: 1
Living Area:	
Upper floor	432 sq. ft.
Main floor	728 sq. ft.
Total Living Area:	**1,160 sq. ft.**
Tuck-under garage	728 sq. ft.
Exterior Wall Framing:	2x4

Foundation Options:

Slab

(All plans can be built with your choice of foundation and framing. A generic conversion diagram is available. See order form.)

BLUEPRINT PRICE CODE: A

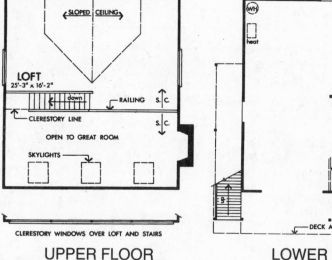

UPPER FLOOR

LOWER FLOOR

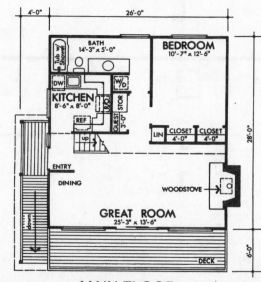

MAIN FLOOR

TO ORDER THIS BLUEPRINT, CALL TOLL-FREE 1-800-547-5570

Plan H-963-2A

PRICES AND DETAILS ON PAGES 12-15

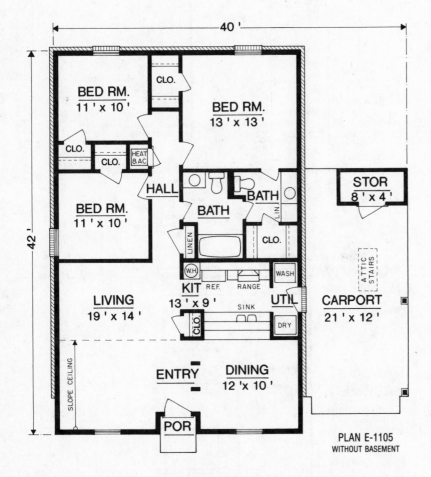

40'

BED RM.
11' x 10'

CLO.

BED RM.
13' x 13'

CLO.

CLO.

HEAT & AC

HALL

BATH

STOR
8' x 4'

BED RM.
11' x 10'

BATH

LINEN

CLO.

42'

LINEN

W.H.

WASH

ATTIC STAIRS

LIVING
19' x 14'

KIT
13' x 9'

REF.   RANGE

SINK

UTIL

DRY

CARPORT
21' x 12'

CLO.

SLOPE CEILING

ENTRY

DINING
12' x 10'

POR

PLAN E-1105
WITHOUT BASEMENT

Simple, Economical to Build

AREAS

Living	1168 sq. ft.
Carport, Storage, Stoops	316 sq. ft.
Total	1484 sq. ft.

Exterior walls are 2x6 construction.
Specify crawlspace or slab foundation.

Suspended Sun Room

- This narrow-lot design is a perfect combination of economical structure and luxurious features.
- The living and dining rooms flow together to create a great space for parties or family gatherings. A 16-ft. sloped ceiling and clerestory windows add drama and brightness. A fabulous deck expands the entertaining area.
- An exciting sun room provides the advantages of passive-solar heating.
- The sunny, efficient kitchen is open to the dining room.
- A full bath serves the two isolated main-floor bedrooms.
- The optional daylight basement includes an additional bedroom and bath as well as a tuck-under garage and storage space.

Plans H-951-1A & -1B

Bedrooms: 2+	Baths: 1-2
Living Area:	
Main floor	1,075 sq. ft.
Sun room	100 sq. ft.
Daylight basement	662 sq. ft.
Total Living Area:	**1,175/1,837 sq. ft.**
Tuck-under garage	311 sq. ft.
Exterior Wall Framing:	2x6
Foundation Options:	**Plan #**
Daylight basement	H-951-1B
Crawlspace	H-951-1A

(All plans can be built with your choice of foundation and framing. A generic conversion diagram is available. See order form.)

BLUEPRINT PRICE CODE:	**A/B**

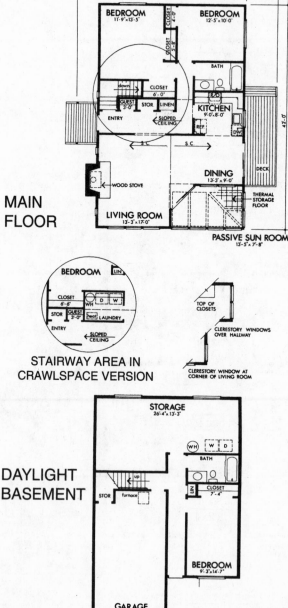

MAIN FLOOR

STAIRWAY AREA IN CRAWLSPACE VERSION

DAYLIGHT BASEMENT

Plans H-951-1A & -1B

PRICES AND DETAILS ON PAGES 12-15

A Perfect Fit

- This country-style home will fit anywhere. Its charming character and narrow width make it ideal for those who value vintage styling along with plenty of yard space.
- The quaint covered front porch opens into the living room, which boasts a 12-ft., 8-in. cathedral ceiling and an inviting fireplace.
- The adjacent bay-windowed dining area features a 9-ft.-high vaulted ceiling and easy access to the efficient, galley-style kitchen.
- Off the kitchen, a handy laundry/utility room is convenient to the back entrance. The carport can accommodate two cars and includes a lockable storage area.
- The master bedroom suite offers a roomy walk-in closet, a private bath and sliding glass doors to a rear patio.
- Another full bath is centrally located for easy service to the rest of the home. Two more nice-sized bedrooms complete the plan.

Plan J-86119

Bedrooms: 3	Baths: 2
Living Area:	
Main floor	1,346 sq. ft.
Total Living Area:	**1,346 sq. ft.**
Standard basement	1,346 sq. ft.
Carport	400 sq. ft.
Exterior Wall Framing:	2x4

Foundation Options:

Standard basement
Crawlspace
Slab

(All plans can be built with your choice of foundation and framing. A generic conversion diagram is available. See order form.)

BLUEPRINT PRICE CODE:	**A**

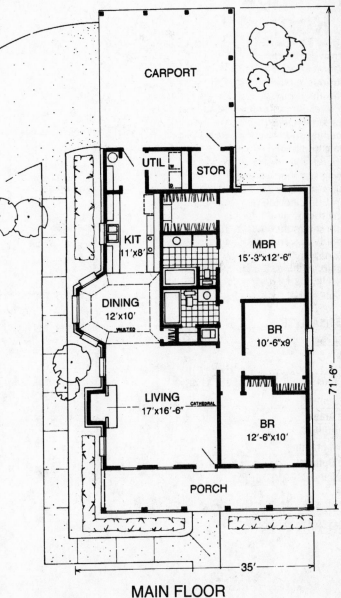

MAIN FLOOR

Appealing Farmhouse

- This appealing farmhouse design features a shady and inviting front porch with decorative railings.
- Inside, 14-ft. vaulted ceilings expand the living and dining rooms.
- This large area is brightened by bay windows and warmed by a unique two-way fireplace. Sliding glass doors lead to a sunny backyard patio.
- The functional kitchen includes a pantry closet, plenty of cabinet space and a serving bar to the dining room.
- The master bedroom boasts a mirrored dressing area, a private bath and abundant closet space.
- Two additional bedrooms share another full bath. The third bedroom includes a cozy window seat.

Plan NW-521

Bedrooms: 3	Baths: 2
Living Area:	
Main floor	1,187 sq. ft.
Total Living Area:	**1,187 sq. ft.**
Garage	448 sq. ft.
Exterior Wall Framing:	2x6

Foundation Options:

Crawlspace

(All plans can be built with your choice of foundation and framing. A generic conversion diagram is available. See order form.)

BLUEPRINT PRICE CODE: A

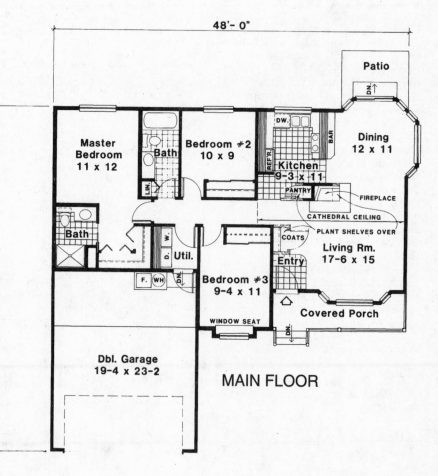

MAIN FLOOR

MAIN FLOOR

BEDROOM 12'-0" × 10'-0"
CLOSET
BATH
shower
CLOS
B.R. OR DEN 12'-5" × 10'-0"
DECK
washer dryer
dn
up
KITCHEN DINING 15'-10" × 11'-5"
LIVING ROOM 19'-5" × 14'-10"
eating counter
DECK

36'-0"
4'-0"
4'-0"
26'-0"
10'-0"

BATH
shower
CLOS
BEDROOM 11'-7" × 11'-5"
dn
DECK

UPPER FLOOR

Multi-Level Design

- This open and attractive design features multi-level construction and efficient use of living space.
- Elevated den and high ceilings with exposed rafters enhance the spacious feeling of the living room.
- Washer/dryer and kitchen are separated from the dining area by an eating counter.
- Third level comprises the master bedroom and bath.
- Garage and storage space are combined in the basement level.

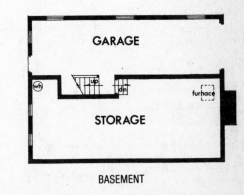

GARAGE

wh
up
dn
furnace

STORAGE

BASEMENT

Plan H-863-2

Bedrooms: 2-3	Baths: 2

Space:
Upper floor: 252 sq. ft.
Main floor: 936 sq. ft.

Total living area: 1,188 sq. ft.
Basement: approx. 936 sq. ft.
(includes garage)

Exterior Wall Framing: 2x4

Foundation options:
Daylight basement only.
(Foundation & framing conversion diagram available — see order form.)

Blueprint Price Code: A

Family Tradition

- This quaint home basks in tradition, with beautiful gables facing the street and vaulted family spaces inside.
- A columned front porch opens to a spacious family room, where a 16-ft. vaulted ceiling soars above a striking fireplace flanked by arched windows. The 16-ft. ceiling continues into the dining room and the kitchen.
- The sunny dining room opens to the backyard through a French door. The walk-through kitchen offers a bright angled sink, a snack bar and a large pantry closet topped by a plant shelf.
- The master suite boasts a 10½-ft. tray ceiling in the bedroom and a 13½-ft. vaulted ceiling in the lush garden bath.
- Two secondary bedrooms share another full bath. A handy laundry closet is close to the bedrooms and the garage.
- For added spaciousness, all ceilings are 9 ft. high unless otherwise specified.

Plan FB-5115-CLAI

Bedrooms: 3	Baths: 2
Living Area:	
Main floor	1,198 sq. ft.
Total Living Area:	**1,198 sq. ft.**
Daylight basement	1,198 sq. ft.
Garage	400 sq. ft.
Exterior Wall Framing:	2x4

Foundation Options:

Daylight basement

Crawlspace

(All plans can be built with your choice of foundation and framing. A generic conversion diagram is available. See order form.)

BLUEPRINT PRICE CODE: A

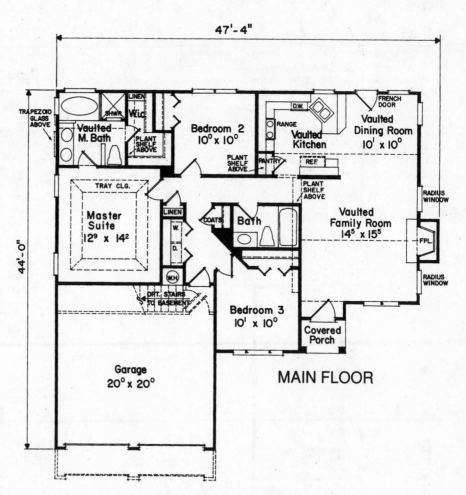

MAIN FLOOR

Plan FB-5115-CLAI

PRICES AND DETAILS ON PAGES 12-15

Super Chalet

- The charming Alpine detailing of the exterior and the open, flexible layout of the interior make this one of our most popular plans.
- In from the large front deck, the living room wraps around a central fireplace or woodstove, providing a warm and expansive multipurpose living space. Sliding glass doors open to the deck for outdoor entertaining.
- The adjoining dining room is easily serviced from the galley-style kitchen. A

convenient full bath serves a nearby bedroom and the remainder of the main floor.
- Two upper-floor bedrooms have 12-ft.-high sloped ceilings, extra closet space and access to another full bath. The larger bedroom offers sliding glass doors to a lofty deck.
- The blueprints recommend finishing the interior walls with solid lumber paneling for a rich, rustic look.
- In addition to a large general-use area and a shop, the optional daylight basement has space for a car or a boat.

Plans H-26-1 & -1A

Bedrooms: 3	Baths: 2
Living Area:	
Upper floor	476 sq. ft.
Main floor	728 sq. ft.
Daylight basement	410 sq. ft.
Total Living Area:	**1,204/1,614 sq. ft.**
Tuck-under garage	318 sq. ft.
Exterior Wall Framing:	2x4
Foundation Options:	**Plan #**
Daylight basement	H-26-1
Crawlspace	H-26-1A

(All plans can be built with your choice of foundation and framing. A generic conversion diagram is available. See order form.)

BLUEPRINT PRICE CODE:	**A/B**

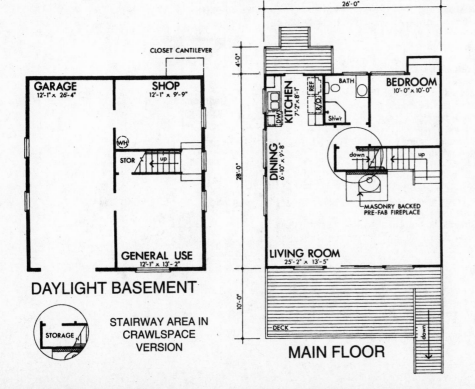

DAYLIGHT BASEMENT

STAIRWAY AREA IN CRAWLSPACE VERSION

MAIN FLOOR

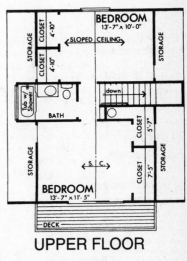

UPPER FLOOR

A-Frame Chalet with Popular Features

Ski chalets bring to mind Alpine comforts and evenings by the hearth. Schussing down nearby slopes is much more enjoyable when you don't have to worry about long drives home. Also, being on hand means you won't miss the fresh snowfall. In addition, summer time finds the mountain setting ideal for refreshing weekends away from the crowds and heat.

This class A-Frame is designed for optimum comfort and minimum cost, yet allows for variety and individual taste in setting and decor. Your home away from home can vary from plush to rustic, depending on personal preferences.

A special feature of this plan is the natural stone fireplace located where it can be enjoyed from indoors and outdoors. It serves the dual function of being a standard fireplace indoors and a handy barbecue outdoors. Two sleeping rooms on the main floor are a further advantage. Upstairs, there is a third bedroom plus a half bath. A balcony room provides space for overflow guests or a playroom for the kids. All the rooms in the house have "knee walls" so the space is usable right to the wall. These walls provide handy storage places as well as space for insulation.

First floor:	845 sq. ft.
Second floor:	375 sq. ft.
Total living area:	1,220 sq. ft.

PLAN H-6
WITHOUT BASEMENT
(CRAWLSPACE FOUNDATION)

SECOND FLOOR
375 SQUARE FEET

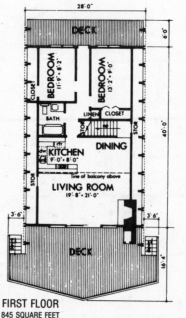

FIRST FLOOR
845 SQUARE FEET

Blueprint Price Code A
Plan H-6

PRICES AND DETAILS
ON PAGES 12-15

Welcoming Facade

- The warm cedar and brick facade of this charming one-story will be a welcome sight at the end of the day.
- An inviting, sidelighted foyer opens directly to the living room, which is warmed by a central fireplace. A stunning 11-ft. cathedral ceiling rises over the living room and the foyer.
- Around an open corner, the kitchen boasts a cheery bayed eating nook with sliding glass doors to a wide, covered porch overlooking the backyard.
- The master bedroom is graced by an elegant 9-ft. tray ceiling and private porch access.
- Down the hall, a large secondary bedroom is serviced by a hall bath that is just steps away.
- A cozy den between the two bedrooms is the perfect prescription for stressful days. A delightful bayed window offers comforting views of the side yard.

Plan GL-1239

Bedrooms: 2+	Baths: 2
Living Area:	
Main floor	1,239 sq. ft.
Total Living Area:	**1,239 sq. ft.**
Standard basement	1,203 sq. ft.
Garage	440 sq. ft.
Exterior Wall Framing:	2x4

Foundation Options:

Standard basement

(All plans can be built with your choice of foundation and framing. A generic conversion diagram is available. See order form.)

BLUEPRINT PRICE CODE: A

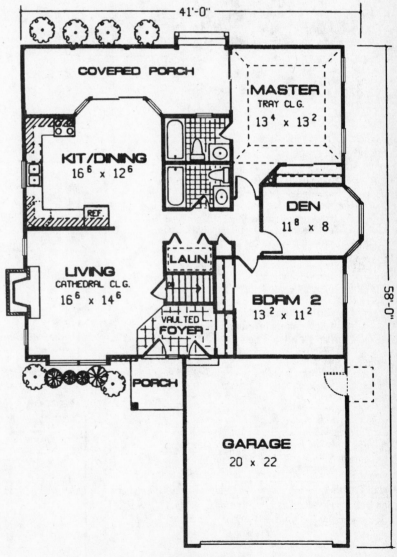

MAIN FLOOR

REAR VIEW

FRONT VIEW

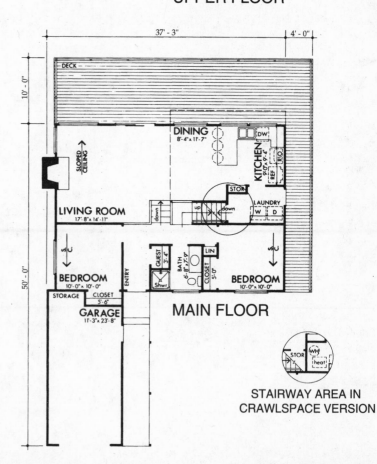

UPPER FLOOR

Easy Living

- The living is easy in this affordable home, which is perfect for a scenic lot.
- Five steps down from the entry, the main living areas look out over an inviting wraparound deck. The living room offers a 16-ft.-high sloped ceiling, a handsome fireplace and deck access. A snack bar separates the sunny kitchen from the spacious dining area. Additional deck access is provided near the laundry area.
- Two bedrooms near the main entrance share a bath and feature 13-ft. sloped ceilings.
- The secluded upper-floor master suite boasts a 14-ft. vaulted ceiling, a walk-in closet, a full bath and a private deck.

Plans H-925-1 & -1A

Bedrooms: 3	Baths: 2
Living Area:	
Upper floor	288 sq. ft.
Main floor	951 sq. ft.
Total Living Area:	**1,239 sq. ft.**
Daylight basement	951 sq. ft.
Garage	266 sq. ft.
Exterior Wall Framing:	2x4
Foundation Options:	**Plan #**
Daylight basement	H-925-1
Crawlspace	H-925-1A

(All plans can be built with your choice of foundation and framing. A generic conversion diagram is available. See order form.)

BLUEPRINT PRICE CODE:	**A**

MAIN FLOOR

STAIRWAY AREA IN CRAWLSPACE VERSION

TO ORDER THIS BLUEPRINT, CALL TOLL-FREE 1-800-547-5570

Plans H-925-1 & -1A

PRICES AND DETAILS ON PAGES 12-15

Comfortable L-Shaped Ranch

- From the covered entry to the beautiful and spacious family gathering areas, this comfortable ranch-style home puts many extras into a compact space.
- Straight off the central foyer, an inviting fireplace and a bright bay window highlight the living and dining area, while sliding glass doors open to a wide backyard terrace.
- The combination kitchen/family room features a large eating bar. The nearby mudroom offers a service entrance, laundry facilities, access to the garage and room for a half-bath.
- In the isolated sleeping wing, the master bedroom boasts a private bath and plenty of closet space. Two additional bedrooms share another full bath.

Plan K-276-R

Bedrooms: 3	Baths: 2+

Living Area:

Main floor	1,245 sq. ft.
Total Living Area:	**1,245 sq. ft.**
Standard basement	1,245 sq. ft.
Garage	499 sq. ft.
Exterior Wall Framing:	2x4 or 2x6

Foundation Options:

Standard basement
Crawlspace
Slab

(All plans can be built with your choice of foundation and framing. A generic conversion diagram is available. See order form.)

BLUEPRINT PRICE CODE: A

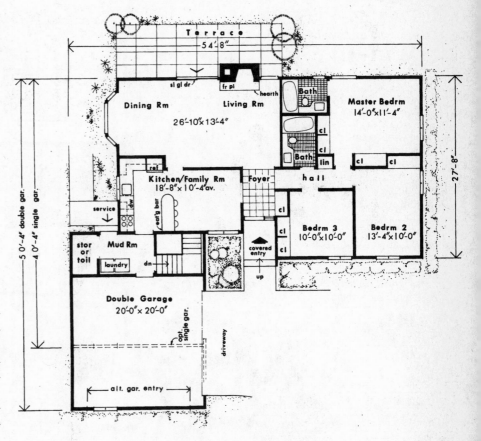

MAIN FLOOR

Compact Three-Bedroom

- Both openness and privacy are possible in this economical three-bedroom home design.
- The bright living room boasts a 17-ft. vaulted ceiling, a warming fireplace and a corner window. A high clerestory window lets in additional natural light.
- The modern, U-shaped kitchen features a handy corner pantry and a versatile snack bar.
- The adjacent open dining area provides access to a backyard deck through sliding glass doors.
- A lovely corner window brightens the secluded master bedroom, which also includes a roomy walk-in closet and private access to a compartmentalized hall bath.
- Upstairs, two good-sized bedrooms share a second split bath.

Plan B-101-8501

Bedrooms: 3	Baths: 2
Living Area:	
Upper floor	400 sq. ft.
Main floor	846 sq. ft.
Total Living Area:	**1,246 sq. ft.**
Garage	400 sq. ft.
Standard basement	846 sq. ft.
Exterior Wall Framing:	2x4

Foundation Options:

Standard basement
(All plans can be built with your choice of foundation and framing. A generic conversion diagram is available. See order form.)

BLUEPRINT PRICE CODE:	A

UPPER FLOOR

Br 2 11-6x10
Upper Living
Dn
Br 3 13x9

MAIN FLOOR

Deck
Dining 9x9-6
K 12x9
P
Mbr 14x12-8
Clerestory Above
Dn
Living 12-4x17 vaulted
Up
Plant Shelf
Garage 20x20
38'-8"
36'-8"

TO ORDER THIS BLUEPRINT, CALL TOLL-FREE 1-800-547-5570

PRICES AND DETAILS ON PAGES 12-15

Plan B-101-8501

Adorable and Affordable

- This charming one-story home has much to offer, despite its modest size and economical bent.
- The lovely full-width porch has old-fashioned detailing, such as the round columns, decorative railings and ornamental molding.
- An open floor plan maximizes the home's square footage. The front door opens to the living room, where a railing creates a hallway effect while using very little space.
- Straight ahead, the dining room adjoins the island kitchen, while offering a compact laundry closet and sliding glass doors to a large rear patio.
- Focusing on quality, the home also offers features such as a 10-ft. tray ceiling in the living room and a 9-ft. stepped ceiling in the dining room.
- The three bedrooms are well proportioned. The master bedroom includes a private bathroom, while the two smaller bedrooms share another full bath. Note that the fixtures are arranged to reduce plumbing runs.

Plan AX-91316

Bedrooms: 3	Baths: 2
Living Area:	
Main floor	1,097 sq. ft.
Total Living Area:	**1,097 sq. ft.**
Basement	1,097 sq. ft.
Garage	461 sq. ft.
Exterior Wall Framing:	2x4

Foundation Options:
Daylight basement
Standard basement
Slab
(All plans can be built with your choice of foundation and framing. A generic conversion diagram is available. See order form.)

BLUEPRINT PRICE CODE: **A**

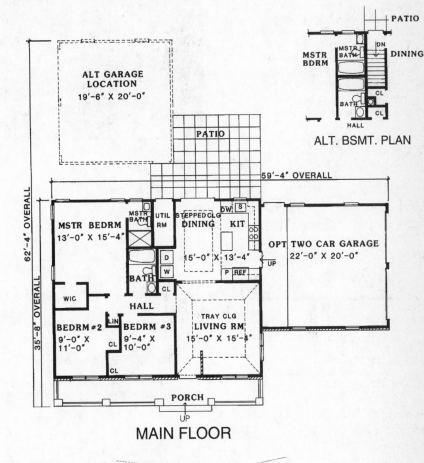

MAIN FLOOR

ALT. BSMT. PLAN

VIEW INTO LIVING ROOM AND DINING ROOM

Narrow-Lot Solar Design

- This design offers your choice of foundation and number of bedrooms, and it can be built on a narrow, sloping lot.
- The passive-solar dining room has windows on three sides and a slate floor for heat storage. A French door leads to a rear deck.
- The living room features a sloped ceiling, a woodstove in ceiling-high masonry, and sliding glass doors to the adjoining deck.
- The kitchen is open to the dining room but separated from the living room by a 7½-ft.-high wall.
- The upper-level variations include a choice of one or two bedrooms. Clerestory windows above the balcony railing add drama to both versions.

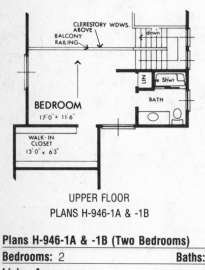

UPPER FLOOR
PLANS H-946-1A & -1B

Plans H-946-1A & -1B (Two Bedrooms)

Bedrooms: 2	Baths: 2
Living Area:	
Upper floor	381 sq. ft.
Main floor	814 sq. ft.
Total Living Area:	**1,195 sq. ft.**
Basement	approx. 814 sq. ft.
Garage	315 sq. ft.
Exterior Wall Framing:	2x6

Foundation Options:
Daylight basement (Plan H-946-1B)
Crawlspace (Plan H-946-1A)
(Typical foundation & framing conversion diagram available—see order form.)

BLUEPRINT PRICE CODE: A

MAIN FLOOR

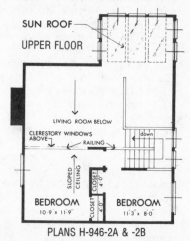

UPPER FLOOR
PLANS H-946-2A & -2B

Plans H-946-2A & -2B (Three Bedrooms)

Bedrooms: 3	Baths: 2
Living Area:	
Upper floor	290 sq. ft.
Main floor	814 sq. ft.
Total Living Area:	**1,104 sq. ft.**
Basement	approx. 814 sq. ft.
Garage	315 sq. ft.
Exterior Wall Framing:	2x6

Foundation Options:
Daylight basement (Plan H-946-2B)
Crawlspace (Plan H-946-2A)
(Typical foundation & framing conversion diagram available—see order form.)

BLUEPRINT PRICE CODE: A

Plans H-946-1A/1B & -2A/2B

PRICES AND DETAILS ON PAGES 12-15

Active Living Made Easy

- This home is perfect for active living. Its rectangular design allows the use of truss roof framing, which makes construction easy and economical.
- The galley-style kitchen and the sunny dining area are kept open to the living room, forming one huge activity space. Two sets of sliding glass doors expand the living area to the large deck.

- The secluded master bedroom offers a private bath, while the remaining bedrooms share a hall bath.
- The two baths, the laundry facilities and the kitchen are clustered to allow common plumbing walls.
- Plan H-921-1A has a standard crawlspace foundation and an optional solar-heating system. Plan H-921-2A has a Plen-Wood system, which utilizes the sealed crawlspace as a chamber for distributing heated or cooled air. Both versions of the design call for energy-efficient 2x6 exterior walls.

Plans H-921-1A & -2A	
Bedrooms: 3	Baths: 2
Living Area:	
Main floor	1,164 sq. ft.
Total Living Area:	**1,164 sq. ft.**
Exterior Wall Framing:	2x6
Foundation Options:	Plan #
Crawlspace	H-921-1A
Plen-Wood crawlspace	H-921-2A

(All plans can be built with your choice of foundation and framing. A generic conversion diagram is available. See order form.)

BLUEPRINT PRICE CODE:	A

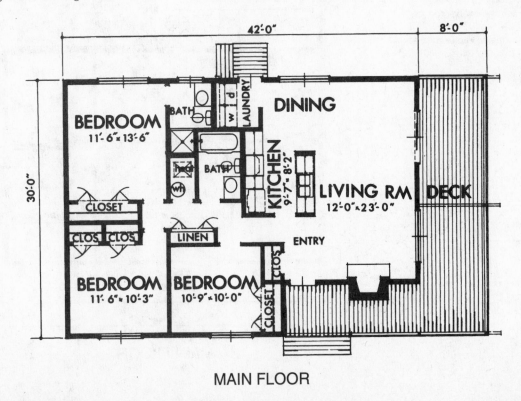

MAIN FLOOR

Cozy, Rustic Country Home

- This cozy, rustic home offers a modern, open interior that efficiently maximizes the square footage.
- The large living room features a 13-ft. sloped ceiling accented by rustic beams and an eye-catching corner fireplace.
- The living room flows into the adjoining dining room and the efficient U-shaped kitchen for a spacious, open feel.
- The master and secondary bedrooms are separated by the activity areas. The master suite includes a private bath and a separate dressing area with a dual-sink vanity.
- The secondary bedrooms share another full bath.

Plan E-1109

Bedrooms: 3	Baths: 2
Living Area:	
Main floor	1,191 sq. ft.
Total Living Area:	**1,191 sq. ft.**
Garage	462 sq. ft.
Storage & utility	55 sq. ft.
Exterior Wall Framing:	2x6

Foundation Options:

Crawlspace
Slab
(All plans can be built with your choice of foundation and framing. A generic conversion diagram is available. See order form.)

BLUEPRINT PRICE CODE:	**A**

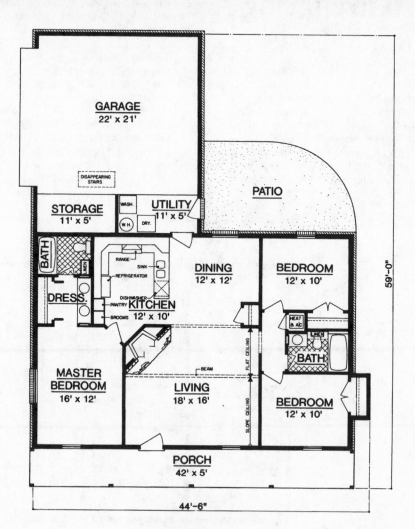

MAIN FLOOR

    Plan E-1109   PRICES AND DETAILS ON PAGES 12-15

Unexpected Amenities

- Surprising interior amenities are found within the casual exterior of this good-looking design.
- A dramatic fireplace warms the comfortable formal areas. The living and dining rooms share a 20-ft. cathedral ceiling and high windows that flank the fireplace. Sliding glass doors access an expansive side patio.

- The efficient walk-through kitchen provides plenty of counter space, in addition to a windowed sink and a pass-through to the living areas.
- A large bedroom, a full bath and an oversized utility room complete the main floor. The utility room offers space for a washer and dryer, plus a sink and an extra freezer.
- Upstairs, the spacious and secluded master suite boasts a walk-in closet, a private bath and lots of storage space. A railed loft area overlooks the living and dining rooms.

Plan I-1249-A	
Bedrooms: 2	**Baths:** 2
Living Area:	
Upper floor	297 sq. ft.
Main floor	952 sq. ft.
Total Living Area:	**1,249 sq. ft.**
Standard basement	952 sq. ft.
Exterior Wall Framing:	2x6
Foundation Options:	
Standard basement	
Crawlspace	

(All plans can be built with your choice of foundation and framing. A generic conversion diagram is available. See order form.)

BLUEPRINT PRICE CODE:	**A**

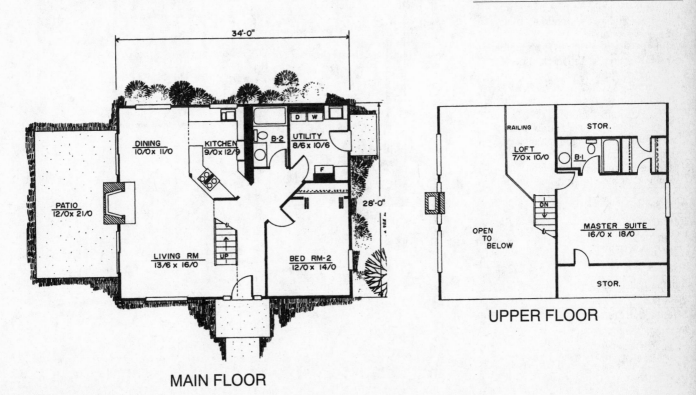

MAIN FLOOR

UPPER FLOOR

Photo by Mark Englund/HomeStyles

Style and Economy

- This attractive one-story home successfully combines a modest square footage with stylish extras such as vaulted ceilings, a fireplace and a relaxing deck.
- The sidelighted entry opens to the spacious living room, which is brightened by a Palladian window arrangement.
- The living room shares a 15-ft. vaulted ceiling and a high plant shelf with the adjoining dining room. A handsome fireplace adds warmth and ambience to the entire area.
- Sliding glass doors open from the dining room to a good-sized deck, a perfect spot for outdoor meals.
- The efficient galley-style kitchen is open to the dining room for easy serving. A pantry closet is a nice feature.
- The quiet master bedroom boasts an 11-ft. vaulted ceiling and a nice private bath. A second bath serves the other two bedrooms, one of which could function as a den or a home office.

Plan B-87106

Bedrooms: 2+	Baths: 2
Living Area:	
Main floor	1,252 sq. ft.
Total Living Area:	**1,252 sq. ft.**
Standard basement	1,252 sq. ft.
Garage	400 sq. ft.
Exterior Wall Framing:	2x4

Foundation Options:

Standard basement

(All plans can be built with your choice of foundation and framing. A generic conversion diagram is available. See order form.)

BLUEPRINT PRICE CODE: A

44'-8"

50'-8"

Br 2
10x10-8

MBr
14-6x11
vaulted

Deck

Dining
10x10-6
vaulted

Kit
8-8x10-6

Den/
Br 3
10-6x9

Plant Shelf

P DN

Living Rm
13-8x16-10
vaulted

Garage
19-4x20-8

NOTE:
The above photographed home may have been modified by the homeowner. Please refer to floor plan and/or drawn elevation shown for actual blueprint details.

MAIN FLOOR

TO ORDER THIS BLUEPRINT, CALL TOLL-FREE 1-800-547-5570

Plan B-87106

PRICES AND DETAILS ON PAGES 12-15

Eye-Catching Chalet

- Steep rooflines, dramatic windows and wide cornices give this chalet a distinctive alpine appearance.
- The large living and dining area offers a striking 20-ft.-high vaulted ceiling and a breathtaking view of the outdoors through a soaring wall of windows. Sliding glass doors access an inviting wood deck.

- The efficient U-shaped kitchen shares an eating bar with the dining area.
- Two main-floor bedrooms share a hall bath, and laundry facilities are nearby.
- The upper floor hosts a master bedroom with a 12-ft. vaulted ceiling, plenty of storage space and easy access to a full bath with a shower.
- The pièce de résistance is a balcony with a 12-ft. vaulted ceiling, offering sweeping outdoor views as well as an overlook into the living/dining area below. Additional storage areas flank the balcony.

Plans H-886-3 & -3A	
Bedrooms: 3	**Baths:** 2
Living Area:	
Upper floor	486 sq. ft.
Main floor	994 sq. ft.
Total Living Area:	**1,480 sq. ft.**
Daylight basement	715 sq. ft.
Tuck-under garage	279 sq. ft.
Exterior Wall Framing:	2x6
Foundation Options:	**Plan #**
Daylight basement	H-886-3
Crawlspace	H-886-3A

(All plans can be built with your choice of foundation and framing. A generic conversion diagram is available. See order form.)

BLUEPRINT PRICE CODE:	**A**

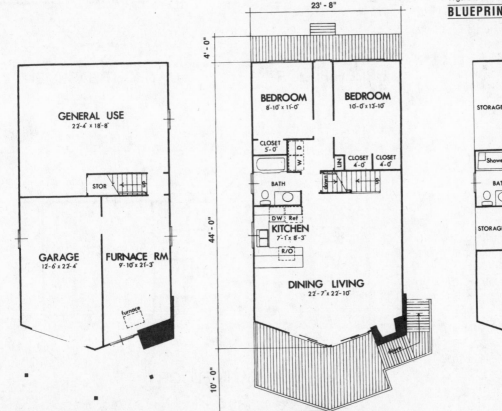

DAYLIGHT BASEMENT

MAIN FLOOR

UPPER FLOOR

Unique and Dramatic

- This home's unique interior and dramatic exterior make it perfect for a sloping, scenic lot.
- The expansive and impressive Great Room, warmed by a woodstove, flows into the island kitchen, which is completely open in design.
- The passive-solar sun room collects and stores heat from the sun, while offering a good view of the surroundings. Its ceiling rises to a height of 16 feet.
- Upstairs, a glamorous, skylighted master suite features an 11-ft. vaulted ceiling, a private bath and a huge walk-in closet.
- A skylighted hall bath serves the bright second bedroom. Both bedrooms open to the vaulted sun room below.
- The daylight basement adds a sunny sitting room, a third bedroom and a large recreation room.

Plans P-536-2A & -2D

Bedrooms: 2+	Baths: 2½-3½
Living Area:	
Upper floor	642 sq. ft.
Main floor	863 sq. ft.
Daylight basement	863 sq. ft.
Total Living Area:	**1,505/2,368 sq. ft.**
Garage	445 sq. ft.
Exterior Wall Framing:	2x6
Foundation Options:	**Plan #**
Daylight basement	P-536-2D
Crawlspace	P-536-2A

(All plans can be built with your choice of foundation and framing. A generic conversion diagram is available. See order form.)

BLUEPRINT PRICE CODE:	**B/C**

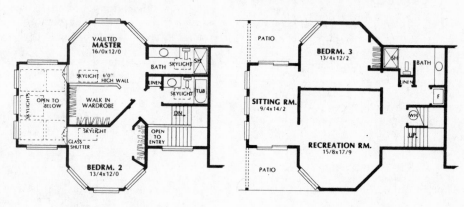

UPPER FLOOR

DAYLIGHT BASEMENT

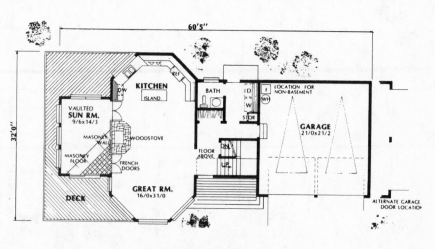

MAIN FLOOR

Luxury in a Small Package

- The elegant exterior of this design sets the tone for the luxurious spaces within.
- The foyer opens to the centrally located living room, which features a 15-ft. cathedral ceiling, a two-way fireplace and access to a lovely rear terrace.
- The unusual kitchen design includes an angled snack bar that lies between the bayed breakfast den and the formal dining room. Sliding glass doors open to another terrace.
- The master suite is a dream come true, with its romantic fireplace, built-in desk and 9-ft.-high tray ceiling. The private bath includes a whirlpool tub and a dual-sink vanity.
- Another full bath serves the remaining two bedrooms, one of which boasts a cathedral ceiling and a tall arched window.

Plan AHP-9300

Bedrooms: 3	Baths: 2
Living Area:	
Main floor	1,513 sq. ft.
Total Living Area:	**1,513 sq. ft.**
Standard basement	1,360 sq. ft.
Garage	400 sq. ft.
Exterior Wall Framing:	2x4 or 2x6

Foundation Options:

Standard basement
Crawlspace
Slab
(All plans can be built with your choice of foundation and framing. A generic conversion diagram is available. See order form.)

BLUEPRINT PRICE CODE: B

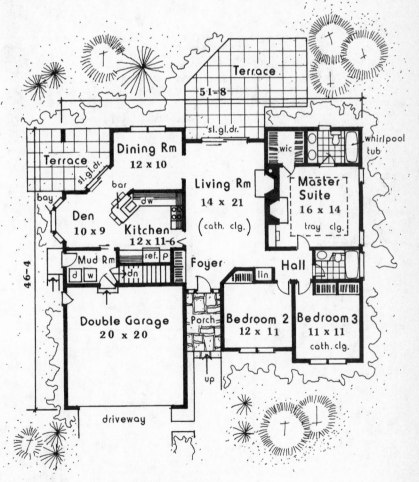

MAIN FLOOR

Romantic Retreat

- The romance and appeal of the Alpine chalet have remained constant over time. With more than 1,500 sq. ft. of living area, this chalet would make a great full-time home or vacation retreat.
- The L-shaped living room, dining room and kitchen flow together for casual living. This huge area is warmed by a freestanding fireplace and surrounded by an ornate deck, which is accessed through sliding glass doors.
- The main-level bedroom, with its twin closets and adjacent bath, could serve as a nice master suite.
- Upstairs, two large bedrooms share another full bath. One bedroom features a walk-in closet, while the other boasts its own private deck.
- The daylight basement offers laundry facilities, plenty of storage space and an extra-long garage.

Plan H-858-2	
Bedrooms: 3	Baths: 2
Living Area:	
Upper floor	576 sq. ft.
Main floor	960 sq. ft.
Total Living Area:	**1,536 sq. ft.**
Daylight basement	530 sq. ft.
Tuck-under garage	430 sq. ft.
Exterior Wall Framing:	2x6

Foundation Options:

Daylight basement
(All plans can be built with your choice of foundation and framing. A generic conversion diagram is available. See order form.)

BLUEPRINT PRICE CODE:	B

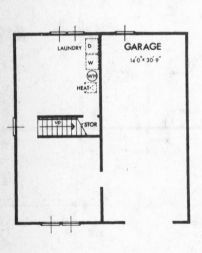

DAYLIGHT BASEMENT

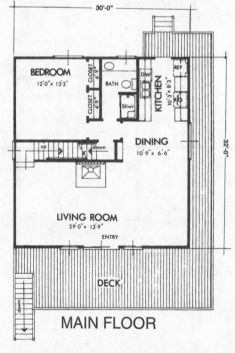

MAIN FLOOR

UPPER FLOOR

Plan H-858-2

PRICES AND DETAILS ON PAGES 12-15

Extra Sparkle

- A lovely front porch with a cameo front door, decorative posts, bay windows and dormers give this country-style home extra sparkle.
- The Great Room is at the center of the floor plan, where it merges with the dining room and the screened porch. The Great Room features a 10-ft. tray ceiling, a fireplace, a built-in wet bar and a wall of windows to the patio.
- The eat-in kitchen has a half-wall that keeps it open to the Great Room and hallway. The dining room offers a half-wall facing the foyer and a bay window overlooking the front porch.
- The delectable master suite is isolated from the other bedrooms and includes a charming bay window, a 10-ft. tray ceiling and a luxurious private bath.
- The two smaller bedrooms are off the main foyer and separated by a full bath.
- A mudroom with a washer and dryer is accessible from the two-car garage.

Plan AX-91312

Bedrooms: 3	Baths: 2
Space:	
Main floor	1,595 sq. ft.
Total Living Area	**1,595 sq. ft.**
Screened Porch	178 sq. ft.
Basement	1,595 sq. ft.
Garage, Storage and Utility	508 sq. ft.
Exterior Wall Framing	2x4

Foundation Options:

Daylight basement

Standard basement

Slab

(All plans can be built with your choice of foundation and framing. A generic conversion diagram is available. See order form.)

Blueprint Price Code	B

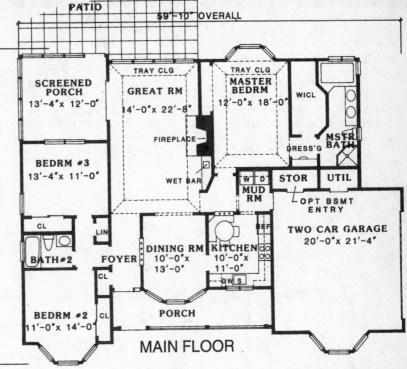

MAIN FLOOR

VIEW INTO GREAT ROOM

Rustic Comfort

- Rustic charm highlights the exterior of this design, while the interior is filled with all the latest comforts.
- The wide, covered porch opens to a roomy entry, where two 7-ft.-high openings with decorative railings view into the dining room.
- Straight ahead lies the sunken living room, which features a 16-ft.-high vaulted ceiling with exposed beams. The fireplace is faced with floor-to-ceiling fieldstone, adding to the rustic look. A rear door opens to a large patio with twin plant areas.

- The large U-shaped kitchen has such nice extras as a china niche with glass shelves. Other bonuses include the adjacent sewing/hobby room, the oversized utility room and the storage area and built-in workbench in the side-entry garage.
- The secluded master suite hosts a sunken sleeping area with built-in bookshelves. One step up is a cozy sitting area that is outlined by brick columns and a railed room divider. Double doors open to the deluxe bath, which offers a niche with glass shelves.
- Double doors conceal two more bedrooms and a full bath.

Plan E-1607

Bedrooms: 3	Baths: 2
Living Area:	
Main floor	1,600 sq. ft.
Total Living Area:	**1,600 sq. ft.**
Standard basement	1,600 sq. ft.
Garage	484 sq. ft.
Storage	132 sq. ft.
Exterior Wall Framing:	2x6

Foundation Options:
Standard basement
Crawlspace
Slab
(All plans can be built with your choice of foundation and framing. A generic conversion diagram is available. See order form.)

BLUEPRINT PRICE CODE: B

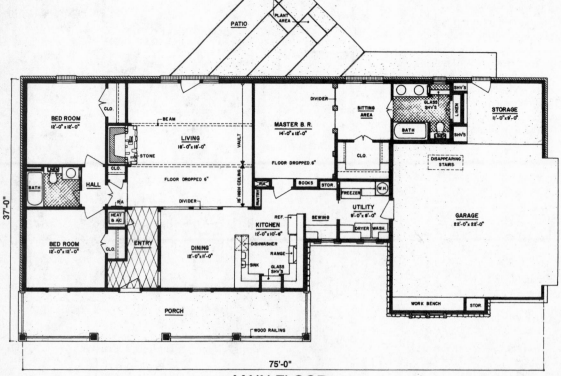

MAIN FLOOR

Plan E-1607

PRICES AND DETAILS ON PAGES 12-15

Photo courtesy of Breland & Farmer Designers, Inc.

Stylish and Compact

- This country-style home has a classic exterior and a space-saving and compact interior.
- A quaint covered porch extends along the front of the home. The oval-glassed front door opens to the entry, which leads to the spacious living room with a handsome fireplace, windows at either end and access to a big screened porch.
- The formal dining room flows from the living room and is easily served by the convenient U-shaped kitchen.
- A nice-sized laundry room and a full bath are nearby. The two-car garage offers a super storage area.
- The deluxe master suite features a huge walk-in closet. A separate dressing area leads to an adjoining, dual-access bath.
- The upper floor offers two more bedrooms and another full bath. Each bedroom has generous closet space and independent access to attic space.

Plan E-1626

Bedrooms: 3	Baths: 2
Living Area:	
Upper floor	464 sq. ft.
Main floor	1,136 sq. ft.
Total Living Area:	**1,600 sq. ft.**
Garage	462 sq. ft.
Exterior Wall Framing:	2x6

Foundation Options:

Crawlspace

Slab

(All plans can be built with your choice of foundation and framing. A generic conversion diagram is available. See order form.)

BLUEPRINT PRICE CODE:	**B**

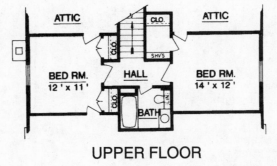

UPPER FLOOR

NOTE:
The above photographed home may have been modified by the homeowner. Please refer to floor plan and/or drawn elevation shown for actual blueprint details.

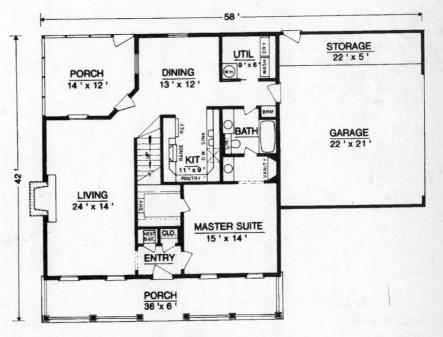

MAIN FLOOR

Photo by Mark Englund/HomeStyles

Luxury and Livability

- Big on style, this modest-sized home features a quaint Colonial exterior and an open interior.
- The covered front porch leads to a two-story foyer that opens to the formal living and dining rooms. A coat closet, an attractive display niche and a powder room are centrally located, as is the stairway to the upper floor.
- The kitchen, breakfast nook and family room are designed so that each room has its own definition yet also functions as part of a whole. The angled sink separates the kitchen from the breakfast nook, which is outlined by a bay window. The large family room includes a fireplace.
- The upper floor has an exceptional master suite, featuring an 8½-ft. tray ceiling in the sleeping area and an 11-ft. vaulted ceiling in the spa bath.
- Two more bedrooms and a balcony hall add to this home's luxury and livability.

Plan FB-1600

Bedrooms: 3	Baths: 2½
Living Area:	
Upper floor	772 sq. ft.
Main floor	828 sq. ft.
Total Living Area:	**1,600 sq. ft.**
Daylight basement	828 sq. ft.
Garage	473 sq. ft.
Exterior Wall Framing:	2x4

Foundation Options:

Daylight basement
Crawlspace
Slab

(All plans can be built with your choice of foundation and framing. A generic conversion diagram is available. See order form.)

BLUEPRINT PRICE CODE: **B**

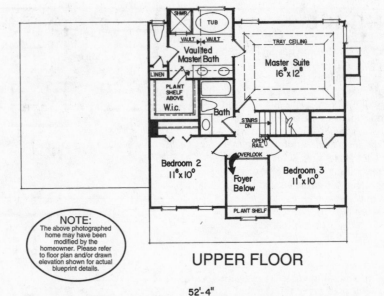

NOTE:
The above photographed home may have been modified by the homeowner. Please refer to floor plan and/or drawn elevation shown for actual blueprint details.

UPPER FLOOR

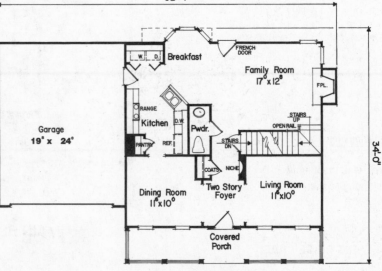

MAIN FLOOR

TO ORDER THIS BLUEPRINT, CALL TOLL-FREE 1-800-547-5570

Plan FB-1600

PRICES AND DETAILS ON PAGES 12-15

Tradition Updated

- The nostalgic exterior of this home gives way to dramatic cathedral ceilings and illuminating skylights inside.
- The covered front porch welcomes guests into the stone-tiled foyer, which flows into the living spaces.
- The living and dining rooms merge, forming a spacious, front-oriented entertaining area.

- A large three-sided fireplace situated between the living room and the family room may be enjoyed in both areas.
- The skylighted family room is also brightened by sliding glass doors that access a rear patio.
- The sunny island kitchen offers a nice breakfast nook and easy access to the laundry room and the garage.
- The master suite boasts a walk-in closet and a skylighted bath with a dual-sink vanity, a soaking tub and a separate shower. Two additional bedrooms share another full bath.

Plan AX-90303-A

Bedrooms: 3	Baths: 2
Living Area:	
Main floor	1,615 sq. ft.
Total Living Area:	**1,615 sq. ft.**
Basement	1,615 sq. ft.
Garage	412 sq. ft.
Exterior Wall Framing:	2x4

Foundation Options:

Daylight basement
Standard basement
Crawlspace
Slab
(All plans can be built with your choice of foundation and framing. A generic conversion diagram is available. See order form.)

BLUEPRINT PRICE CODE: B

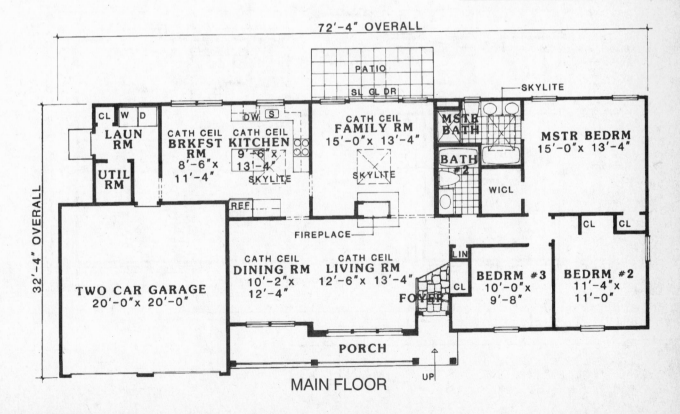

MAIN FLOOR

Friendly Country Charm

- An inviting front porch welcomes you to this friendly one-story home.
- The porch opens to a spacious central living room with a warm fireplace and functional built-in storage shelves.
- The bay window of the adjoining dining room allows a view of the backyard.

The dining area also enjoys an eating bar provided by the adjacent walk-through kitchen.
- The nice-sized kitchen also has a windowed sink and easy access to the laundry room and carport.
- Three bedrooms and two baths occupy the sleeping wing. The oversized master bedroom features a lovely boxed-out window, two walk-in closets and a private bath. The secondary bedrooms share the second full bath.

Plan J-8692	
Bedrooms: 3	**Baths:** 2
Living Area:	
Main floor	1,633 sq. ft.
Total Living Area:	**1,633 sq. ft.**
Standard basement	1,633 sq. ft.
Carport	380 sq. ft.
Exterior Wall Framing:	2x4

Foundation Options:

Standard basement
Crawlspace
Slab

(All plans can be built with your choice of foundation and framing. A generic conversion diagram is available. See order form.)

BLUEPRINT PRICE CODE:	B

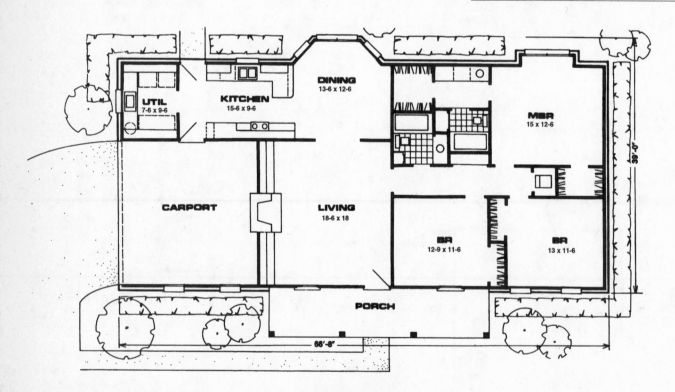

MAIN FLOOR

TO ORDER THIS BLUEPRINT, CALL TOLL-FREE 1-800-547-5570

Plan J-8692

PRICES AND DETAILS ON PAGES 12-15

Affordable Country Charm

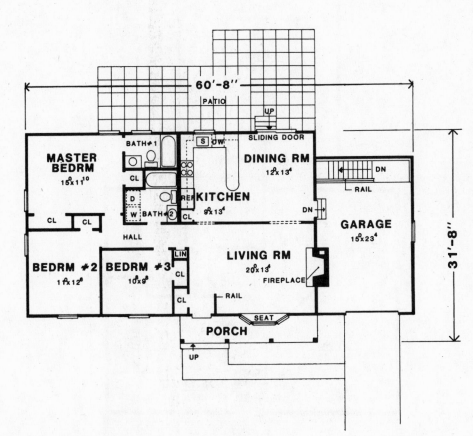

- A covered front porch, attached garage, and bay window add appeal to this efficient, affordable home.
- A spacious living room with fireplace and window seat offer plenty of family living space.
- The kitchen/dining room opens to a rear patio for indoor/outdoor living.
- The attached garage incorporates stairs for the optional basement.
- The plan includes three bedrooms and two baths on the same level, a plus for young families.

Plan AX-98602

Bedrooms: 3	Baths: 2

Space:	
Total living area:	1,253 sq. ft.
Basement:	1,253 sq. ft.
Garage:	368 sq. ft.

Exterior Wall Framing:	2x4

Foundation options:
Standard basement.
Slab.
(Foundation & framing conversion
diagram available — see order form.)

Blueprint Price Code:	A

Covered Porch
Invites Visitors

- This nice home welcomes visitors with its covered front porch and its wide-open living areas.
- Detailed columns, railings and shutters decorate the front porch that guides guests to the central entry.
- Just off the entry, the bright living room merges with the dining room. The side wall is lined with glass, including a glass door that opens to the yard.
- The angled kitchen features a serving counter facing the dining room. A handry laundry closet and access to a storage area and the garage is nearby.
- An angled hall leads to the bedroom wing. The master suite offers a private bath, a walk-in closet and a dressing area with a vanity. Two additional bedrooms and another full bath are located down the hall.

Plan E-1217

Bedrooms: 3	Baths: 2
Living Area:	
Main floor	1,266 sq. ft.
Total Living Area:	**1,266 sq. ft.**
Garage and storage	550 sq. ft.
Exterior Wall Framing:	2x6

Foundation Options:

Crawlspace
Slab
(All plans can be built with your choice of foundation and framing. A generic conversion diagram is available. See order form.)

BLUEPRINT PRICE CODE: **A**

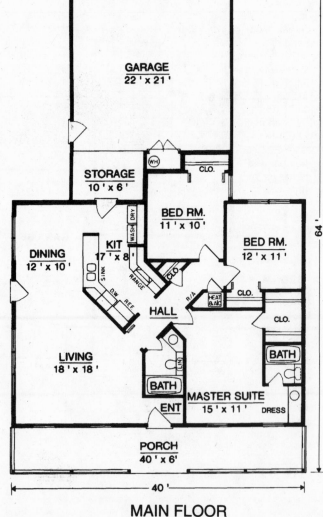

MAIN FLOOR

Plan E-1217

PRICES AND DETAILS
ON PAGES 12-15

Comfortable Ranch Design

- This affordable ranch design offers numerous amenities and is ideally structured for comfortable living, both indoors and out.
- A tiled reception hall leads into the spacious living and dining rooms, which feature a handsome brick fireplace, an 11-ft. sloped ceiling and two sets of sliding glass doors to access a lovely backyard terrace.
- The adjacent family room, designed for privacy, showcases a large boxed-out window with a built-in seat. The kitchen features an efficient U-shaped counter, an eating bar and a pantry.
- The master suite has its own terrace and private bath with a whirlpool tub.
- Two additional bedrooms share a second full bath.
- The garage has two separate storage areas—one accessible from the interior and the other from the backyard.

VIEW INTO LIVING ROOM AND DINING ROOM

Plan K-518-A

Bedrooms: 3	Baths: 2
Living Area:	
Main floor	1,276 sq. ft.
Total Living Area:	**1,276 sq. ft.**
Standard basement	1,247 sq. ft.
Garage and storage	579 sq. ft.
Exterior Wall Framing:	2x4 or 2x6

Foundation Options:
Standard basement
Slab
(All plans can be built with your choice of foundation and framing. A generic conversion diagram is available. See order form.)

BLUEPRINT PRICE CODE: A

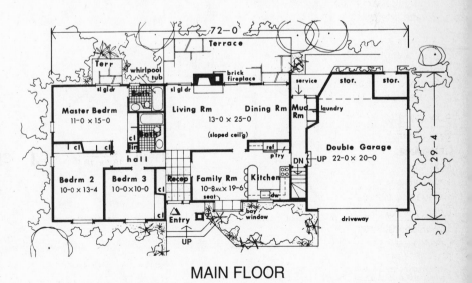

MAIN FLOOR

Angled Solar One-Story

- Captivating angles, solar efficiency and an open floor plan highlight this contemporary home.
- A covered entry leads into the reception area, which is dramatically brightened by a clerestory window.
- The spacious living room features a majestic sloped ceiling, an inviting high-efficiency fireplace and sliding glass doors to a backyard terrace.
- Glazed roof panels in the dining room capture the sun's warmth for winter heating, and adjustable shades promote summertime cooling.
- The kitchen features a generous angled counter, a skylight, a full pantry and a dinette area for family dining.
- The expansive master suite has its own private terrace and whirlpool bath.
- Two additional bedrooms share a second full bath.

Plan K-523-C

Bedrooms: 3	Baths: 2
Living Area:	
Main floor	1,285 sq. ft.
Total Living Area:	**1,285 sq. ft.**
Standard basement	1,264 sq. ft.
Garage and storage	477 sq. ft.
Exterior Wall Framing:	2x4 or 2x6

Foundation Options:
Standard basement
Slab
(All plans can be built with your choice of foundation and framing. A generic conversion diagram is available. See order form.)

BLUEPRINT PRICE CODE: A

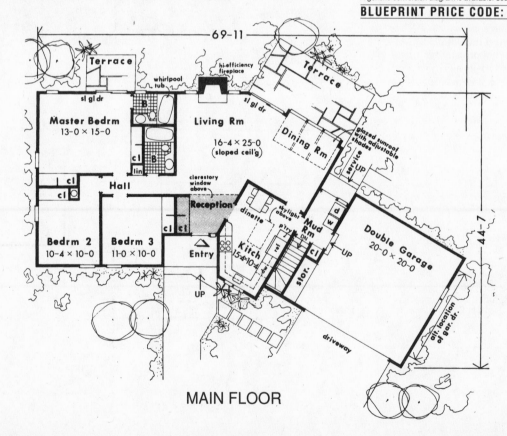

MAIN FLOOR

TO ORDER THIS BLUEPRINT, CALL TOLL-FREE 1-800-547-5570

Plan K-523-C

PRICES AND DETAILS ON PAGES 12-15

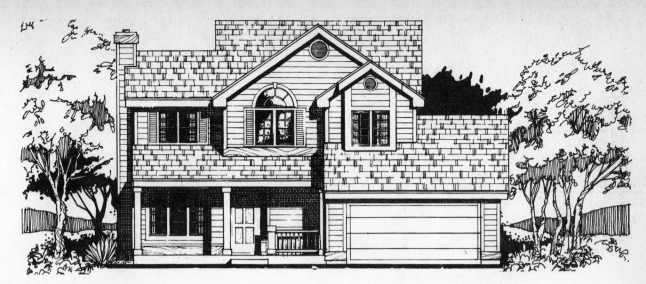

Fancy Country Styling

- With a covered front porch and gables above, this affordable two-story home fancies country styling.
- Off the lovely covered porch is a soaring entry, open to the upper level and featuring an angled stairway focal point.
- A large living area with a fireplace and a patio view adjoins the dining room, which opens to the outdoors.
- Convenient main-floor laundry facilities and a half-bath are located near the garage entrance.
- The upper level includes a master bedroom with a private bath, a walk-in closet and an 11-ft.-high vaulted ceiling. Another full bath with a dual-sink vanity serves the two secondary bedrooms.

Plan AG-1201

Bedrooms: 3	Baths: 2½
Living Area:	
Upper floor	668 sq. ft.
Main floor	620 sq. ft.
Total Living Area:	**1,288 sq. ft.**
Standard basement	620 sq. ft.
Garage	420 sq. ft.
Exterior Wall Framing:	2x4

Foundation Options:

Standard basement
(All plans can be built with your choice of foundation and framing. A generic conversion diagram is available. See order form.)

BLUEPRINT PRICE CODE:	**A**

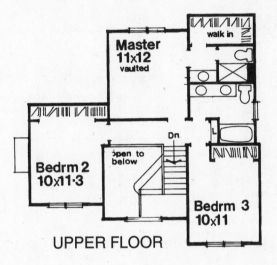

UPPER FLOOR

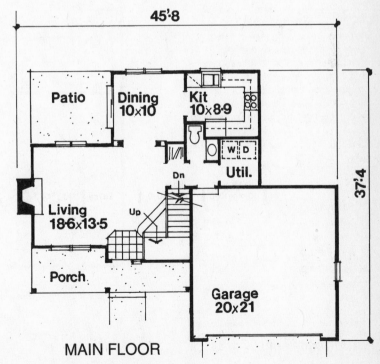

MAIN FLOOR

Eye-Catching Details

- This eye-catching home features a handsome exterior and an exciting floor plan that maximizes square footage.
- The covered porch leads into a vaulted foyer with an angled coat closet. Straight ahead, the 16½-ft.-high vaulted Great Room combines with the dining room and kitchen to create one expansive living and entertaining area.
- The Great Room offers a fireplace and access to the backyard. The galley-style kitchen has a 16½-ft.-high ceiling and is bordered by the vaulted dining room on one side and a breakfast area with a laundry closet on the other.
- The master suite boasts a 15-ft., 8-in. tray ceiling. The 13-ft.-high vaulted bath has a garden tub, a separate shower and a vanity with knee space.
- The two remaining bedrooms are located on the opposite side of the home and share a full bath. A plant shelf is an attention-getting detail found here.

Plan FB-1289

Bedrooms: 3	Baths: 2
Living Area:	
Main floor	1,289 sq. ft.
Total Living Area:	**1,289 sq. ft.**
Daylight basement	1,289 sq. ft.
Garage	430 sq. ft.
Exterior Wall Framing:	2x4

Foundation Options:
Daylight basement
Crawlspace
Slab
(All plans can be built with your choice of foundation and framing. A generic conversion diagram is available. See order form.)

BLUEPRINT PRICE CODE: **A**

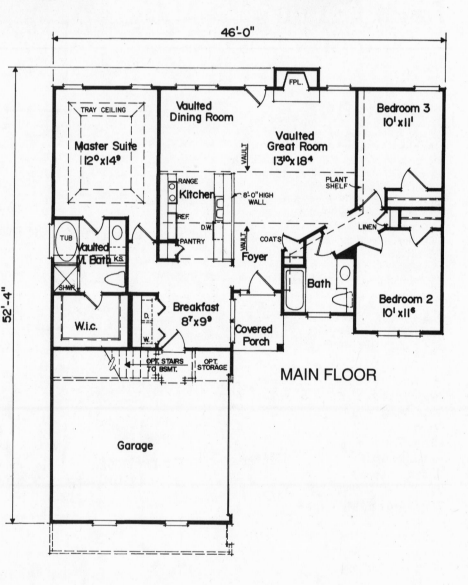

MAIN FLOOR

46'-0"

52'-4"

TRAY CEILING
Master Suite 12⁰x14⁹
Vaulted Dining Room
Vaulted Great Room 13¹⁰x18⁴
Bedroom 3 10'x11'
RANGE
Kitchen
8'-0" HIGH WALL
REF.
D.W.
PLANT SHELF
LINEN
TUB
Vaulted M. Bath
K.S.
PANTRY
VAULT
COATS
Foyer
Bath
SHMR
W.i.c.
Breakfast 8⁷x9⁹
Covered Porch
Bedroom 2 10'x11⁶
OPT. STAIRS TO BSMT.
OPT. STORAGE
Garage

Simple and Balanced

- Balanced living and sleeping areas are found in this quaint, country ranch.
- Overlooking the front covered porch through a bay window are the living and dining rooms, with fireplace, snack counter and adjoining covered deck at the rear.
- The open kitchen has a view of both rooms, as well as the deck; convenient laundry facilities are just steps away.
- The master bedroom, secluded to the rear, has a walk-in closet, separate dressing area and private deck access.
- Two additional bedrooms share a second bath.

Plan NW-258

Bedrooms: 3	Baths: 2
Space:	
Main floor	1,289 sq. ft.
Total Living Area	**1,289 sq. ft.**
Garage	430 sq. ft.
Exterior Wall Framing	2x6

Foundation options:

Crawlspace
(Foundation & framing conversion diagram available—see order form.)

Blueprint Price Code	**A**

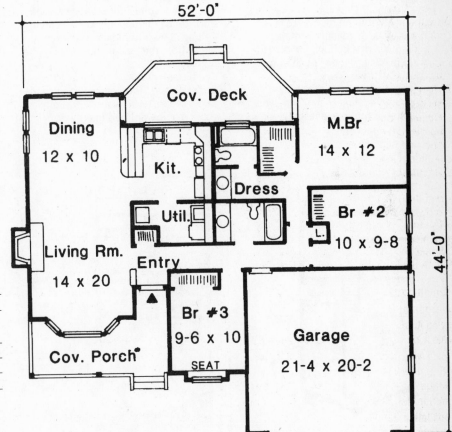

A Chalet for Today

- With its wraparound deck and soaring windows, this chalet-style home is ideal for recreational living and scenic sites.
- The living and dining rooms are combined to take advantage of the dramatic cathedral ceiling, the rugged stone fireplace and the view through the spectacular windows.
- A quaint balcony above adds to the warm country feeling of the living area, which extends to the expansive deck.

- The open kitchen features a bright corner sink and a nifty breakfast bar that adjoins the living area.
- The handy main-floor laundry area is close to two bedrooms and a full bath.
- The study is a feature rarely found in a home of this size and style.
- The master suite and a storage area encompass the upper floor. A cathedral ceiling, a whirlpool bath and sweeping views from the balcony give this space an elegant feel.
- The basement option includes a tuck-under garage, additional storage space and a separate utility area. A family room may be finished later.

Plan AHP-9340

Bedrooms: 3+	Baths: 2
Living Area:	
Upper floor	332 sq. ft.
Main floor	974 sq. ft.
Total Living Area:	**1,306 sq. ft.**
Basement	624 sq. ft.
Tuck-under garage	350 sq. ft.
Exterior Wall Framing:	2x4 or 2x6

Foundation Options:
Standard basement
Daylight basement
Crawlspace
Slab
(All plans can be built with your choice of foundation and framing. A generic conversion diagram is available. See order form.)

BLUEPRINT PRICE CODE:	A

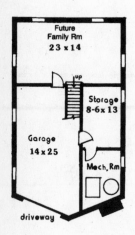

BASEMENT

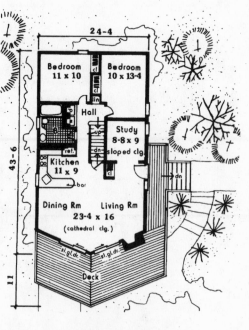

MAIN FLOOR

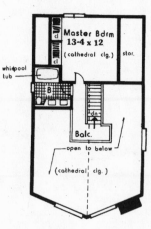

UPPER FLOOR

Intriguing Great Room

- The focal point of this open, economical home is its comfortable Great Room and dining area. An inviting fireplace, a dramatic arched window and a 13-ft. vaulted ceiling spark conversation.
- The roomy kitchen incorporates a sunny breakfast room with a 10-ft. vaulted ceiling. Sliding glass doors open to the backyard deck. The kitchen also has a pantry and a handy pass-through to the dining room.
- The bedroom wing includes a lovely master suite and two secondary bedrooms. The master suite boasts a private bath with a separate tub and shower, while the secondary bedrooms share another full bath.
- The washer and dryer are conveniently located near the bedroom wing and the entrance from the garage.

Plan B-90008

Bedrooms: 3	Baths: 2
Living Area:	
Main floor	1,325 sq. ft.
Total Living Area:	**1,325 sq. ft.**
Standard basement	1,325 sq. ft.
Garage	390 sq. ft.
Exterior Wall Framing:	2x6

Foundation Options:

Standard basement

(All plans can be built with your choice of foundation and framing. A generic conversion diagram is available. See order form.)

BLUEPRINT PRICE CODE:	**A**

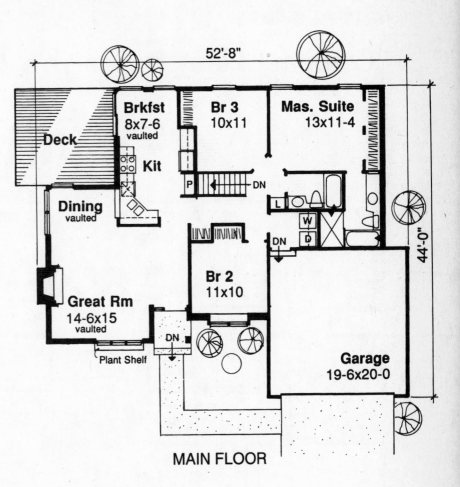

MAIN FLOOR

FRONT VIEW

Compact Plan Fits Narrow Building Site

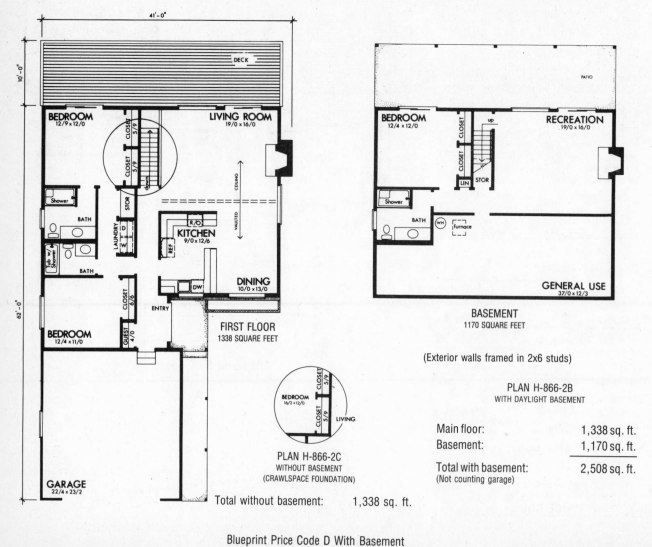

41'-0"

10'-0"

DECK

BEDROOM
12/9 x 12/0

CLOSET 5/9
CLOSET 5/9

LIVING ROOM
19/0 x 16/0

Shower

STOR

down

CEILING

VAULTED

BATH

LAUNDRY
D
W

R/O

KITCHEN
9/0 x 12/6

REF

Tub w/ Shower

BATH

CLOSET 5/6

DW

DINING
10/0 x 13/0

GUEST 4/0

ENTRY

BEDROOM
12/4 x 11/0

62'-0"

FIRST FLOOR
1338 SQUARE FEET

GARAGE
22/4 x 23/2

BEDROOM
12/4 x 12/0

CLOSET
CLOSET

up

RECREATION
19/0 x 16/0

PATIO

LIN STOR

Shower

BATH

WH

furnace

GENERAL USE
37/0 x 12/3

BASEMENT
1170 SQUARE FEET

(Exterior walls framed in 2x6 studs)

PLAN H-866-2B
WITH DAYLIGHT BASEMENT

Main floor:	1,338 sq. ft.
Basement:	1,170 sq. ft.
Total with basement: (Not counting garage)	2,508 sq. ft.

BEDROOM
16/2 x 12/0

CLOSET 5/9
CLOSET 5/9

LIVING

PLAN H-866-2C
WITHOUT BASEMENT
(CRAWLSPACE FOUNDATION)

Total without basement: 1,338 sq. ft.

Blueprint Price Code D With Basement
Blueprint Price Code A Without Basement

**TO ORDER THIS BLUEPRINT,
CALL TOLL-FREE 1-800-547-5570**

Plans H-866-2B & -2C

**PRICES AND DETAILS
ON PAGES 12-15**

High-Profile Contemporary

- This design does away with wasted space, putting the emphasis on quality rather than on size.
- The angled floor plan minimizes hall space and creates smooth traffic flow while adding architectural appeal. The roof framing is square, however, to allow for economical construction.
- The spectacular living and dining rooms share a 16-ft. cathedral ceiling and a fireplace. Both rooms have lots of glass overlooking an angled rear terrace.
- The dining room includes a glass-filled alcove and sliding patio doors topped by transom windows. Tall windows frame the living room fireplace and trace the slope of the ceiling.
- A pass-through joins the dining room to the combination kitchen and family room, which features a snack bar and a clerestory window.
- The sleeping wing provides a super master suite, which boasts a skylighted dressing area and a luxurious bath. The optional den, or third bedroom, shares a second full bath with another bedroom that offers a 14-ft. sloped ceiling.

Plan K-688-D

Bedrooms: 2+	Baths: 2½
Living Area:	
Main floor	1,340 sq. ft.
Total Living Area:	**1,340 sq. ft.**
Standard basement	1,235 sq. ft.
Garage	484 sq. ft.
Exterior Wall Framing:	2x4 or 2x6

Foundation Options:

Standard basement

Slab

(All plans can be built with your choice of foundation and framing. A generic conversion diagram is available. See order form.)

BLUEPRINT PRICE CODE: A

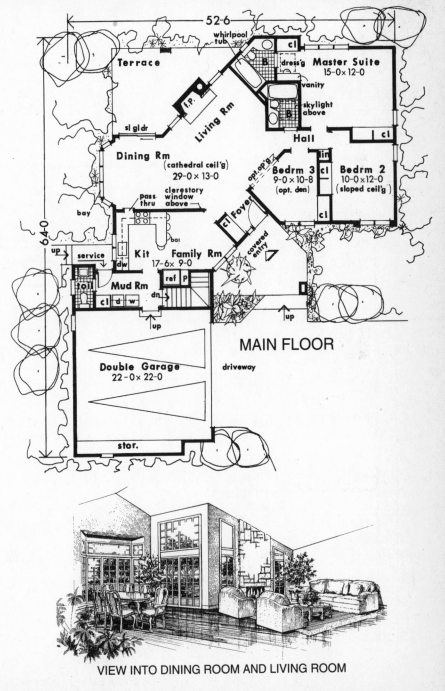

MAIN FLOOR

VIEW INTO DINING ROOM AND LIVING ROOM

Maximum Livability

- Compact and easy to build, this appealing ranch-style home is big on charm and livability.
- The entry of the home opens to a dramatic 13-ft. vaulted living room with exposed beams, a handsome fireplace and access to a backyard patio.
- Wood post dividers set off the large raised dining room, which is brightened by a stunning window wall.
- The adjoining kitchen offers a spacious snack bar and easy access to the utility room and the two-car garage. A nice storage area is also included.
- Three bedrooms and two baths occupy the sleeping wing. One of the baths is private to the master suite, which features a walk-in closet and a dressing area with a sit-down make-up table. The two remaining bedrooms also have walk-in closets.

Plan E-1305

Bedrooms: 3	Baths: 2
Living Area:	
Main floor	1,346 sq. ft.
Total Living Area:	**1,346 sq. ft.**
Garage	441 sq. ft.
Storage	44 sq. ft.
Exterior Wall Framing:	2x4

Foundation Options:

Crawlspace

Slab

(All plans can be built with your choice of foundation and framing. A generic conversion diagram is available. See order form.)

BLUEPRINT PRICE CODE: A

MAIN FLOOR

TO ORDER THIS BLUEPRINT, CALL TOLL-FREE 1-800-547-5570

Plan E-1305

PRICES AND DETAILS ON PAGES 12-15

Roomy One-Story Home

- Economical to build and maintain, this home includes many luxurious features.
- The large living room includes a massive fireplace and a beamed, vaulted ceiling, and visually flows into the raised dining room. A French door provides access to an inviting patio.
- The U-shaped kitchen offers a windowed sink and an adjoining utility room with a washer and dryer.
- The master suite features a large walk-in closet and a private bath.
- The two secondary bedrooms also have walk-in closets and share a hall bath.

Plan E-1307

Bedrooms: 3	Baths: 2
Living Area:	
Main floor	1,346 sq. ft.
Total Living Area:	**1,346 sq. ft.**
Garage	441 sq. ft.
Storage & utility	88 sq. ft.
Exterior Wall Framing:	2x4

Foundation Options:

Crawlspace

Slab

(All plans can be built with your choice of foundation and framing. A generic conversion diagram is available. See order form.)

BLUEPRINT PRICE CODE: **A**

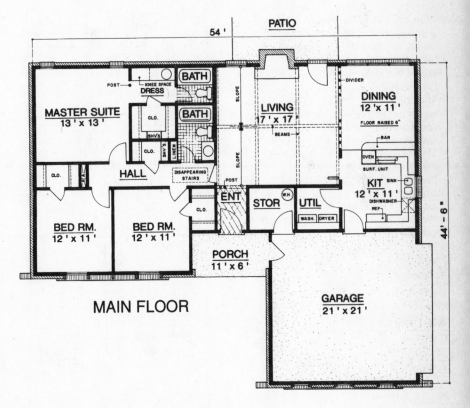

MAIN FLOOR

Spacious Swiss Chalet

- Three decks, lots of views and Swiss styling make this three-bedroom chalet the perfect design for that special site.
- A stone-faced fireplace is the focal point of the huge central living area. Sliding glass doors between the living room and the dining room lead to the large main-level deck. The space-saving kitchen conveniently serves the entire entertaining area.
- The main-floor bedroom is close to a full bath. The oversized laundry room doubles as a mudroom.
- Upstairs, each of the two bedrooms has a sloped ceiling, accessible attic storage space and a private deck.
- The optional daylight basement provides space for utilities as well as the opportunity for expansion. In the crawlspace version of the design, the furnace and water heater are located in the laundry room.

Plans H-755-5E & -6E

Bedrooms: 3	Baths: 2
Living Area:	
Upper floor	454 sq. ft.
Main floor	896 sq. ft.
Daylight basement	896 sq. ft.
Total Living Area:	**1,350/2,246 sq. ft.**
Exterior Wall Framing:	2x4
Foundation Options:	**Plan #**
Daylight basement	H-755-6E
Crawlspace	H-755-5E

(All plans can be built with your choice of foundation and framing. A generic conversion diagram is available. See order form.)

BLUEPRINT PRICE CODE:	**A/C**

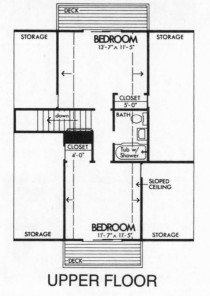

UPPER FLOOR

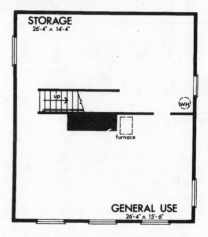

DAYLIGHT BASEMENT

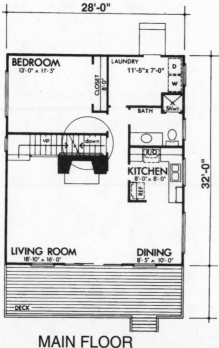

MAIN FLOOR

STAIRWAY AREA IN CRAWLSPACE VERSION

Plans H-755-5E & -6E

PRICES AND DETAILS ON PAGES 12-15

Striking
Stone Chimney

- With tall windows and a rustic stone chimney, the striking facade of this home demands attention.
- The sheltered entry leads into a raised foyer, which steps down to the sunny living room and its dramatic 16-ft. vaulted ceiling.
- A handsome fireplace warms the living room and the adjoining dining room, which offers access to an inviting deck.
- A cozy breakfast nook is included in the efficient, open-design kitchen. A special feature is the convenient pass-through to the dining room.
- A skylighted staircase leads upstairs to the master suite, with its private bath and large walk-in closet.
- A second bedroom shares another full bath with a loft or third bedroom.
- A dramatic balcony overlooks the living room below.

Plan B-224-8512

Bedrooms: 2+	Baths: 2½
Living Area:	
Upper floor	691 sq. ft.
Main floor	668 sq. ft.
Total Living Area:	**1,359 sq. ft.**
Standard basement	668 sq. ft.
Garage	458 sq. ft.
Exterior Wall Framing:	2x4

Foundation Options:

Standard basement
(All plans can be built with your choice of foundation and framing. A generic conversion diagram is available. See order form.)

BLUEPRINT PRICE CODE:	**A**

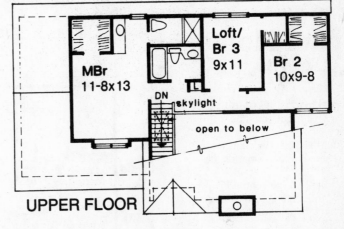

UPPER FLOOR

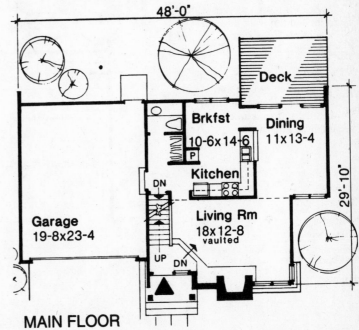

MAIN FLOOR

Compact Home Big on Style

- While compact in size, this stylish one-story offers lots of room and little wasted space.
- Staggered rooflines, brick accents and beautiful arched windows smarten the exterior.
- The interior offers a large central living room with a 10-ft. ceiling, a warming fireplace flanked by windows and an adjoining patio.
- The spacious breakfast area merges with the living room and the walk-through kitchen. The formal dining room is located on the opposite end of the kitchen.
- Separated from the other two bedrooms, the master suite is both private and spacious. It offers its own garden bath with twin vanities and walk-in closets, plus a separate tub and shower.

DD-1296

Bedrooms: 3	**Baths:** 2

Space:	
Main floor	1,364 sq. ft.
Total Living Area	**1,364 sq. ft.**
Standard basement	1,364 sq. ft.
Garage	443 sq. ft.
Exterior Wall Framing	2x4

Foundation options:
Standard Basement
Crawlspace
Slab
(Foundation & framing conversion diagram available—see order form.)

Blueprint Price Code	**A**

All in One!

- This plan puts all of today's most luxurious home-design features into one attractive, economical package.
- The covered front porch and the gabled roofline, accented by an arched window and a round louver vent, give the exterior a homey yet stylish appeal.
- Just inside the front door, the ceiling rises up to 11 ft., making an impressive greeting. A skylight and French doors framing the fireplace flood the living room with light.
- The living room flows into a nice-sized dining room, also with an 11-ft. ceiling, which in turn leads to the large eat-in kitchen. Here you'll find lots of counter space, a handy laundry closet and a eating area that opens to a terrace.
- The bedroom wing includes a wonderful master suite, with a sizable sleeping area and a dressing area with two closets. Glass blocks above the dual-sink vanity let in light yet maintain privacy. A whirlpool tub and a separate shower complete the suite.
- The larger of the two remaining bedrooms boasts an 11-ft.-high ceiling and an arched window.

Plan HFL-1680-FL

Bedrooms: 3	Baths: 2
Living Area:	
Main floor	1,367 sq. ft.
Total Living Area:	**1,367 sq. ft.**
Standard basement	1,367 sq. ft.
Garage	431 sq. ft.
Exterior Wall Framing:	2x6

Foundation Options:

Standard basement

(All plans can be built with your choice of foundation and framing. A generic conversion diagram is available. See order form.)

BLUEPRINT PRICE CODE: A

VIEW INTO LIVING ROOM

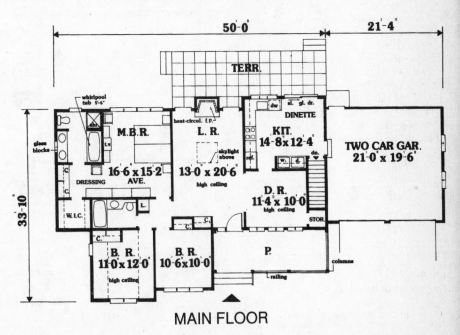

MAIN FLOOR

Inviting
Windows

- This comfortable home presents an impressive facade, with its large and inviting front window arrangement.
- A step down from the front entry, the Great Room boasts a 12-ft. vaulted ceiling with a barrel-vaulted area that outlines the half-round front window. The striking angled fireplace can be enjoyed from the adjoining dining area.
- The galley-style kitchen hosts a half-round cutout above the sink and a breakfast area that accesses a backyard deck and patio. The kitchen, breakfast area and dining area also are enhanced by 12-ft. vaulted ceilings.
- The master bedroom features a boxed-out window, a walk-in closet and a ceiling that vaults to 12 feet. The private bath includes a garden tub, a separate shower and a private toilet compartment.
- Another full bath serves the two remaining bedrooms, one of which has sliding glass doors to the deck and would make an ideal den.

Plan B-902

Bedrooms: 2+	Baths: 2
Living Area:	
Main floor	1,368 sq. ft.
Total Living Area:	**1,368 sq. ft.**
Standard basement	1,368 sq. ft.
Garage	412 sq. ft.
Exterior Wall Framing:	2x4

Foundation Options:

Standard basement

(All plans can be built with your choice of foundation and framing. A generic conversion diagram is available. See order form.)

BLUEPRINT PRICE CODE: A

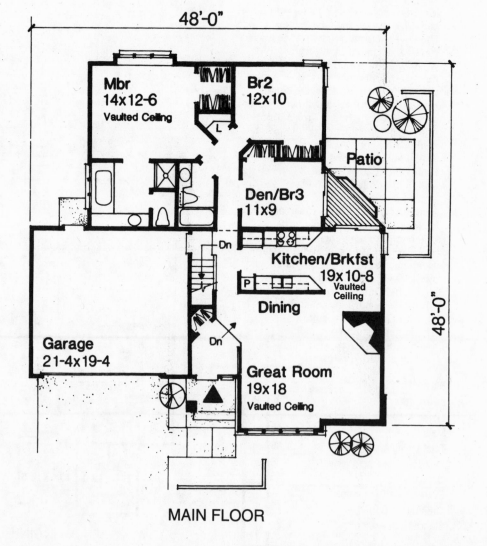

48'-0"

48'-0"

Mbr 14x12-6 Vaulted Ceiling

Br2 12x10

L

Patio

Den/Br3 11x9

Dn

Kitchen/Brkfst 19x10-8 Vaulted Ceiling

P

Dining

Dn

Garage 21-4x19-4

Great Room 19x18 Vaulted Ceiling

MAIN FLOOR

Family-Style Leisure Living

- This handsome ranch-style home features a floor plan that is great for family living and entertaining.
- In from the quaint covered porch, the spacious formal areas flow together for a dramatic impact. The living room is enhanced by a fireplace and a sloped ceiling. A patio door in the dining room extends activities to the outdoors.
- The efficient U-shaped kitchen opens to the dining room and offers a pantry, a

window above the sink and abundant counter space.
- A good-sized utility room with convenient laundry facilities opens to the carport. This area also includes a large storage room and disappearing stairs to even more storage space.
- Three bedrooms and two baths occupy the sleeping wing. The master suite features a large walk-in closet and a private bath.
- The two remaining bedrooms are well proportioned and share a hall bath. Storage space is well accounted for here as well, with two linen closets and a coat closet in the bedroom hall.

Plan E-1308	
Bedrooms: 3	**Baths:** 2
Living Area:	
Main floor	1,375 sq. ft.
Total Living Area:	**1,375 sq. ft.**
Carport	430 sq. ft.
Storage	95 sq. ft.
Exterior Wall Framing:	2x4

Foundation Options:
Crawlspace
Slab
(All plans can be built with your choice of foundation and framing. A generic conversion diagram is available. See order form.)

BLUEPRINT PRICE CODE: A

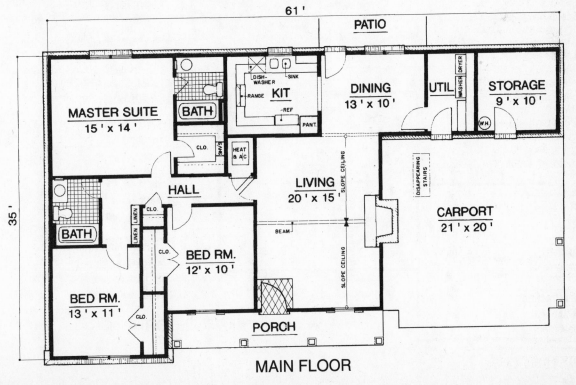

MAIN FLOOR

MASTER BEDROOM
13' × 11'4"

BEDROOM 3
12'8" × 10'4"

Bedroom 2
11'8" × 12'

UPPER FLOOR

48'-0"

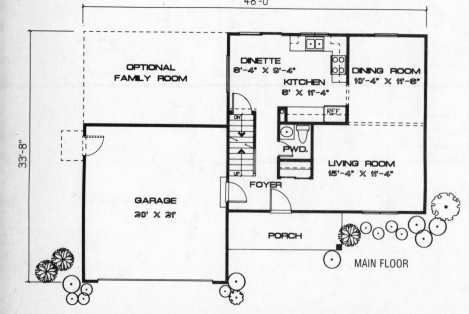

OPTIONAL
FAMILY ROOM

DINETTE
8'-4" × 9'-4"

KITCHEN
8' × 11'-4"

DINING ROOM
10'-4" × 11'-8"

DN

REF.

PWD.

UP

LIVING ROOM
15'-4" × 11'-4"

FOYER

33'-8"

GARAGE
20' × 21'

PORCH

MAIN FLOOR

Stylish
Two-Story

- This two-story home boasts contemporary and traditional elements.
- The open main floor offers a large front living room and attached dining room.
- A sunny breakfast dinette with sliders joins a functional kitchen with plenty of counter space.
- A family room bordered by the dinette and garage may be added later. The blueprints do not show the family room.
- Three nice-sized bedrooms occupy the upper level.

Plan GL-1382

Bedrooms: 3		**Baths:** 2 ½
Space:		
Upper floor		710 sq. ft.
Main floor		672 sq. ft.
Total Living Area		**1,382 sq. ft.**
Basement		672 sq. ft.
Garage		420 sq. ft.
Exterior Wall Framing		2x6
Foundation options:		
Standard Basement		
(Foundation & framing conversion diagram available—see order form.)		
Blueprint Price Code		A

Plan GL-1382

PRICES AND DETAILS
ON PAGES 12-15

Stylish Exterior, Open Floor Plan

- With its simple yet stylish exterior, this modest-sized design is suitable for country or urban settings.
- A covered front porch and a gabled roof extension accent the facade while providing plenty of sheltered space for outdoor relaxation.
- Inside, the open floor plan puts available space to efficient use.
- The living room, which offers an inviting fireplace, is expanded by a cathedral ceiling. The adjoining dining area is open to the island kitchen, and all three rooms combine to create one huge gathering place.
- The master suite features a private bath and a large walk-in closet.
- Two more good-sized bedrooms share a second full bath.
- A convenient utility area leads to the carport, which incorporates extra storage space.

Plan J-86155

Bedrooms: 3	Baths: 2
Living Area:	
Main floor	1,385 sq. ft.
Total Living Area:	**1,385 sq. ft.**
Standard basement	1,385 sq. ft.
Carport	380 sq. ft.
Exterior Wall Framing:	2x4

Foundation Options:

Standard basement
Crawlspace
Slab

(All plans can be built with your choice of foundation and framing. A generic conversion diagram is available. See order form.)

BLUEPRINT PRICE CODE: A

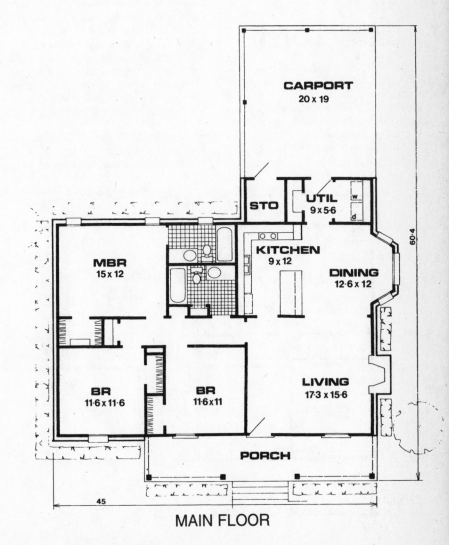

MAIN FLOOR

Inviting Country Porch

- A columned porch with double doors invites you into the rustic living areas of this ranch-style home.
- Inside, the entry allows views back to the expansive, central living room and the backyard beyond.
- The living room boasts an exposed-beam ceiling and a massive fireplace with a wide stone hearth, a wood box and built-in bookshelves. A sunny patio offers additional entertaining space.
- The dining room and the efficient kitchen combine for easy meal service, with a serving bar separating the two.
- The main hallway leads to the sleeping wing, which offers a large master bedroom with a walk-in closet and a private bath.
- Two additional bedrooms share another full bath, and a laundry closet is accessible to the entire bedroom wing.

Plan E-1304

Bedrooms: 3	**Baths:** 2

Living Area:	
Main floor	1,395 sq. ft.
Total Living Area:	**1,395 sq. ft.**
Garage & storage	481 sq. ft.
Exterior Wall Framing:	2x4

Foundation Options:

Crawlspace
Slab
(All plans can be built with your choice of foundation and framing. A generic conversion diagram is available. See order form.)

BLUEPRINT PRICE CODE: **A**

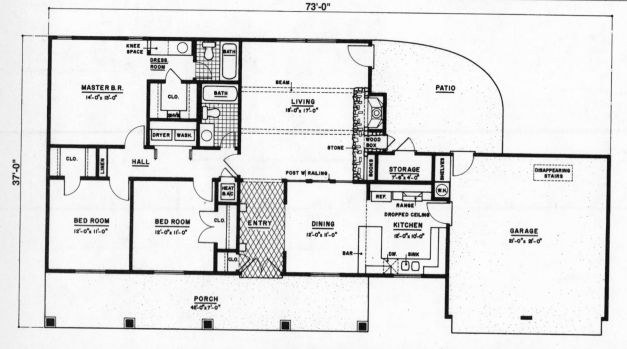

MAIN FLOOR

TO ORDER THIS BLUEPRINT,
CALL TOLL-FREE 1-800-547-5570

Plan E-1304

PRICES AND DETAILS
ON P...ES 12-15

Vacation Home with Views

- The octagonal shape and window-filled walls of this home create a powerful interior packed with panoramic views.
- Straight back from the angled entry, the Great Room is brightened by expansive windows and sliding glass doors to a huge wraparound deck. An impressive spiral staircase at the center of the floor plan lends even more character.
- The walk-through kitchen offers a handy pantry. A nice storage closet and a coat closet are located between the entry and the two-car garage.
- The main-floor bedroom is conveniently located near a full bath.
- The upper-floor master suite is a sanctuary, featuring lots of glass, a walk-in closet, a private bath and access to concealed storage rooms.
- The optional daylight basement offers an extra bedroom, a full bath, a laundry area and a large recreation room.

Plans H-964-1A & -1B

Bedrooms: 2+	Baths: 2-3
Living Area:	
Upper floor	346 sq. ft.
Main floor	1,067 sq. ft.
Daylight basement	1,045 sq. ft.
Total Living Area:	**1,413/2,458 sq. ft.**
Garage	512 sq. ft.
Storage (upper floor)	134 sq. ft.
Exterior Wall Framing:	2x6
Foundation Options:	**Plan #**
Daylight basement	H-964-1B
Crawlspace	H-964-1A

(All plans can be built with your choice of foundation and framing. A generic conversion diagram is available. See order form.)

BLUEPRINT PRICE CODE:	**A/C**

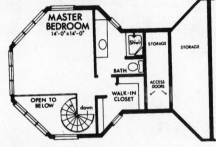

UPPER FLOOR

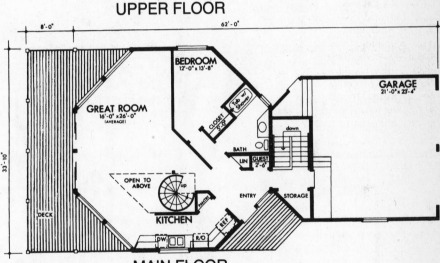

MAIN FLOOR

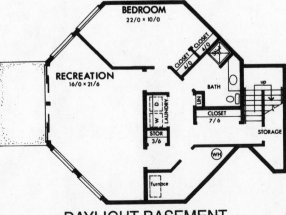

DAYLIGHT BASEMENT

One-Story with Dimension

- An eye-catching front window and half-hipped roofs add dimension to this feature-filled one-story.
- The covered entry opens to a tiled foyer, where the living and dining rooms merge to the left.
- The living room showcases a lovely window seat set into a 10-ft.-high vaulted alcove that is topped by a half-round transom. The dining room includes an angled china niche.
- The open kitchen faces a sunny nook with a bay window and access to a backyard patio. The cooktop island has a snack bar that easily services the adjoining family room, where a corner woodstove warms the entire area.
- Double doors open to the elegant master suite, which boasts a split bath with a skylighted dressing area.
- A second full bath serves the two remaining bedrooms.

Plan R-1063

Bedrooms: 3	Baths: 2
Living Area:	
Main floor	1,585 sq. ft.
Total Living Area:	**1,585 sq. ft.**
Garage	408 sq. ft.
Exterior Wall Framing:	2x6

Foundation Options:

Crawlspace
(All plans can be built with your choice of foundation and framing. A generic conversion diagram is available. See order form.)

BLUEPRINT PRICE CODE: B

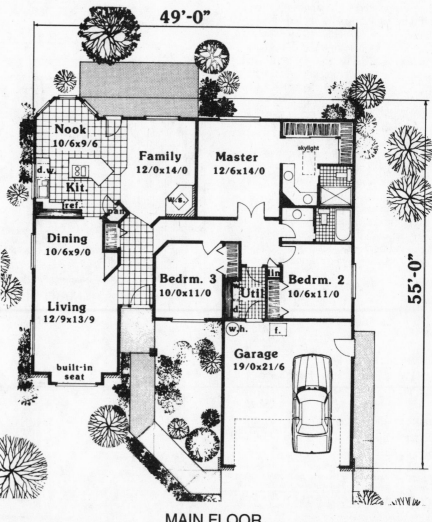

MAIN FLOOR

49'-0"

55'-0"

Nook 10/6x9/6

Family 12/0x14/0

Master 12/6x14/0

skylight

d.w.

Kit.

ref.

pan

w.s.

Dining 10/6x9/0

Living 12/9x13/9

Bedrm. 3 10/0x11/0

Util.

Bedrm. 2 10/6x11/0

w.h.

f.

Garage 19/0x21/6

built-in seat

Plan R-1063

PRICES AND DETAILS ON PAGES 12-15

Charming Traditional

- The attractive facade of this traditional home features decorative fretwork and louvers in the gables, plus eye-catching window and door treatments.
- The entry area features a commanding view of the living room, which boasts a 12½-ft. ceiling and a corner fireplace. A rear porch and patio are visible through French doors.
- The bayed dining room shares an eating bar with the U-shaped kitchen. The nearby utility room includes a pantry and laundry facilities.
- The quiet master suite includes a big walk-in closet and a private bath with a dual-sink vanity.
- On the other side of the home, double doors close off the two secondary bedrooms from the living areas. A full bath services this wing.

Plan E-1428

Bedrooms: 3	Baths: 2
Living Area:	
Main floor	1,415 sq. ft.
Total Living Area:	**1,415 sq. ft.**
Garage	484 sq. ft.
Storage	60 sq. ft.
Exterior Wall Framing:	2x6

Foundation Options:

Crawlspace
Slab

(All plans can be built with your choice of foundation and framing. A generic conversion diagram is available. See order form.)

BLUEPRINT PRICE CODE: A

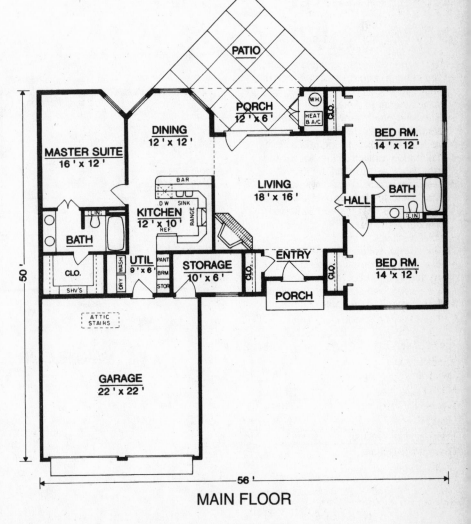

MAIN FLOOR

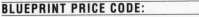

Rustic Ranch-Style Design

- This ranch-style home offers a rustic facade that is warm and inviting. The railed front porch and stone accents are especially appealing.
- The interior is warm as well, with the focal point being the attractive living room. Features here include an eye-catching fireplace, patio access and a dramatic 14-ft. sloped ceiling with exposed beams.
- The open dining room lies off the foyer and adjoins the efficient U-shaped kitchen, which includes a pantry and a broom closet.
- The master suite features a large walk-in closet and a roomy master bath.
- At the other end of the home, two secondary bedrooms with abundant closet space share another full bath.

Plan E-1410

Bedrooms: 3	Baths: 2
Living Area:	
Main floor	1,418 sq. ft.
Total Living Area:	**1,418 sq. ft.**
Garage	484 sq. ft.
Storage	38 sq. ft.
Exterior Wall Framing:	2x4

Foundation Options:

Crawlspace

Slab

(All plans can be built with your choice of foundation and framing. A generic conversion diagram is available. See order form.)

BLUEPRINT PRICE CODE: A

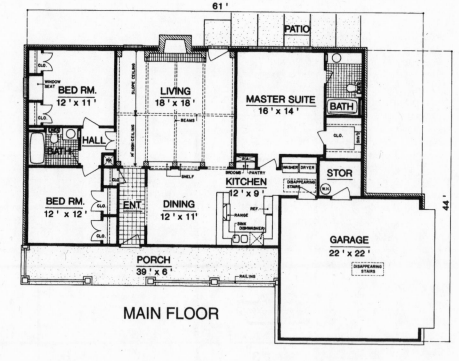

MAIN FLOOR

Splendid Split-Foyer

- This popular split-foyer home offers soaring vaulted formal areas and a splendid master suite.
- The foyer leads up to the airy living room, which is brightened by broad windows and warmed by a fireplace
- The adjoining dining room merges with the breakfast area and accesses the back deck though sliding glass doors.

- Double windows warm the breakfast nook and provide views to the backyard. The kitchen also boasts an angled sink area with a plant shelf.
- The master suite features a large closet, a corner window and a deluxe master bath that boasts another closet, a step-up spa tub and a separate shower. Two additional bedrooms share a full bath.
- The lower level provides space for expansion with the inclusion of an unfinished family room. The tuck-under garage and the laundry room share this level.

Plan APS-1410

Bedrooms: 3	Baths: 2
Living Area:	
Main floor	1,428 sq. ft.
Total Living Area:	**1,428 sq. ft.**
Daylight basement	458 sq. ft.
Tuck-under garage	480 sq. ft.
Exterior Wall Framing:	2x4

Foundation Options:

Daylight basement
(All plans can be built with your choice of foundation and framing. A generic conversion diagram is available. See order form.)

BLUEPRINT PRICE CODE: A

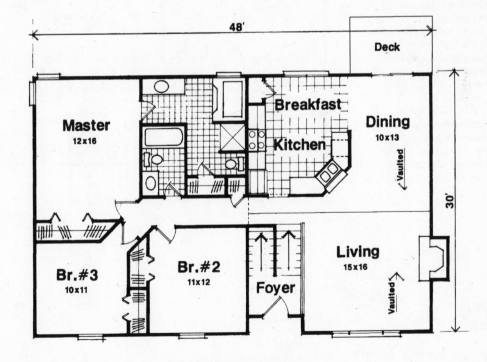

MAIN FLOOR

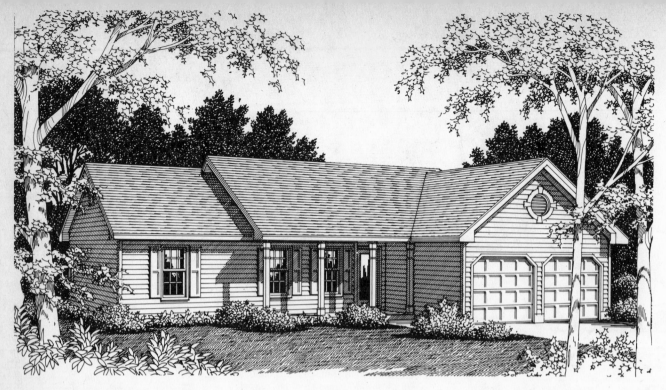

Appealing and Affordable

- This affordable 1,428-sq.-ft. home has an exterior available in a choice of brick, stucco or siding.
- Its simple yet appealing interior design offers three bedrooms, two full baths and open living spaces.
- The spacious living room at the center of the home has a vaulted ceiling and a rear fireplace flanked by windows.
- A spacious bay with French doors to a rear patio highlights the adjoining dining room.
- A large, sunny eat-in kitchen has generous counter space and a handy washer/dryer closet near the garage entrance.
- The master bedroom features a dramatic corner window and a private, vaulted bath with luxury tub.

Plan APS-1413

Bedrooms: 3	Baths: 2
Space:	
Main floor	1,428 sq. ft.
Total Living Area	**1,428 sq. ft.**
Garage	387 sq. ft.
Exterior Wall Framing	2x4

Foundation options:

Slab

(Foundation & framing conversion diagram available—see order form.)

Blueprint Price Code	A

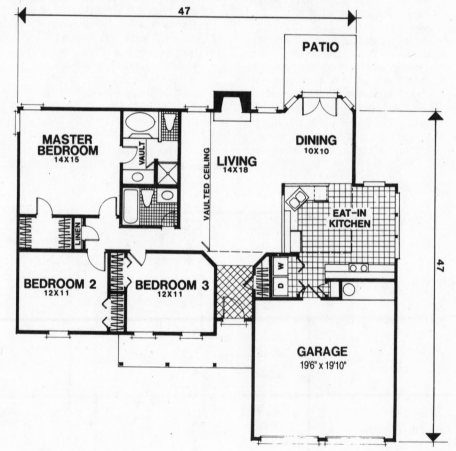

TO ORDER THIS BLUEPRINT, CALL TOLL-FREE 1-800-547-5570

PRICES AND DETAILS ON PAGES 12-15

Plan APS-1413

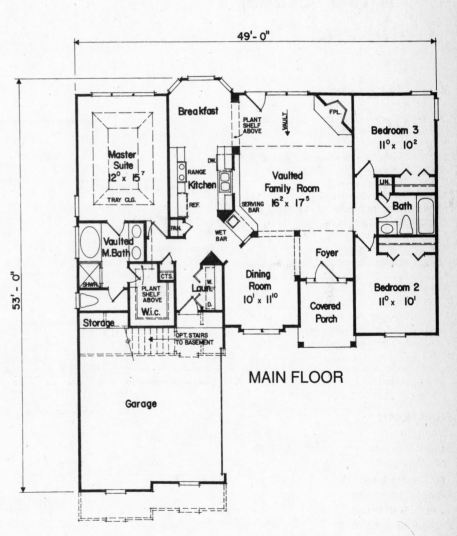

Distinctive
Inside and Out

- A decorative columned entry, shuttered windows and a facade of stucco and stone offer a distinct look to this economical one-story home.
- The focal point of the interior is the huge, central family room. The room is enhanced with a dramatic corner fireplace, a vaulted ceiling and a neat serving bar that extends from the kitchen and includes a wet bar.
- A decorative plant shelf adorns the entrance to the adjoining breakfast room, which features a lovely bay window. The kitchen offers a pantry and a pass-through to the serving bar.
- The formal dining room is easy to reach from both the kitchen and the family room, and is highlighted by a raised ceiling and a tall window.
- The secluded master suite boasts a vaulted private bath with dual sinks, an oval garden tub, a separate toilet room and a large walk-in closet.
- Two more bedrooms share a second bath at the other end of the home.

Plan FB-5001-SAVA

Bedrooms: 3	Baths: 2
Living Area:	
Main floor	1,429 sq. ft.
Total Living Area:	**1,429 sq. ft.**
Daylight basement	1,429 sq. ft.
Garage	250 sq. ft.
Storage	14 sq. ft.
Exterior Wall Framing:	2x4

Foundation Options:

Daylight basement
Crawlspace
Slab
(Typical foundation & framing conversion diagram available—see order form.)

BLUEPRINT PRICE CODE: A

MAIN FLOOR

49'- 0"

53'- 0"

Quality Details Inside and Out

- A sparkling stucco finish, an eye-catching roofline and elegant window treatments hint at the quality features found inside this exquisite home.
- The airy entry opens to a large, central living room, which is embellished with a 10-ft. ceiling and a dramatic fireplace.
- The living room flows into a nice-sized dining area. A covered side porch expands the entertaining area.
- A functional eating bar and pantry are featured in the adjoining U-shaped kitchen. The nearby hallway to the garage neatly stores a washer, a dryer and a laundry sink.
- Secluded to the back of the home is a private master suite with a romantic sitting area and a large walk-in closet. The master bath offers dual sinks and an exciting oval tub.
- Two secondary bedrooms and another bath are located on the other side of the living room and entry.

Plan E-1435

Bedrooms: 3	Baths: 2
Living Area:	
Main floor	1,442 sq. ft.
Total Living Area:	**1,442 sq. ft.**
Garage and storage	516 sq. ft.
Exterior Wall Framing:	2x4

Foundation Options:

Crawlspace
Slab
(All plans can be built with your choice of foundation and framing. A generic conversion diagram is available. See order form.)

BLUEPRINT PRICE CODE: A

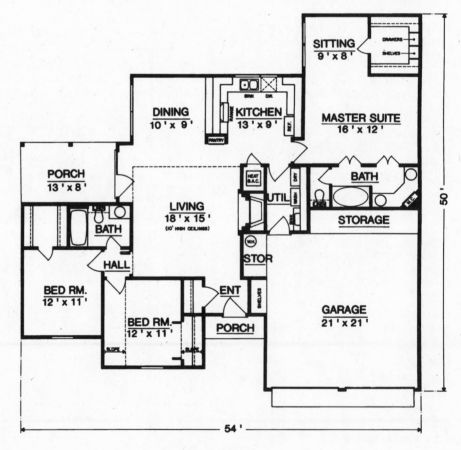

MAIN FLOOR

Sleek One-Story

- Steep, sleek rooflines and a trio of French doors with half-round transoms give this one-story a look of distinction.
- The covered front porch opens to the spacious living room, where a central fireplace cleverly incorporates a wet bar, bookshelves and a coat closet.
- Behind the fireplace, the adjoining dining room offers views to the backyard through an arched window arrangement. The two rooms are expanded by 11-ft. ceilings and a covered back porch.
- A snack bar connects the dining room to the U-shaped kitchen, which offers a pantry closet and large windows over the sink. Laundry facilities are nearby.
- The secluded master suite features a large walk-in closet and a private bath. Across the home, the secondary bedrooms each have a walk-in closet and share another full bath.

Plan E-1427

Bedrooms: 3	Baths: 2

Living Area:	
Main floor	1,444 sq. ft.
Total Living Area:	**1,444 sq. ft.**
Garage and storage	540 sq. ft.

Exterior Wall Framing: 2x4

Foundation Options:

Crawlspace

Slab

(All plans can be built with your choice of foundation and framing. A generic conversion diagram is available. See order form.)

BLUEPRINT PRICE CODE: A

MAIN FLOOR

Traditional Retreat

- This traditional vacation retreat maximizes space by offering an open, flowing floor plan.
- The spacious living room's luxurious features include a cathedral ceiling, fireplace and wet bar; its openness is extended by an exciting adjoining covered deck.
- Sweeping diagonally from the living room is the formal dining room with both front-facing and roof windows.
- The merging kitchen is separated from the living areas by a counter bar.
- The first floor bedroom features a unique triangular window seat, a dressing area and a full bath.
- The second floor is devoted entirely to a private master suite, complete with a lovely window seat, walk-in closet and attached bath.

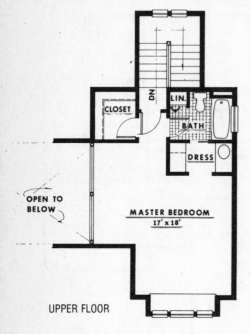

UPPER FLOOR

Plan NW-334

Bedrooms: 2	Baths: 2

Space:

Upper floor:	438 sq. ft.
Main floor:	1,015 sq. ft.
Total living area:	**1,453 sq. ft.**
Carport:	336 sq. ft.
Exterior Wall Framing:	**2x6**

Foundation options:
Crawlspace.
(Foundation & framing conversion diagram available — see order form.)

Blueprint Price Code:	**A**

MAIN FLOOR

Plan NW-334

**PRICES AND DETAILS
ON PAGES 12-15**

Contemporary Blends with Site

The striking contemporary silhouette of this home paradoxically blends with the rustic setting. Perhaps it is the way the shed rooflines repeat the spreading limbs of the surrounding evergreens, or the way the foundation conforms to the grade much as do the rocks in the foreground. Whatever the reason, the home "belongs."

Aesthetics aside, one must examine the floor plan to determine genuine livability. From the weather-protected entry there is access to any part of the house without annoying cross traffic. Kitchen, dining and living room, the active "waking-hours" section of the residence, are enlarged and enhanced by the convenient outdoor deck. Laundry and bath are located inconspicuously along the hall leading to the main floor bedroom. A huge linen closet is convenient to this area. The additional bedrooms are located upstairs on the 517 sq. ft. second level. A romantic feature of the second floor is the balcony overlooking the living area.

Plans including a full basement are available at your option. A large double garage completes the plan and is an important adjunct, especially if the home is built without a basement, because it can provide much needed storage space.

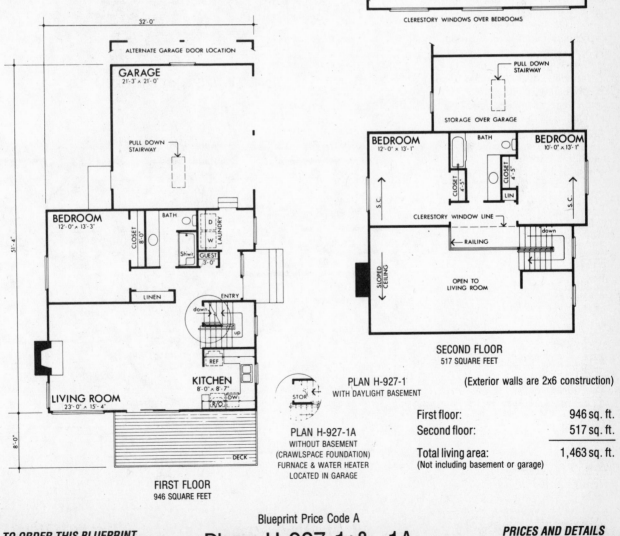

FIRST FLOOR
946 SQUARE FEET

SECOND FLOOR
517 SQUARE FEET

PLAN H-927-1
WITH DAYLIGHT BASEMENT

PLAN H-927-1A
WITHOUT BASEMENT
(CRAWLSPACE FOUNDATION)
FURNACE & WATER HEATER
LOCATED IN GARAGE

(Exterior walls are 2x6 construction)

First floor:	946 sq. ft.
Second floor:	517 sq. ft.
Total living area:	1,463 sq. ft.
(Not including basement or garage)	

Blueprint Price Code A

Victorian Form

- This beautiful home flaunts true-to-form Victorian styling in a modest one-story.
- A delightful, covered front porch and a stunning, sidelighted entry give way to the welcoming foyer.
- The foyer flows into the Great Room, which is warmed by a corner fireplace and topped by a 10-ft. stepped ceiling.
- Sliding French doors open to the backyard from both the Great Room and the adjoining formal dining room.
- On the other side of the open kitchen, a turreted breakfast room overlooks the front porch with cheery windows under an incredible 16-ft. ceiling!
- The restful master suite is graced by a charming window seat and crowned by a 10-ft. stepped ceiling. A dressing area leads to the master bath, which offers a separate tub and shower.
- To the right of the foyer, two more bedrooms share a hall bath. One bedroom features an impressive 11-ft. vaulted ceiling.
- Unless otherwise specified, all rooms have 9-ft. ceilings.

Plan AX-94319

Bedrooms: 3	Baths: 2
Living Area:	
Main floor	1,466 sq. ft.
Total Living Area:	**1,466 sq. ft.**
Standard basement	1,498 sq. ft.
Garage, storage and utility	483 sq. ft.
Exterior Wall Framing:	2x4

Foundation Options:

Standard basement

Crawlspace

Slab

(All plans can be built with your choice of foundation and framing. A generic conversion diagram is available. See order form.)

BLUEPRINT PRICE CODE: A

VIEW INTO BREAKFAST ROOM

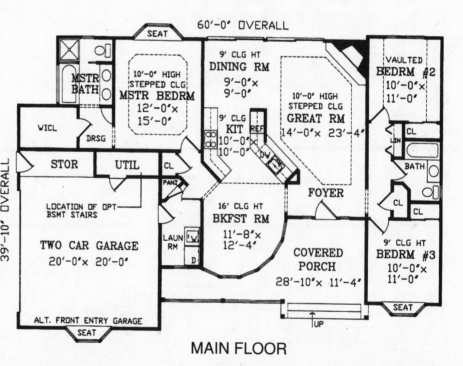

MAIN FLOOR

Pleasantly Peaceful

- The covered front porch of this lovely two-story traditional home offers a pleasant and peaceful welcome.
- Off the open foyer is an oversized family room, drenched with sunlight through a French door and surrounding windows. A handsome fireplace adds further warmth.
- The neatly arranged kitchen is conveniently nestled between the formal dining room and the sunny breakfast room. A pantry and a powder room are also within easy reach.
- A stairway off the family room accesses the upper floor, which houses three bedrooms. The isolated master bedroom features a 10-ft. tray ceiling, a huge walk-in closet and a private bath offering a vaulted ceiling, an oval garden tub and a separate shower.
- The two secondary bedrooms share another full bath.

Plan FB-1466

Bedrooms: 3	Baths: 2½
Living Area:	
Upper floor	703 sq. ft.
Main floor	763 sq. ft.
Total Living Area:	**1,466 sq. ft.**
Daylight basement	763 sq. ft.
Garage	426 sq. ft.
Storage	72 sq. ft.
Exterior Wall Framing:	2x4

Foundation Options:

Daylight basement

Crawlspace

(All plans can be built with your choice of foundation and framing. A generic conversion diagram is available. See order form.)

BLUEPRINT PRICE CODE: **A**

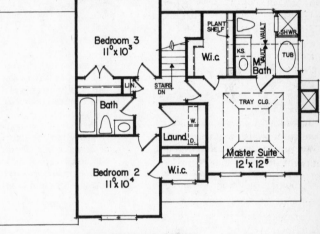

UPPER FLOOR

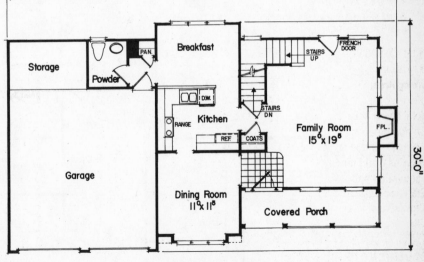

MAIN FLOOR

All-Season Chalet

A guided tour from the front entry of this home takes you into the central hallway that serves as the hub of traffic to the main floor level. From here, convenience extends in every direction and each room is connected in a step-saving manner. Besides the master bedroom with twin closets, a full bathroom with stall shower is placed adjacent to a common wall that also serves the laundry equipment.

The living room and dining area are connected to allow for the expandable use of the dining table should the need arise for additional seating. The kitchen is open ended onto the dining area and has all the modern conveniences and built-in details.

A raised deck flanks the gable end of the living zone and extends outward for a distance of 8'.

A full basement is reached via a stairway connecting with the central hallway. The basement provides ample storage plus room for the central heating system. Another interesting feature is the garage placed under the home where the owner may not only store his automobile but such things as a boat and trailer and other sporting equipment.

First floor: 1,008 sq. ft.
Second floor: 462 sq. ft.

Total living area: 1,470 sq. ft.
(Not counting basement or garage)

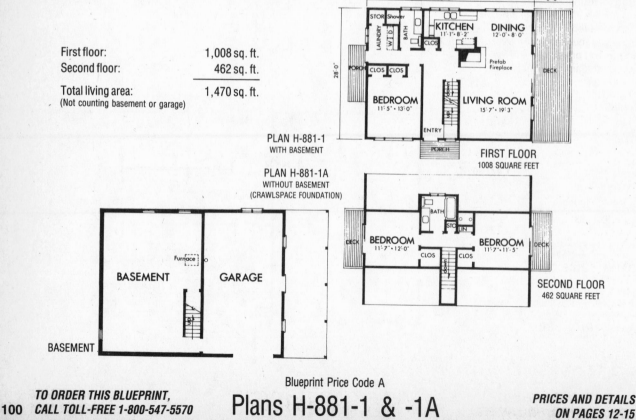

PLAN H-881-1
WITH BASEMENT

PLAN H-881-1A
WITHOUT BASEMENT
(CRAWLSPACE FOUNDATION)

FIRST FLOOR
1008 SQUARE FEET

SECOND FLOOR
462 SQUARE FEET

BASEMENT

Blueprint Price Code A

TO ORDER THIS BLUEPRINT,
CALL TOLL-FREE 1-800-547-5570

Plans H-881-1 & -1A

PRICES AND DETAILS
ON PAGES 12-15

REAR VIEW

All Decked Out!

- All decked out to take full advantage of the outdoors, this stylish home is perfect for a scenic site.
- Entered through a front vestibule, the bright and open floor plan provides an ideal setting for casual lifestyles.
- The sunken living room features a handsome fireplace, a skylighted 19-ft. ceiling and three sets of sliding glass doors that open to an expansive backyard deck.
- The efficient kitchen has a sunny sink and a pass-through with bi-fold doors to the adjoining dining room.
- The main-floor bedroom has a walk-in closet and sliding glass doors to the deck. A half-bath is nearby.
- Upstairs, a railed balcony overlooks the living room. The smaller of the two bedrooms has private access to the bathroom and another deck.

Plan CAR-81007

Bedrooms: 2+	Baths: 1½
Living Area:	
Upper floor	560 sq. ft.
Main floor	911 sq. ft.
Total Living Area:	**1,471 sq. ft.**
Standard basement	911 sq. ft.
Exterior Wall Framing:	2x6

Foundation Options:

Standard basement

(All plans can be built with your choice of foundation and framing. A generic conversion diagram is available. See order form.)

BLUEPRINT PRICE CODE:	**A**

UPPER FLOOR

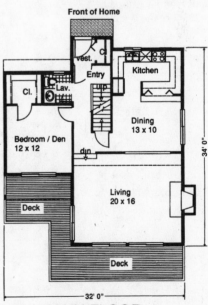

MAIN FLOOR

FRONT VIEW

REAR VIEW

More for Less

- Big in function but small in square footage, this passive-solar plan can be built as a single-family home or as part of a multiple-unit complex.
- The floor plan flows visually from its open foyer to its high-ceilinged Great Room, where a high-efficiency fireplace is flanked by glass. Sliding glass doors open to a brilliant south-facing sun room that overlooks a backyard terrace.
- The eat-in kitchen has a pass-through to a bright dining area that opens to a nice side terrace.
- The master bedroom boasts a pair of tall windows, a deluxe private bath and two roomy closets.
- A handy laundry closet and a half-bath are located at the center of the floor plan, near the garage.
- Upstairs, a skylighted bath serves two more bedrooms, one with a private, rear-facing balcony.

Plan K-507-S

Bedrooms: 3	Baths: 2½
Living Area:	
Upper floor	397 sq. ft.
Main floor	915 sq. ft.
Sun room	162 sq. ft.
Total Living Area:	**1,474 sq. ft.**
Standard basement	915 sq. ft.
Garage	400 sq. ft.
Exterior Wall Framing:	2x4 or 2x6

Foundation Options:

Standard basement

Slab

(All plans can be built with your choice of foundation and framing. A generic conversion diagram is available. See order form.)

BLUEPRINT PRICE CODE: A

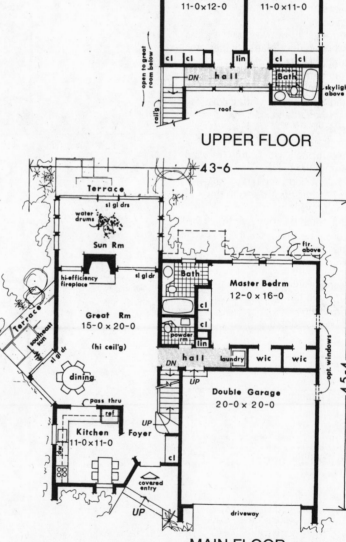

UPPER FLOOR

MAIN FLOOR

Farmhouse for the Family

- This farmhouse design's covered porch, backyard deck and spacious family room promote warm family closeness.
- The front entry opens directly into the family room, which is warmed by a delightful corner fireplace and features a 10-ft. ceiling.
- The roomy island kitchen flaunts a 12-ft. vaulted ceiling and a lovely arched window arrangement. A cozy, informal dining area offers a nice view of the backyard deck.
- A covered walkway provides easy access to the two-car garage.
- Down the skylighted hall from the family room, two secondary bedrooms boast ample walk-in closets and share a full bath.
- The quietly isolated master bedroom is enhanced by a large walk-in closet and a private bath with a dual-sink vanity. An alternate master bath plan adds more space and the convenience of a separate shower.
- Unless otherwise noted, all rooms have 9-ft. ceilings.

Plan GMA-1475

Bedrooms: 3	Baths: 2
Living Area:	
Main floor	1,475 sq. ft.
Total Living Area:	**1,475 sq. ft.**
Garage	455 sq. ft.
Exterior Wall Framing:	2x4

Foundation Options:

Crawlspace

Slab

(All plans can be built with your choice of foundation and framing. A generic conversion diagram is available. See order form.)

BLUEPRINT PRICE CODE: A

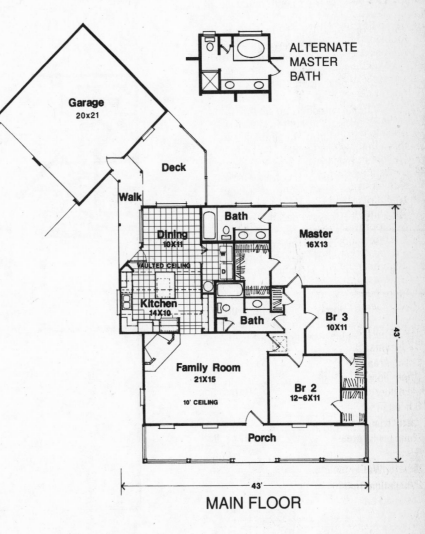

ALTERNATE MASTER BATH

MAIN FLOOR

Clever Touches

- This attractive one-story was designed for comfortable living, with many clever interior touches.
- Just beyond the 11-ft., 10-in. vaulted entry, the living room is warmed by a rustic fireplace. A gorgeous round-top window arrangement is set into a boxed-out area with a 10-ft. sloped ceiling.
- The dining room offers an 11-ft., 10-in. vaulted ceiling and built-in shelves.
- Easily accessed from the dining room, the walk-through kitchen is topped by a 10-ft., 5-in. vaulted ceiling and boasts a cute breakfast bar and corner windows.
- The adjoining family room suits large gatherings well and offers French-door access to a backyard porch. An 11-ft., 10-in. vaulted ceiling rises overhead.
- In a secluded corner, the master suite boasts private porch access through a French door. The skylighted master bath flaunts a dual-sink vanity and a spacious walk-in closet.
- Two more bedrooms across the hall share a skylighted bath. One bedroom sports a bright study alcove for reading or homework.

Plan LMB-4119-CDB

Bedrooms: 3	Baths: 2

Living Area:

Main floor	1,477 sq. ft.
Total Living Area:	**1,477 sq. ft.**
Garage	400 sq. ft.
Exterior Wall Framing:	2x4

Foundation Options:

Crawlspace

(All plans can be built with your choice of foundation and framing. A generic conversion diagram is available. See order form.)

BLUEPRINT PRICE CODE: A

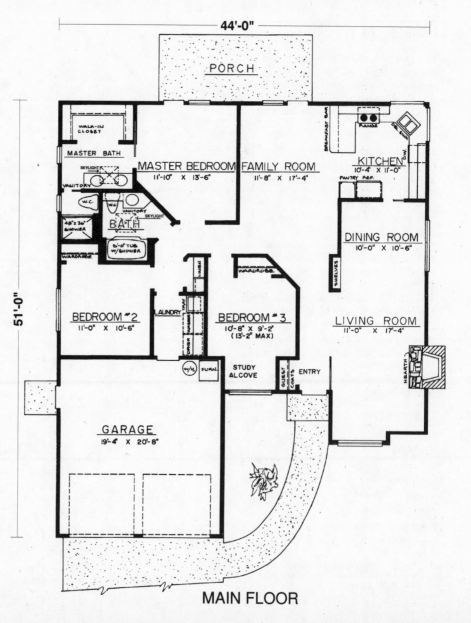

MAIN FLOOR

TO ORDER THIS BLUEPRINT, CALL TOLL-FREE 1-800-547-5570   Plan LMB-4119-CDB   **PRICES AND DETAILS ON PAGES 12-15**

Classic Country-Style

- The classic covered front porch with decorative railings and columns make this home reminiscent of an early 20th-century farmhouse.
- Dormers give the home the appearance of a two-story, even though it is designed for single-level living.
- The huge living room features a ceiling that slopes up to 13 feet. A corner fireplace radiates warmth to both the living room and the dining room.
- The dining room overlooks a backyard patio and shares a versatile serving bar with the open kitchen. A large utility room is just steps away.
- The master bedroom boasts a roomy bath with a dual-sink vanity. The two smaller bedrooms at the other end of the home share a full bath.

Plan E-1412

Bedrooms: 3	Baths: 2
Living Area:	
Main floor	1,484 sq. ft.
Total Living Area:	**1,484 sq. ft.**
Garage	440 sq. ft.
Exterior Wall Framing:	2x6

Foundation Options:

Crawlspace

Slab

(All plans can be built with your choice of foundation and framing. A generic conversion diagram is available. See order form.)

BLUEPRINT PRICE CODE: **A**

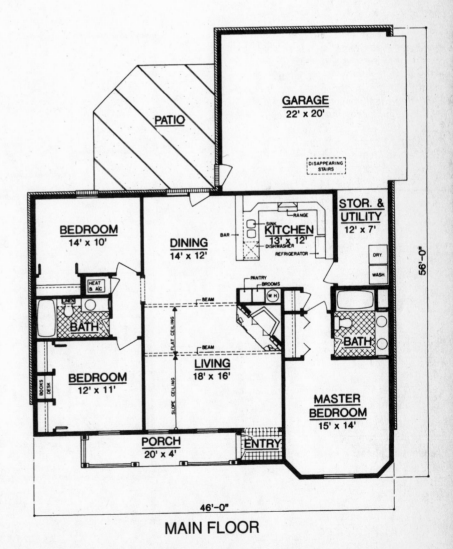

MAIN FLOOR

Compact, Cozy, Inviting

- Full-width porches at the front and the rear of this home add plenty of space for outdoor living and entertaining.
- The huge, centrally located living room is the core of this three-bedroom home. The room features a corner fireplace, a 16-ft. sloped, open-beam ceiling and access to the back porch.
- The dining room combines with the kitchen to create an open, more spacious atmosphere. A long, central work island and a compact laundry closet are other space-saving features.
- The main-floor master suite offers a private bath with dual vanities and a large walk-in closet. Two additional bedrooms, a full bath and an intimate sitting area that overlooks the living room and entry are upstairs.
- A separate two-car garage is included with the blueprints.

Plan E-1421

Bedrooms: 3	Baths: 2
Living Area:	
Upper floor	561 sq. ft.
Main floor	924 sq. ft.
Total Living Area:	**1,485 sq. ft.**
Standard basement	924 sq. ft.
Exterior Wall Framing:	2x6

Foundation Options:

Standard basement

Crawlspace

Slab

(All plans can be built with your choice of foundation and framing. A generic conversion diagram is available. See order form.)

BLUEPRINT PRICE CODE:	**A**

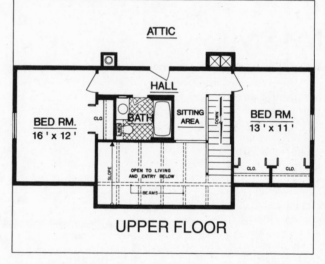

UPPER FLOOR

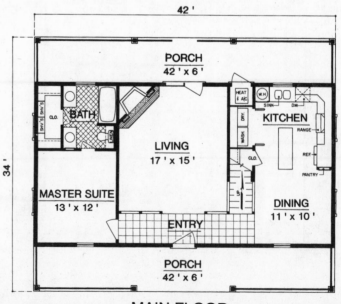

MAIN FLOOR

TO ORDER THIS BLUEPRINT, CALL TOLL-FREE 1-800-547-5570

Plan E-1421

PRICES AND DETAILS ON PAGES 12-15

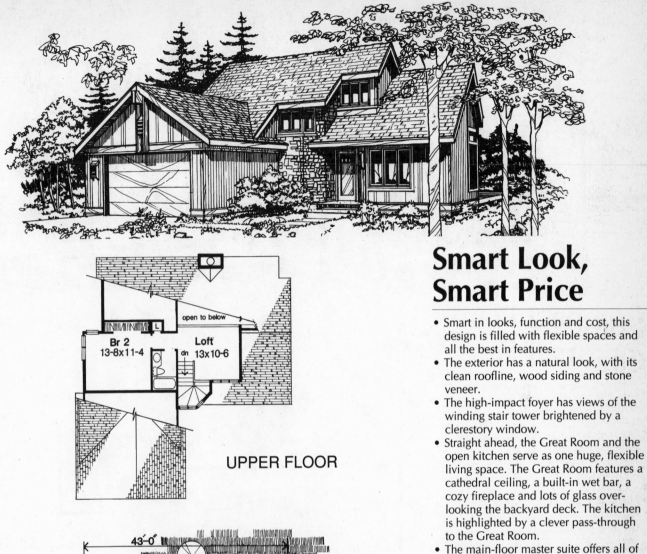

UPPER FLOOR

MAIN FLOOR

Smart Look, Smart Price

- Smart in looks, function and cost, this design is filled with flexible spaces and all the best in features.
- The exterior has a natural look, with its clean roofline, wood siding and stone veneer.
- The high-impact foyer has views of the winding stair tower brightened by a clerestory window.
- Straight ahead, the Great Room and the open kitchen serve as one huge, flexible living space. The Great Room features a cathedral ceiling, a built-in wet bar, a cozy fireplace and lots of glass over-looking the backyard deck. The kitchen is highlighted by a clever pass-through to the Great Room.
- The main-floor master suite offers all of today's amenities, including a window seat facing the backyard, a walk-in closet and a private bath.
- Another full bathroom, a roomy bedroom and a multipurpose loft are on the upper floor.

Plan B-711	
Bedrooms: 2-3	**Baths:** 2½
Living Area:	
Upper floor	454 sq. ft.
Main floor	1,044 sq. ft.
Total Living Area:	**1,498 sq. ft.**
Standard basement	1,044 sq. ft.
Garage	380 sq. ft.
Exterior Wall Framing:	2x6
Foundation Options:	
Standard basement	
(Typical foundation & framing conversion diagram available—see order form.)	
BLUEPRINT PRICE CODE:	**A**

Compact Plan for Small Lot

- Luxury is not forgotten in this compact one-story home, which is perfect for a small or narrow lot.
- Off the entry, the living room boasts a 13-ft.-high vaulted ceiling and a boxed-out window. The adjoining dining area features a half-wall opening to the hall.
- The kitchen is separated from the family room by a functional eating bar. The family room is brightened by sliding glass doors that open to a patio.
- The master bedroom offers generous closet space and a private bath with a dual-sink vanity. Two additional bedrooms share another full bath.

Plans P-7699-2A & -2D

Bedrooms: 3	Baths: 2
Living Area:	
Main floor (crawlspace version)	1,460 sq. ft.
Main floor (basement version)	1,509 sq. ft.
Total Living Area:	**1,460/1,509 sq. ft.**
Daylight basement	1,530 sq. ft.
Garage	383 sq. ft.
Exterior Wall Framing:	2x4
Foundation Options:	**Plan #**
Daylight basement	P-7699-2D
Crawlspace	P-7699-2A

(All plans can be built with your choice of foundation and framing. A generic conversion diagram is available. See order form.)

BLUEPRINT PRICE CODE:	A/B

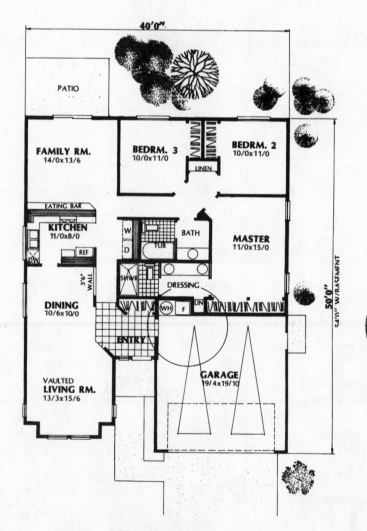

MAIN FLOOR

BASEMENT STAIRWAY LOCATION

Plans P-7699-2A & -2D
PRICES AND DETAILS ON PAGES 12-15

Cozy and Energy-Efficient

Planned for year-round comfort and energy efficiency, this passive solar design boasts a highly livable floor plan. Vertical wood siding and deep overhang give the exterior a natural appeal. Inside, the open plan is carefully designed to provide ample natural light with a minimum heat loss; windows and sliding doors are double-paned; heavy insulation is specified. In summer, operable clerestory windows aid in air circulation, cooling the house by convection.

The high-ceilinged reception hall neatly channels traffic. To the right is the family room/kitchen, equipped with an eating bar. Straight ahead are the living and dining rooms, dramatically accented by a sloped ceiling, a wood-burning fireplace and a light-filled sunroom. Sliding glass doors lead to a rear terrace.

Isolated on the left side are the quiet sleeping quarters, with three bedrooms. Master bedroom has a private terrace, a walk-in closet and a personal bath that features a whirlpool tub.

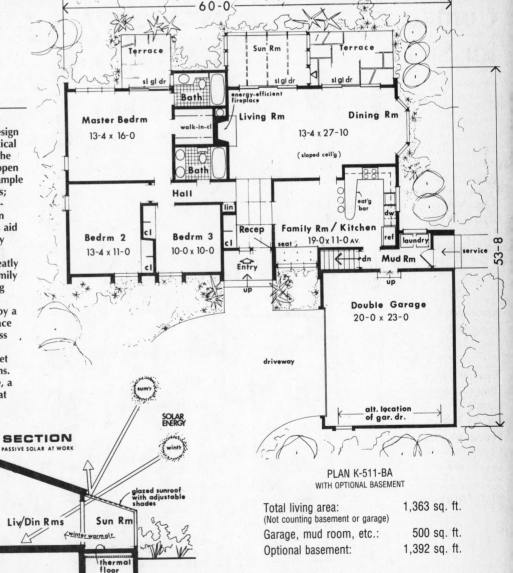

SECTION
PASSIVE SOLAR AT WORK

PLAN K-511-BA
WITH OPTIONAL BASEMENT

Total living area:	1,363 sq. ft.
(Not counting basement or garage)	
Garage, mud room, etc.:	500 sq. ft.
Optional basement:	1,392 sq. ft.

Blueprint Price Code A

Plan K-511-BA

Split-Level Vacation Home

By opting for a smaller than average lot, a family choosing a split-level design such as this will benefit from the space-savings and their attending cost savings. Notice, for example, the overall width of 68' includes the projection of the double-sized garage on one side and the location of a sun deck that flanks the sliding doors of the den. Since most leisure home building sites have some slope, the three-level design of this dwelling will fit many situations.

This plan is an example of a design for seclusion, with all the primary living areas oriented to the rear of the home. Notice how the living room, dining area and U-shaped kitchen face the rear wall and have access to the spacious raised deck. The recreation room at the basement level and a third bedroom also face the rear garden.

The main floor area of 1,200 sq. ft. is actually on two elevations. The entry hall is on the same level as the adjacent den and bedroom with bath. A dramatic effect is achieved by the placement of the living room four steps below. The soaring height

of the vaulted ceiling, with exposed beams extending from the central ridge to the exterior wall, adds to the feeling of openness to the outdoors, framed by the window wall and sliding glass doors.

The kitchen itself is convenient to both the dining area and informal portions of the home, and has a work-saving U-shaped design.

The spacious master bedroom suite offers the unencumbered view of an eagle's nest, and also boasts a walk-in

closet and private bath with shower stall. Another added luxury is the 4' cantilevered sun deck, accessible through sliding glass doors. This raised portion of the home that includes the master bedroom contains 320 additional sq. ft.

Other features which should be pointed out include the two massive fireplaces. One is located in the recreation room and the other is the focal point of the end wall of the living room. A third full bath is also placed at the basement level.

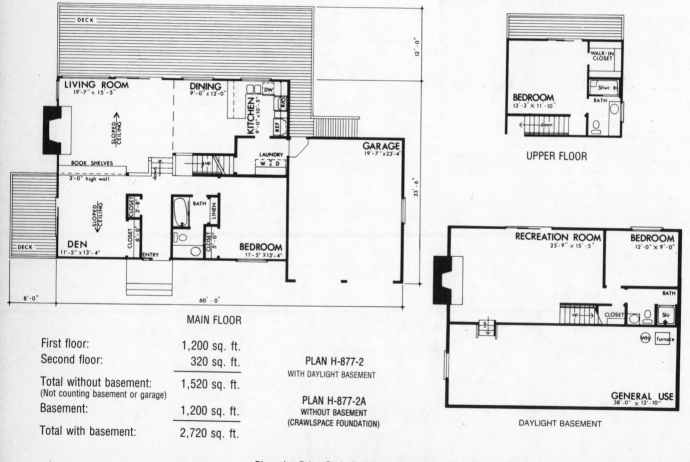

MAIN FLOOR

UPPER FLOOR

DAYLIGHT BASEMENT

First floor:	1,200 sq. ft.
Second floor:	320 sq. ft.
Total without basement:	1,520 sq. ft.
(Not counting basement or garage)	
Basement:	1,200 sq. ft.
Total with basement:	2,720 sq. ft.

PLAN H-877-2
WITH DAYLIGHT BASEMENT

PLAN H-877-2A
WITHOUT BASEMENT
(CRAWLSPACE FOUNDATION)

Blueprint Price Code D With Basement
Blueprint Price Code B Without Basement

TO ORDER THIS BLUEPRINT, CALL TOLL-FREE 1-800-547-5570

Plans H-877-2 & -2A

PRICES AND DETAILS ON PAGES 12-15

Rustic Styling, Comfortable Interior

- Front-to-back split level with large decks lends itself to steep sloping site, particularly in a scenic area.
- Compact, space-efficient design makes for economical construction.
- Great Room design concept utilizes the entire 36' width of home for the kitchen/dining/living area.
- Two bedrooms and a bath are up three steps, on the entry level.
- Upper level bedroom includes a compact bath and a private deck.

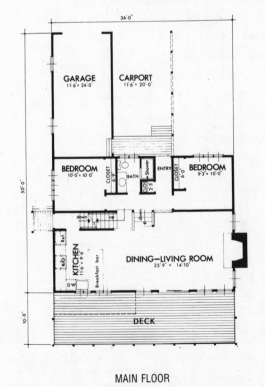

GARAGE
11-6 × 24-0

CARPORT
11-6 × 20-0

BEDROOM
10-0 × 10-0

CLOSET
6-3

BATH

ENTRY

CLOSET
6-0

BEDROOM
9-3 × 10-0

down

up

KITCHEN
11-6 × 9-6

Breakfast bar

DW

Ref.

DINING—LIVING ROOM
25-9 × 14-10

DECK

36-0

50-0

10-0

MAIN FLOOR

BATH

BEDROOM
11-8 × 11-5

CLOSET
4-0×3-0

Shwr

down

DECK

UPPER FLOOR

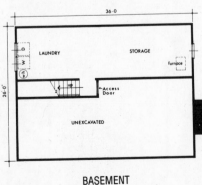

36-0

26-0

LAUNDRY

STORAGE

furnace

up

Access Door

UNEXCAVATED

BASEMENT

Plan H-25-C

Bedrooms: 3	Baths: 2

Space:	
Upper floor:	222 sq. ft.
Main floor:	936 sq. ft.
Basement:	365 sq. ft.
Total living area:	**1,523 sq. ft.**
Garage:	276 sq. ft.

Exterior Wall Framing:	2x4

Foundation options:
Daylight basement only.
(Foundation & framing conversion diagram available — see order form.)

Blueprint Price Code:	B

Hillside Design Fits Contours

- The daylight-basement version of this popular plan is perfect for a scenic, sloping lot.
- A large, wraparound deck embraces the rear-oriented living areas, accessed through sliding glass doors.
- The spectacular living room boasts a corner fireplace and a 19-ft. vaulted ceiling with three clerestory windows.
- The secluded master suite upstairs offers a walk-in closet, a private bath and sliding doors to a sun deck.
- The daylight basement (not shown) includes a fourth bedroom with a private bath and a walk-in closet, as well as a recreation room with a fireplace and access to a rear patio.
- The standard basement (not shown) includes a recreation room with a fireplace and a room for hobbies or child's play.
- Both basements also have a large unfinished area below the main-floor bedrooms.

REAR VIEW

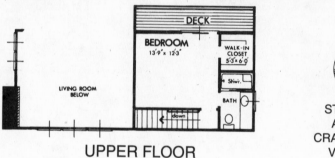

UPPER FLOOR

STAIRWAY AREA IN CRAWLSPACE VERSION

Plans H-877-4, -4A & -4B	
Bedrooms: 3+	Baths: 2-3
Living Area:	
Upper floor	333 sq. ft.
Main floor	1,200 sq. ft.
Basement (finished area)	591 sq. ft.
Total Living Area:	**1,533/2,124 sq. ft.**
Basement (unfinished area)	493 sq. ft.
Garage	480 sq. ft.
Exterior Wall Framing:	2x6
Foundation Options:	**Plan #**
Daylight basement	H-877-4B
Standard basement	H-877-4
Crawlspace	H-877-4A

(All plans can be built with your choice of foundation and framing. A generic conversion diagram is available. See order form.)

BLUEPRINT PRICE CODE: B/C

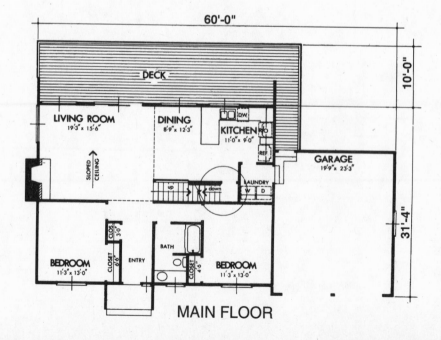

MAIN FLOOR

Vaulted Living Room Featured

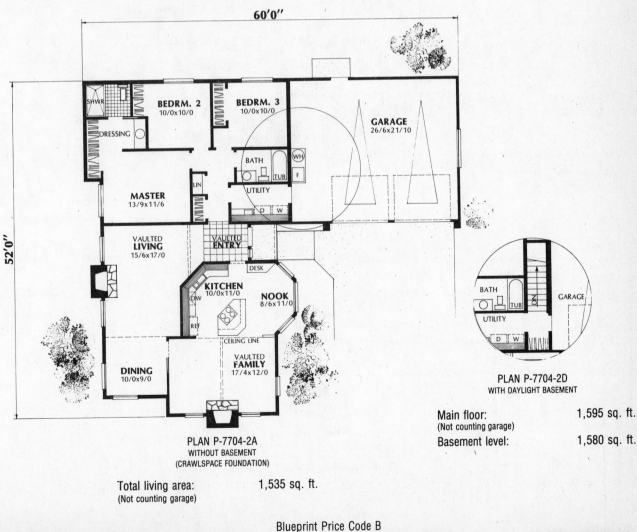

60'0"

52'0"

SHWR

DRESSING

BEDRM. 2
10/0x10/0

BEDRM. 3
10/0x10/0

GARAGE
26/6x21/10

MASTER
13/9x11/6

LIN

BATH

UTILITY

WH
F

D   W

TUB

**VAULTED
LIVING**
15/6x17/0

**VAULTED
ENTRY**

DESK

KITCHEN
10/0x11/0

DW

REF

NOOK
8/6x11/0

CEILING LINE

DINING
10/0x9/0

**VAULTED
FAMILY**
17/4x12/0

PLAN P-7704-2A
WITHOUT BASEMENT
(CRAWLSPACE FOUNDATION)

Total living area:
(Not counting garage)   1,535 sq. ft.

BATH

UTILITY

TUB

DN

GARAGE

D   W

PLAN P-7704-2D
WITH DAYLIGHT BASEMENT

Main floor: 1,595 sq. ft.
(Not counting garage)
Basement level: 1,580 sq. ft.

Blueprint Price Code B

Plans P-7704-2A & -2D

Space-Saving Floor Plan

- Easy, affordable living is the basis for this great town and country design.
- The welcoming porch and the graceful arched window give the home its curb appeal. Inside, the floor plan provides large, highly livable spaces rather than several specialized rooms.
- The foyer opens to the spacious living room. A column separates the foyer from the formal dining room, which features a bay window and an alcove that is perfect for a china hutch. The country kitchen is large enough to accommodate family and guests alike.
- A beautiful open staircase leads to the second floor, where there are three bedrooms and two baths. The master bedroom offers a tray ceiling and a luxurious bath with a sloped ceiling and a corner shower.

Plan AX-92320

Bedrooms: 3	Baths: 2½
Living Area:	
Upper floor	706 sq. ft.
Main floor	830 sq. ft.
Total Living Area:	**1,536 sq. ft.**
Standard basement	754 sq. ft.
Garage	510 sq. ft.
Exterior Wall Framing:	2x6

Foundation Options:
Standard basement
Slab

(Typical foundation & framing conversion diagram available—see order form.)

BLUEPRINT PRICE CODE:	B

FRONT VIEW

REAR VIEW

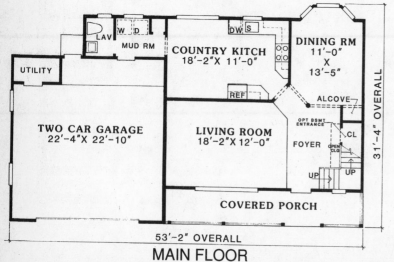

MAIN FLOOR

- LAV
- W
- D
- MUD RM
- UTILITY
- DW
- S
- COUNTRY KITCH 18'-2" X 11'-0"
- REF
- DINING RM 11'-0" X 13'-5"
- ALCOVE
- OPT BSMT ENTRANCE
- CL
- FOYER
- OPEN CLG
- TWO CAR GARAGE 22'-4" X 22'-10"
- LIVING ROOM 18'-2" X 12'-0"
- UP
- UP
- COVERED PORCH
- 31'-4" OVERALL
- 53'-2" OVERALL

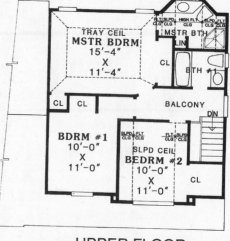

UPPER FLOOR

- TRAY CEIL MSTR BDRM 15'-4" X 11'-4"
- MSTR BTH
- LIN
- BTH #1
- CL
- CL
- CL
- BALCONY
- BDRM #1 10'-0" X 11'-0"
- SLPD CEIL BEDRM #2 10'-0" X 11'-0"
- CL
- DN

Traditional Heritage

- A distinctive roofline and a covered wraparound porch reflect this charming home's traditional heritage.
- The roomy entry flows directly into the spacious, open living area. Enhanced by a cathedral ceiling, the living room is warmed by a fireplace and offers a French door to a backyard patio. A good-sized laundry room is nearby.

- The adjoining dining area shares porch access with the stylish gourmet kitchen, which includes an eating bar and a garden window over the sink.
- The master bedroom suite features a lavish private bath with a garden spa tub, a separate shower, a dual-sink vanity and a big walk-in closet.
- A second full bath, located at the end of the bedroom hallway, is convenient to the two remaining bedrooms.
- The double carport includes a separate lockable storage area.

Plan J-86142

Bedrooms: 3	**Baths:** 2
Living Area:	
Main floor	1,536 sq. ft.
Total Living Area:	**1,536 sq. ft.**
Standard basement	1,536 sq. ft.
Carport and storage	520 sq. ft.
Exterior Wall Framing:	2x4

Foundation Options:

Standard basement
Crawlspace
Slab
(All plans can be built with your choice of foundation and framing. A generic conversion diagram is available. See order form.)

BLUEPRINT PRICE CODE: B

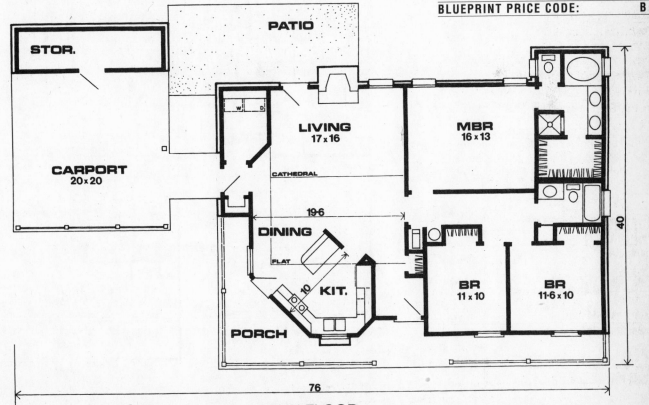

MAIN FLOOR

Fabulous Facade

- A decorative railing atop the roof and a columned entry with an arched transom window introduce this fabulous home.
- French doors open from the arched entry to the foyer, where a 12-ft., 8-in. ceiling directs light to the expansive Great Room beyond. All other areas are enhanced by 10-ft. ceilings.
- To the left of the foyer, the dining room has views to the front yard and is easily serviced from the kitchen.
- The spacious Great Room is highlighted by a striking corner fireplace, a media center and sliding glass doors to a covered backyard patio.
- An angled snack bar in the gourmet kitchen serves both the Great Room and the sunny breakfast area. A pantry closet and a utility/laundry room with garage access are nearby.
- A step from the breakfast room, the master suite has private patio access and a large bath with a garden shower, a dual-sink vanity and a walk-in closet.
- Across the home, two additional bedrooms share another full bath.

Plan HDS-99-173

Bedrooms: 3	Baths: 2

Living Area:

Main floor	1,550 sq. ft.
Total Living Area:	**1,550 sq. ft.**
Garage	387 sq. ft.
Exterior Wall Framing:	2x4

Foundation Options:

Slab

(All plans can be built with your choice of foundation and framing. A generic conversion diagram is available. See order form.)

BLUEPRINT PRICE CODE:	B

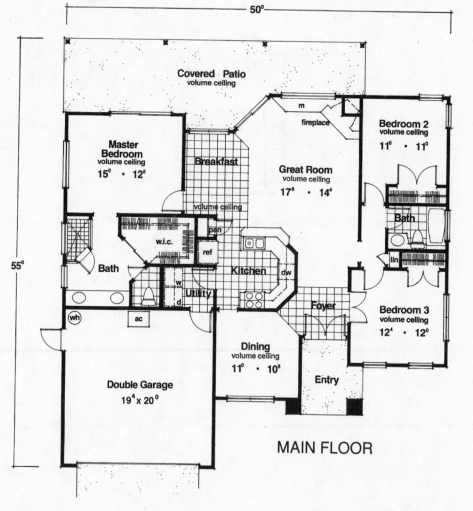

MAIN FLOOR

TO ORDER THIS BLUEPRINT, CALL TOLL-FREE 1-800-547-5570   Plan HDS-99-173   *PRICES AND DETAILS ON PAGES 12-15*

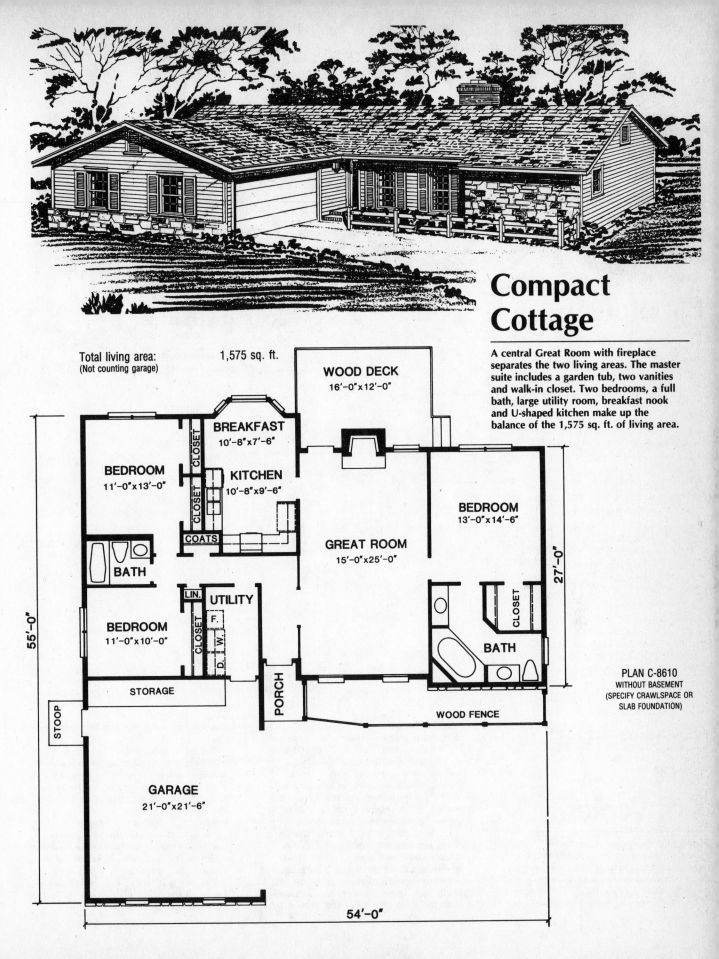

Compact Cottage

A central Great Room with fireplace separates the two living areas. The master suite includes a garden tub, two vanities and walk-in closet. Two bedrooms, a full bath, large utility room, breakfast nook and U-shaped kitchen make up the balance of the 1,575 sq. ft. of living area.

Total living area:
(Not counting garage)

1,575 sq. ft.

WOOD DECK
16'-0"x12'-0"

BREAKFAST
10'-8"x7'-6"

CLOSET

CLOSET

CLOSET

KITCHEN
10'-8"x9'-6"

COATS

BEDROOM
11'-0"x13'-0"

BATH

BEDROOM
13'-0"x14'-6"

27'-0"

GREAT ROOM
15'-0"x25'-0"

LIN.

UTILITY

F.

D.W.

CLOSET

BEDROOM
11'-0"x10'-0"

CLOSET

BATH

55'-0"

STORAGE

STOOP

PORCH

WOOD FENCE

PLAN C-8610
WITHOUT BASEMENT
(SPECIFY CRAWLSPACE OR
SLAB FOUNDATION)

GARAGE
21'-0"x21'-6"

54'-0"

Blueprint Price Code B

Plan C-8610

TO ORDER THIS BLUEPRINT,
CALL TOLL-FREE 1-800-547-5570

PRICES AND DETAILS
ON PAGES 12-15   117

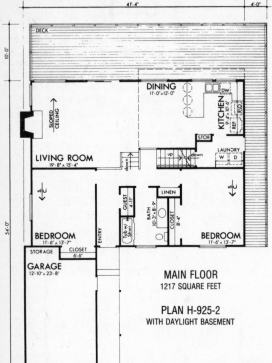

DECK

DINING
11'-0"x12'-0"

KITCHEN
9'-4"x10'-6"

DW

REF.

STOR

SLOPED CEILING

LIVING ROOM
19'-8"x15'-4"

down

down

LAUNDRY
W D

GUEST
4'-11"

LINEN

BATH
10'-3"x8'-9"

Tub w/ Shwr

CLOSET
8'-4"

ENTRY

BEDROOM
11'-6"x13'-7"

STORAGE

CLOSET
6'-6"

BEDROOM
11'-6"x13'-7"

GARAGE
12'-10"x23'-8"

MAIN FLOOR
1217 SQUARE FEET

PLAN H-925-2
WITH DAYLIGHT BASEMENT

DECK

SLOPED CEILING

WALK-IN CLOSET
7'-5"x5'-0"

Shwr

BEDROOM
14'-0"x14'-0"

down

BATH
9'-6"x5'-0"

SECOND FLOOR
360 SQUARE FEET

First floor:	1,217 sq. ft.
Second floor:	360 sq. ft.
Total living area: (Not counting basement or garage)	1,577 sq. ft.

STOR

WH heat

PLAN H-925-2A
WITHOUT BASEMENT
(CRAWLSPACE FOUNDATION)

Economical and Convenient

In an effort to merge the financial possibilities and the space requirements of the greatest number of families, the designers of this home restricted themselves to just over 1,200 sq. ft. of ground cover (exclusive of garage), and still managed to develop a superior three-bedroom design.

From a covered walkway, one approaches a centralized entry hall which effectively distributes traffic throughout the home without causing interruptions. Two main floor bedrooms and bath as well as the stairway to the second floor master suite are immediately accessible to the entry. Directly forward and four steps down finds one in the main living area, consisting of a large living room with vaulted ceiling and a dining-kitchen combination with conventional ceiling height. All these rooms have direct access to an outdoor living deck of over 400 sq. ft. Thus, though modest and unassuming from the street side, this home evolves into eye-popping expansion and luxury toward the rear.

To ease homemaking chores, whether this is to be a permanent or vacation home, the working equipment, including laundry space, is all on the main floor. Yet the homemaker remains part of the family scene because there is only a breakfast counter separating the work space from the living area.

Tucked away upstairs, in complete privacy, one finds a master bedroom suite equipped with separate bath, walk-in wardrobe and a romantic private deck.

The plan is available with or without a basement and is best suited to a lot that slopes gently down from the road.

Striking One-Story Home

- Eye-catching angles, both inside and out, are the keynotes of this luxurious one-story home.
- The striking double-door entry is illuminated by a skylight. The foyer is just as impressive, with its cathedral ceiling and skylight.
- The sunken living room also features a cathedral ceiling, and a bay-window alcove faces the front.
- A low partition separates the living room from the formal dining room. Here, too, a cathedral ceiling and bay windows add interesting angles and spaciousness to the room.
- The open family room, breakfast room and kitchen offer plenty of space for casual family living. The family room includes a corner fireplace with adjacent built-in shelves. The bayed breakfast area boasts a cathedral ceiling and French doors to the backyard. An angled snack counter faces the U-shaped kitchen.
- The master bedroom also has a bay window facing the backyard, plus a large walk-in closet. Also included is a private bath with a whirlpool tub.
- Two more bedrooms, another full bath and a utility area complete the design.

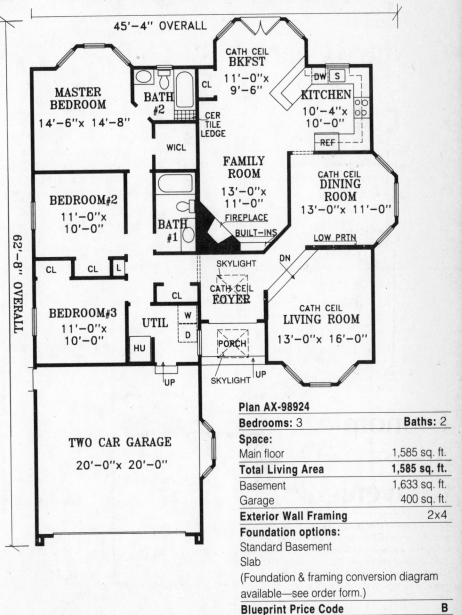

Plan AX-98924

Bedrooms: 3	Baths: 2

Space:

Main floor	1,585 sq. ft.
Total Living Area	**1,585 sq. ft.**
Basement	1,633 sq. ft.
Garage	400 sq. ft.
Exterior Wall Framing	2x4

Foundation options:

Standard Basement

Slab

(Foundation & framing conversion diagram available—see order form.)

Blueprint Price Code	B

TO ORDER THIS BLUEPRINT,
CALL TOLL-FREE 1-800-547-5570

Plan AX-98924

PRICES AND DETAILS
ON PAGES 12-15

119

Modern Country Charm

- Charming window treatments, a covered porch and detailed railings give this modern home a country feeling.
- The inviting entry flows into the elegant living room, which features a 10-ft. ceiling and a striking corner fireplace.
- The sunny kitchen is built into a beautiful bay and easily serves the formal dining room.

- The spacious sunken family room enjoys bright windows and offers sliding glass doors to a backyard patio.
- A half-bath, a laundry/utility room and a storage area are conveniently located off the garage entrance.
- Upstairs, the master bedroom includes a private garden bath, a walk-in closet and a separate dressing area with a dual-sink vanity.
- Two additional upper-floor bedrooms share a full bath and a linen closet. Both rooms are enhanced by sizable closets and cozy window seats.

Plan NW-836	
Bedrooms: 3	**Baths:** 2½
Living Area:	
Upper floor	684 sq. ft.
Main floor	934 sq. ft.
Total Living Area:	**1,618 sq. ft.**
Garage	419 sq. ft.
Exterior Wall Framing:	2x6
Foundation Options:	
Crawlspace	

(All plans can be built with your choice of foundation and framing. A generic conversion diagram is available. See order form.)

BLUEPRINT PRICE CODE:	B

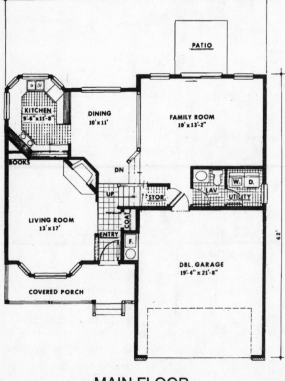

MAIN FLOOR

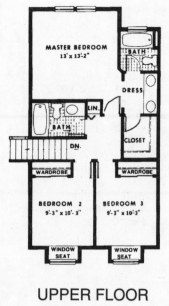

UPPER FLOOR

Plan NW-836

Indoor/Outdoor Pleasure

- For a sloping, scenic lake or mountain lot, this spectacular design hugs the hill and takes full advantage of the views.
- A three-sided wraparound deck makes indoor/outdoor living a pleasure.
- The sunken living room—with a 19-ft. cathedral ceiling, a skylight, a beautiful fireplace and glass galore—is the heart of the floor plan.
- The formal dining room and the kitchen both overlook the living room and the surrounding deck beyond.
- The main-floor master bedroom has a 12-ft. cathedral ceiling and private access to the deck and hall bath.
- Two more bedrooms upstairs share a skylighted bath and flank a dramatic balcony sitting area overlooking the living room below.

Plan AX-98607

Bedrooms: 3	**Baths:** 2

Living Area:	
Upper floor	531 sq. ft.
Main floor	1,098 sq. ft.
Total Living Area:	**1,629 sq. ft.**
Standard basement	894 sq. ft.
Garage	327 sq. ft.
Exterior Wall Framing:	2x4

Foundation Options:

Standard basement

Slab

(All plans can be built with your choice of foundation and framing. A generic conversion diagram is available. See order form.)

BLUEPRINT PRICE CODE:	B

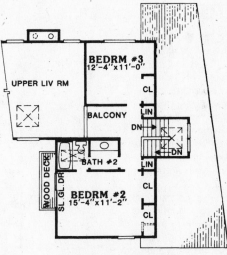

UPPER FLOOR

◀ 45'-0" ▶

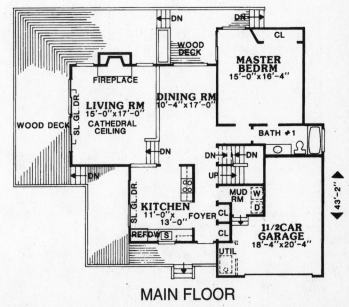

MAIN FLOOR

Delightful Backyard Views

- This home embraces easy living with its huge backyard deck, which may be accessed from three areas of the home.
- The sidelighted entry opens to the spacious vaulted living room, where a fireplace is centered between windows.
- The adjoining dining room is adorned with decorative columns, and sliding glass doors access the expansive deck.
- The angled kitchen has a corner sink, plenty of counter space and a sunny breakfast nook that opens to the deck.
- The vaulted master suite boasts a bright sitting area with private deck access. The skylighted master bath features a large walk-in closet, a dual-sink vanity, a spa tub and a private toilet.
- Another full bath serves the two additional bedrooms. One of the bedrooms could serve as a den and boasts a high-ceilinged area that showcases a half-round transom.
- A two-car garage and a bright laundry room round out the floor plan.

Plan B-87127

Bedrooms: 2+	Baths: 2
Living Area:	
Main floor	1,630 sq. ft.
Total Living Area:	**1,630 sq. ft.**
Standard basement	1,630 sq. ft.
Garage	448 sq. ft.
Exterior Wall Framing:	2x4

Foundation Options:

Standard basement
(All plans can be built with your choice of foundation and framing. A generic conversion diagram is available. See order form.)

BLUEPRINT PRICE CODE:	**B**

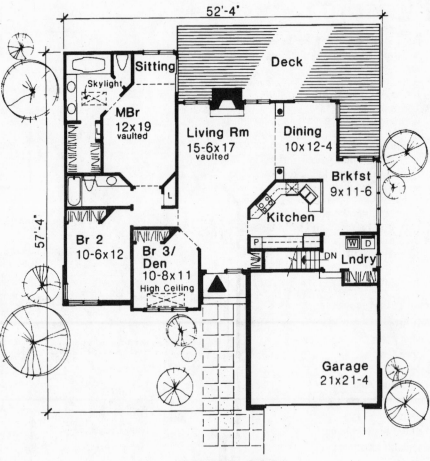

MAIN FLOOR

Distinctive Design

- This well-designed home is neatly laid out to provide distinctive formal and informal living areas.
- The entry guides guests into the combination living and dining room. Straight ahead, double doors open to a large family room that overlooks an inviting patio. An 11-ft. vaulted ceiling with exposed beams and a dramatic fireplace with a raised hearth give the room added appeal.
- The galley-style kitchen offers easy service to the dining room and the bayed eating area. Nearby, a deluxe utility room features laundry facilities and access to the garage.
- Three bedrooms, each with a walk-in closet, make up the sleeping wing. The master suite offers a private bath with a separate dressing area set off by a decorative half-wall.

Plan E-1601	
Bedrooms: 3	**Baths:** 2
Living Area:	
Main floor	1,630 sq. ft.
Total Living Area:	**1,630 sq. ft.**
Garage and storage	610 sq. ft.
Exterior Wall Framing:	2x4

Foundation Options:

Crawlspace
Slab
(All plans can be built with your choice of foundation and framing. A generic conversion diagram is available. See order form.)

BLUEPRINT PRICE CODE:	B

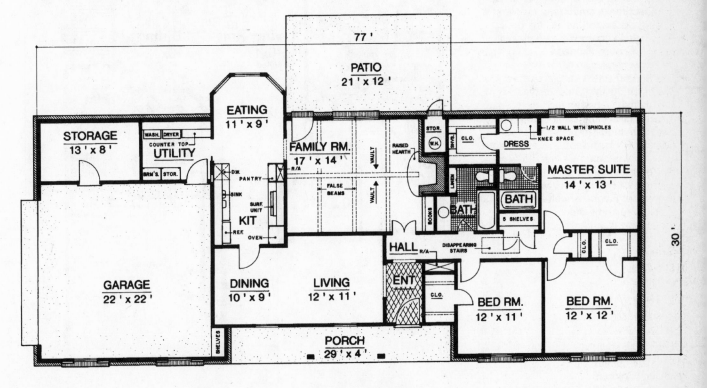

MAIN FLOOR

Affordable Luxury

- This stylish and enticing home combines luxury and affordability in one compact package.
- The foyer offers an immediate view of the living room's impressive fireplace and the wraparound deck beyond. The spacious living room also features a dramatic 15-ft. vaulted ceiling.
- The adjoining formal dining room is outlined by decorative wood columns. Sliding glass doors access the deck.
- A corner sink framed by a half-wall keeps the well-planned kitchen open to the sunny breakfast nook.
- The master suite is spectacular, with a bright sitting area and a distinctive ceiling that slopes up to 10 feet. A large walk-in closet and a sumptuous master bath with a dual-sink vanity, a whirlpool tub and a corner shower are other highlights.
- The third bedroom, with its beautiful Palladian window and vaulted ceiling, would serve equally well as a den or an impressive home office.

Plan B-89020

Bedrooms: 2+	Baths: 2
Living Area:	
Main floor	1,642 sq. ft.
Total Living Area:	**1,642 sq. ft.**
Standard basement	1,642 sq. ft.
Garage	455 sq. ft.
Exterior Wall Framing:	2x4

Foundation Options:

Standard basement

(All plans can be built with your choice of foundation and framing. A generic conversion diagram is available. See order form.)

BLUEPRINT PRICE CODE:	**B**

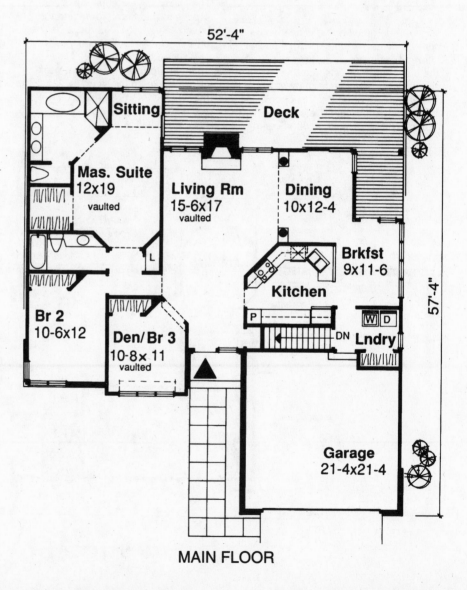

MAIN FLOOR

Plan B-89020

PRICES AND DETAILS
ON PAGES 12-15

Southwestern Standout

- Contemporary styling with a traditional touch makes this house a standout in any neighborhood.
- The generously sized kitchen contains abundant counter space, a handy pantry and corner windows overlooking an enticing backyard patio. The kitchen is open to the family room and nook for informal living.
- The family room and kitchen can be totally closed off to provide extra privacy for the formal dining and living rooms. Both the family room and the living room feature fireplaces.
- The master bedroom has a private bath and is highlighted by a sunny alcove with a French door that opens to the patio.
- The laundry room is handy to the garage and to the bedrooms.

Plan R-1039

Bedrooms: 3	Baths: 2
Space:	
Main floor	1,642 sq. ft.
Total Living Area	**1,642 sq. ft.**
Garage	517 sq. ft.
Exterior Wall Framing	2x6

Foundation options:

Slab

Crawlspace

(Foundation & framing conversion diagram available—see order form.)

Blueprint Price Code	B

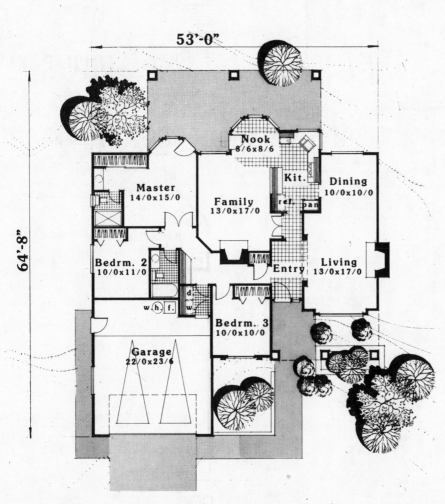

53'-0"

64'-8"

Master 14/0x15/0

Nook 8/6x8/6

Family 13/0x17/0

Kit.

ref. pan

Dining 10/0x10/0

Bedrm. 2 10/0x11/0

Entry

Living 13/0x17/0

w h f.

d w

Bedrm. 3 10/0x10/0

Garage 22/0x23/6

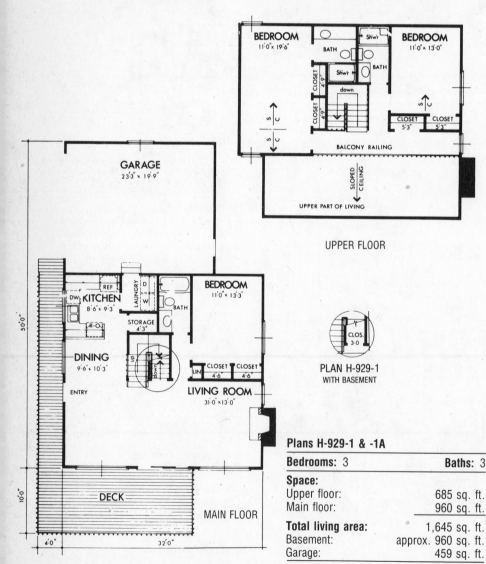

GARAGE
23'-3" x 19'-9"

UPPER FLOOR

BEDROOM
11'-0" x 19'-6"

BATH

Sh'w'r

BEDROOM
11'-0" x 13'-0"

BATH

CLOSET 4'-9"

CLOSET 4'-9"

Sh'w'r

down

CLOSET 5'-3"

CLOSET 5'-3"

SLOPED CEILING

BALCONY RAILING

UPPER PART OF LIVING

REF

DW

KITCHEN
8'-6" x 9'-3"

LAUNDRY

D
W

BATH

BEDROOM
11'-0" x 13'-3"

STORAGE 4'-3"

R-O

DINING
9'-6" x 10'-3"

ENTRY

down

LIN

CLOSET 4'-6"

CLOSET 4'-6"

LIVING ROOM
31'-0" x 13'-0"

DECK

50'-0"

10'-0"

10'-0"

4'-0"

32'-0"

MAIN FLOOR

CLOS. 3'-0"

PLAN H-929-1
WITH BASEMENT

Contemporary Retreat

- Main floor plan revolves around an open, centrally located stairway.
- Spaciousness prevails throughout entire home with open kitchen and combination dining/living room.
- Living room features a great-sized fireplace and access to two-sided deck.
- Separate baths accommodate each bedroom.
- Upstairs hallway reveals an open balcony railing to oversee activities below.

Plans H-929-1 & -1A

Bedrooms: 3	Baths: 3
Space:	
Upper floor:	685 sq. ft.
Main floor:	960 sq. ft.
Total living area:	1,645 sq. ft.
Basement:	approx. 960 sq. ft.
Garage:	459 sq. ft.

Exterior Wall Framing: 2x6

Foundation options:
Daylight basement (Plan H-929-1).
Crawlspace (Plan H-929-1A).
(Foundation & framing conversion diagram available — see order form.)

Blueprint Price Code: B

Angled Solar Design

- This passive-solar design with a six-sided core is angled to capture as much sunlight as possible.
- Finished in natural vertical cedar planks and stone veneer, this contemporary three-bedroom requires a minimum of maintenance.
- Double doors at the entry open into the spacious living and dining areas.

- The formal area features a 14-ft. domed ceiling with skylights, a freestanding fireplace and three sets of sliding glass doors. The central sliding doors lead to a glass-enclosed sun room.
- The bright eat-in kitchen merges with the den, where sliding glass doors lead to one of three backyard terraces.
- The master bedroom, in the quiet sleeping wing, boasts ample closets, a private terrace and a luxurious bath, complete with a whirlpool tub.
- The two secondary bedrooms share a convenient hall bath.

Plan K-534-L	
Bedrooms: 3	**Baths:** 2
Living Area:	
Main floor	1,647 sq. ft.
Total Living Area:	**1,647 sq. ft.**
Standard basement	1,505 sq. ft.
Garage	400 sq. ft.
Exterior Wall Framing:	2x4 or 2x6

Foundation Options:

Standard basement

Slab

(All plans can be built with your choice of foundation and framing. A generic conversion diagram is available. See order form.)

BLUEPRINT PRICE CODE: **B**

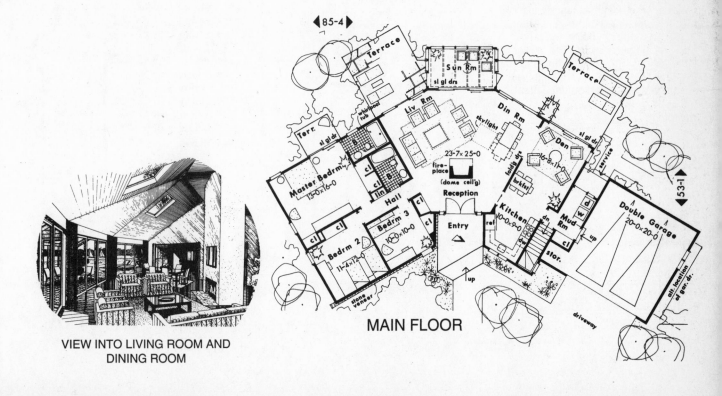

VIEW INTO LIVING ROOM AND DINING ROOM

MAIN FLOOR

Smashing Master Suite!

- Corniced gables accented with arched louvers and a covered front porch with striking columns take this one-story design beyond the ordinary.
- The vaulted ceiling in the foyer rises to join the 19-ft. vaulted ceiling in the family room. A central fireplace heats the casual areas and is framed by a window and a French door.
- An angled serving bar/snack counter connects the family room to the sunny dining room and kitchen. The adjoining breakfast room has easy access to the garage, the optional basement and the laundry room with a plant shelf.
- The master suite is simply smashing, with a 10-ft. tray ceiling and private access to the backyard. The master bath has an 11½-ft. vaulted ceiling and all the amenities, while the 13-ft.-high vaulted sitting area offers an optional fireplace.

Plan FB-1671

Bedrooms: 3	Baths: 2
Living Area:	
Main floor	1,671 sq. ft.
Total Living Area:	**1,671 sq. ft.**
Daylight basement	1,671 sq. ft.
Garage	240 sq. ft.
Exterior Wall Framing:	2x4

Foundation Options:

Daylight basement
Crawlspace
(All plans can be built with your choice of foundation and framing. A generic conversion diagram is available. See order form.)

BLUEPRINT PRICE CODE: B

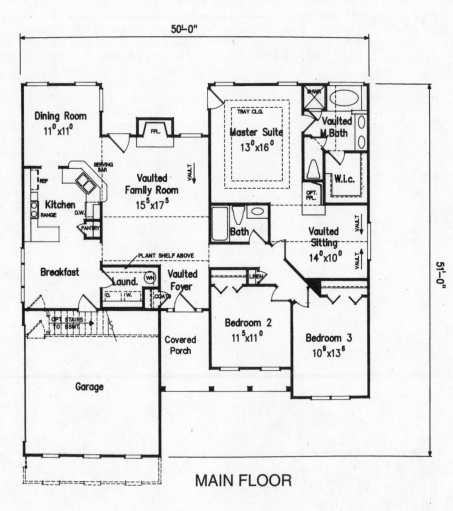

MAIN FLOOR

   Plan FB-1671   *PRICES AND DETAILS* *ON PAGES 12-15*

FRONT VIEW

Gracious Indoor/ Outdoor Living

- A clean design makes this plan adaptable to almost any climate or setting.
- Perfect for a scenic, hillside lot, the structure and wrap-around deck offers a spanning view.
- Kitchen is flanked by family and dining rooms, allowing easy entrance from both.
- Foundation options include a daylight basement on concrete slab (H-2083-1), a wood-framed lower level (H-2083-1B), and a crawlspace (H-2083-1A).

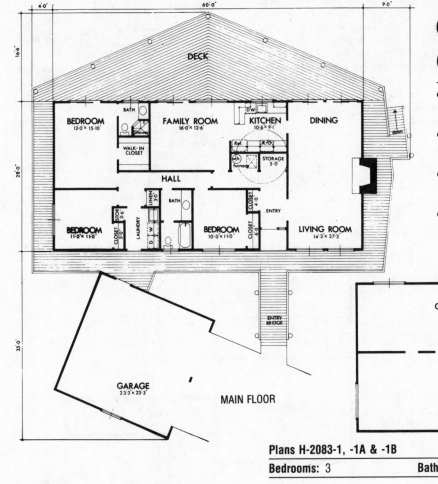

MAIN FLOOR

PLAN H-2083-1
WITH DAYLIGHT BASEMENT
(ON CONCRETE SLAB)

PLAN H-2083-1B
(WITH WOOD-FRAMED LOWER LEVEL)

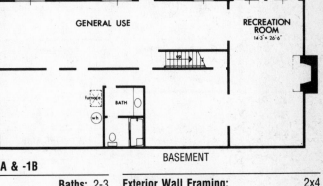

BASEMENT

Plans H-2083-1, -1A & -1B

Bedrooms: 3	Baths: 2-3

Space:

Main floor:	1,660 sq. ft.
Basement:	1,660 sq. ft.

Total living area:

with basement:	3,320 sq. ft.
Garage:	541 sq. ft.

Exterior Wall Framing: 2x4

Foundation options:
Daylight basement (Plan H-2083-1 or -1B).
Crawlspace (Plan H-2083-1A).
(Foundation & framing conversion diagram available — see order form.)

Blueprint Price Code:

Without basement:	B
With basement:	E

Comfortable, Open Plan

- This comfortable home defines function and style, with a sharp window wall to brighten the central living areas.
- In from the broad front deck, the living/family room boasts a fireplace, a cathedral ceiling and soaring views. The fireplace visually sets off the dining room, which extends to the backyard patio through sliding doors.
- The galley-style kitchen offers a bright sink and an abundance of counter space, with a laundry closet and carport access nearby.
- The secluded and spacious master bedroom features private deck access, a walk-in closet and a private bath.
- On the other side of the home, two good-sized secondary bedrooms share another full bath.

Plan C-8160

Bedrooms: 3	Baths: 2
Living Area:	
Main floor	1,669 sq. ft.
Total Living Area:	**1,669 sq. ft.**
Daylight basement	1,660 sq. ft.
Carport	413 sq. ft.
Storage	85 sq. ft.
Exterior Wall Framing:	2x4

Foundation Options:

Daylight basement
Crawlspace
Slab

(All plans can be built with your choice of foundation and framing. A generic conversion diagram is available. See order form.)

BLUEPRINT PRICE CODE:	B

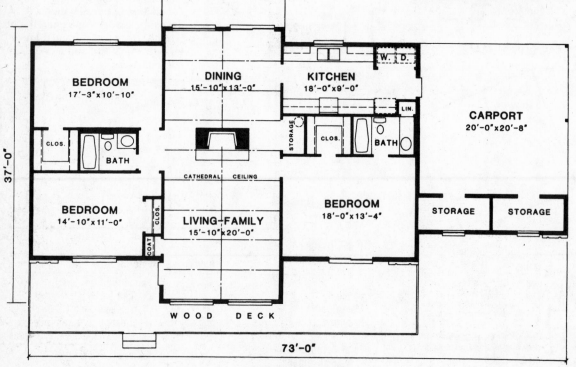

MAIN FLOOR

Plan C-8160

PRICES AND DETAILS ON PAGES 12-15

Porch Offers Three Entries

- Showy window treatments, stately columns and three sets of French doors give this Plantation-style home an inviting exterior.
- High 12-ft. ceilings in the living room, dining room and kitchen add volume to the economically-sized home.
- A corner fireplace and a view to the back porch are found in the living room. The porch is accessed from a door in the dining room.
- The adjoining kitchen features an angled snack bar that easily serves the dining room and the casual eating area.
- The secluded master suite offers a cathedral ceiling, a walk-in closet and a luxurious private bath with a spa tub and a separate shower.
- Across the home, two additional bedrooms share a second full bath.

Plan E-1602

Bedrooms: 3	Baths: 2
Living Area:	
Main floor	1,672 sq. ft.
Total Living Area:	**1,672 sq. ft.**
Standard basement	1,672 sq. ft.
Garage	484 sq. ft.
Exterior Wall Framing:	2x6

Foundation Options:

Standard basement

Crawlspace

Slab

(All plans can be built with your choice of foundation and framing. A generic conversion diagram is available. See order form.)

BLUEPRINT PRICE CODE: B

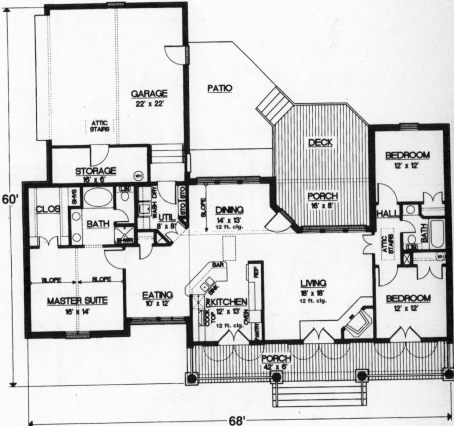

MAIN FLOOR

Smart Design for Sloping Lot

- This design boasts stunning windows and a gorgeous deck, and is perfect for a narrow, sloping lot.
- The main entry opens to the spacious living areas. The Great Room shows off a soaring 12-ft. vaulted ceiling, a cozy woodstove and a boxed-out window arrangement. An 11½-ft. vaulted ceiling presides over the dining area and the

kitchen. The dining area offers sliding glass doors to the deck.
- Two bedrooms and two skylighted baths are located at the back of the home. The master bedroom also has a walk-in wardrobe, a lovely window seat and deck access.
- A vaulted, skylighted hall approaches the stairway to the basement, which hosts a third bedroom and another full bath. A very large shop/storage area and a two-car garage are also included. An extra bonus is the carport/storage area below the deck.

Plan P-529-2D

Bedrooms: 3	**Baths:** 3

Living Area:	
Main floor	1,076 sq. ft.
Daylight basement	597 sq. ft.
Total Living Area:	**1,673 sq. ft.**
Tuck-under garage	425 sq. ft.
Exterior Wall Framing:	2x6

Foundation Options:

Daylight basement

(All plans can be built with your choice of foundation and framing. A generic conversion diagram is available. See order form.)

BLUEPRINT PRICE CODE: B

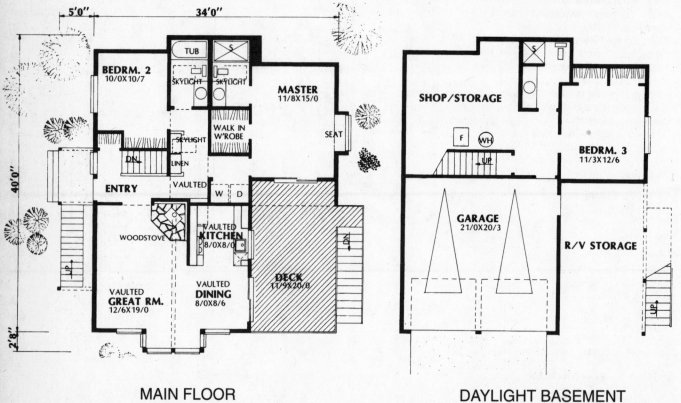

MAIN FLOOR   DAYLIGHT BASEMENT

Surprising Features!

- The exciting exterior of this charming home reflects traditional country style, while its enticing interior is filled with surprising luxurious features.
- The bright foyer boasts a 17-ft. vaulted ceiling highlighted by a high plant shelf set into a classy dormer.
- The adjacent formal dining room enjoys an elegant 10 ft., 10-in. tray ceiling.
- The efficient galley-style kitchen includes a pantry and a sunny breakfast area. A powder room and a laundry closet are nearby.
- Graced by a 17-ft. vaulted ceiling, the Great Room offers a fireplace and a French door to the backyard.
- The deluxe master suite features a 9½-ft. tray ceiling. The master bath has a 13-ft. vaulted ceiling and offers a spa tub, a separate shower and a dual-sink vanity.
- Upstairs, a second full bath is shared by two additional bedrooms. The bonus room may be finished as an extra bedroom, a den or a playroom.

Plan FB-5231-NAPL

Bedrooms: 3+	Baths: 2½
Living Area:	
Upper floor	435 sq. ft.
Main floor	1,065 sq. ft.
Bonus room	175 sq. ft.
Total Living Area:	**1,675 sq. ft.**
Daylight basement	1,065 sq. ft.
Garage and storage	458 sq. ft.
Exterior Wall Framing:	2x4

Foundation Options:

Daylight basement

(All plans can be built with your choice of foundation and framing. A generic conversion diagram is available. See order form.)

BLUEPRINT PRICE CODE:	B

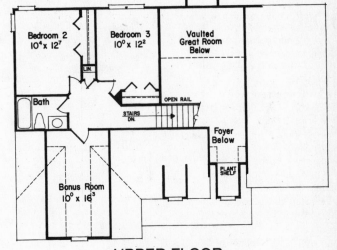

UPPER FLOOR

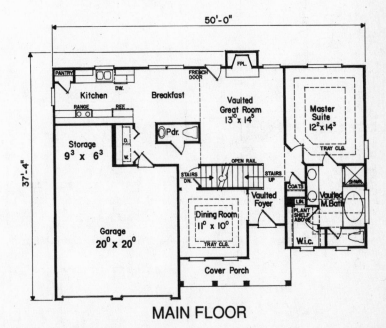

MAIN FLOOR

REAR VIEW

Deck and Spa!

- Designed for relaxation as well as for active indoor/outdoor living, this popular home offers a gigantic deck and an irresistible spa room.
- A covered porch welcomes guests into the entry hall, which flows past the central, open-railed stairway to the spectacular Great Room.
- Sliding glass doors on each side of the Great Room extend the living space to the huge V-shaped deck. The 22-ft. sloped ceiling and a woodstove add to the stunning effect.
- The master suite features a cozy window seat, a walk-in closet and private access to a full bath.
- The passive-solar spa room can be reached from the master suite as well as the backyard deck.
- The upper floor hosts two additional bedrooms, a full bath and a balcony hall that overlooks the Great Room.

Plans H-952-1A & -1B

Bedrooms: 3+	Baths: 2-3
Living Area:	
Upper floor	470 sq. ft.
Main floor	1,207 sq. ft.
Passive spa room	102 sq. ft.
Daylight basement	1,105 sq. ft.
Total Living Area:	**1,779/2,884 sq. ft.**
Garage	496 sq. ft.
Exterior Wall Framing:	2x6
Foundation Options:	Plan #
Daylight basement	H-952-1B
Crawlspace	H-952-1A

(All plans can be built with your choice of foundation and framing. A generic conversion diagram is available. See order form.)

BLUEPRINT PRICE CODE:	**B/D**

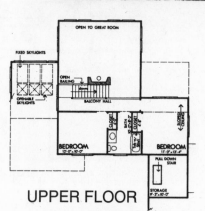

UPPER FLOOR

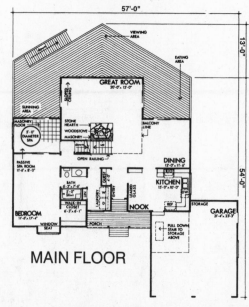

MAIN FLOOR

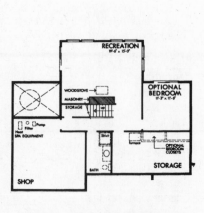

DAYLIGHT BASEMENT

Plans H-952-1A & -1B

PRICES AND DETAILS ON PAGES 12-15

FRONT VIEW

Sunny Family Living

- Pleasant-looking and unassuming from the front, this plan breaks into striking, sun-catching angles at the rear.
- The living room sun roof gathers passive solar heat, which is stored in the tile floor and the two-story high masonry backdrop to the wood stove.
- A 516-square-foot master suite with private bath and balcony makes up the second floor.
- The main floor offers two more bedrooms and a full bath.

UPPER FLOOR

WITHOUT BASEMENT
(CRAWLSPACE FOUNDATION)

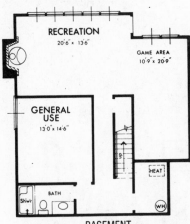

BASEMENT

Main Floor

PASSIVE SUN ROOM

40'-0"

THERMAL STORAGE FLOOR

DINING
10'-3" x 12'-0"

DECK

WOOD STOVE

LIVING ROOM
20'-9" x 13'-6"

SLOPED CEILING

BEDROOM
11'-0" x 10'-0"

KITCHEN
9'-0" x 10'-0"

GARAGE
11'-9" x 23'-9"

BATH

ENTRY

LAUNDRY

BEDROOM
11'-0" x 10'-0"

56'-0"

MAIN FLOOR

Plans H-947-1A & -1B

Bedrooms: 3	Baths: 2-3
Space:	
Upper floor:	516 sq. ft.
Main floor:	1,162 sq. ft.
Total without basement:	1,678 sq. ft.
Daylight basement:	966 sq. ft.
Total with basement:	2,644 sq. ft.
Garage:	279 sq. ft.
Exterior Wall Framing:	2x6

Foundation options:
Daylight basement (H-947-1B).
Crawlspace (H-947-1A).
(Foundation & framing conversion diagram available — see order form.)

Blueprint Price Code:
Without basement:	B
With basement:	D

REAR VIEW

Spacious Economy

- This economical country cottage features wide, angled spaces and 9-ft., 4-in. ceilings in both the Great Room and the master bedroom for roomy appeal and year-round comfort.
- The Great Room boasts a cozy fireplace with a raised hearth and a built-in niche for a TV, making this room perfect for winter gatherings. On warm nights, a homey covered porch at the rear can be accessed through sliding glass doors.
- Amenities in the luxurious master bedroom include a large walk-in closet, a private whirlpool bath and a dual-sink vanity.
- The nicely appointed kitchen offers nearby laundry facilities and porch access. A serving bar allows for casual dining and relaxed conversation.
- The optional daylight basement includes a tuck-under, two-car garage.

Plan AX-94322

Bedrooms: 3	Baths: 2½
Living Area:	
Upper floor	545 sq. ft.
Main floor	1,134 sq. ft.
Total Living Area:	**1,679 sq. ft.**
Daylight basement	618 sq. ft.
Standard basement	1,134 sq. ft.
Tuck-under garage	516 sq. ft.
Exterior Wall Framing:	2x4

Foundation Options:
Daylight basement
Standard basement
Crawlspace
Slab
(All plans can be built with your choice of foundation and framing. A generic conversion diagram is available. See order form.)

BLUEPRINT PRICE CODE: **B**

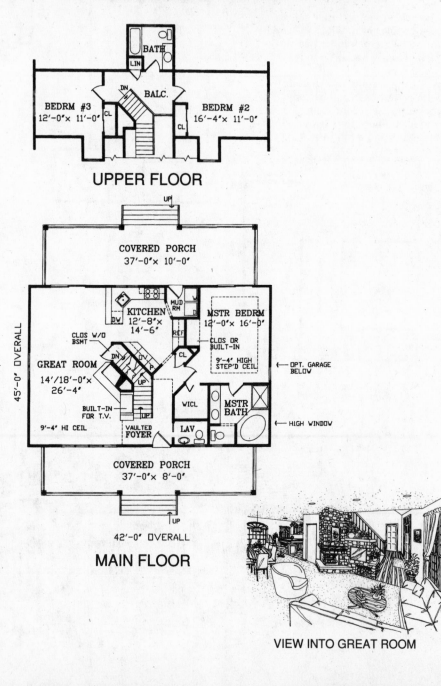

UPPER FLOOR

MAIN FLOOR

VIEW INTO GREAT ROOM

Plenty of Presence

- A stucco facade complemented by fieldstone, a dramatic roofline and handsome keystones accenting the window treatments gives this home plenty of presence.
- Inside, the two-story foyer boasts an open stairway with a balcony overlook. Straight ahead, the huge family room is expanded by a 16½-ft. vaulted ceiling, plus a tall window and a French door that frame the fireplace.
- The adjoining dining room flows into the kitchen and breakfast room, which feature an angled serving bar, a bright window wall and a French door that opens to a covered patio.
- The main-floor master suite is the pride of the floor plan, offering a 10-ft. tray ceiling. The deluxe master bath has a 14-ft. vaulted ceiling, a garden tub and a spacious walk-in closet.
- The upper floor offers two more bedrooms, a full bath and attic space.

Plan FB-1681

Bedrooms: 3	Baths: 2½
Living Area:	
Upper floor	449 sq. ft.
Main floor	1,232 sq. ft.
Total Living Area:	**1,681 sq. ft.**
Daylight basement	1,232 sq. ft.
Garage and storage	435 sq. ft.
Exterior Wall Framing:	2x4

Foundation Options:

Daylight basement
Crawlspace

(All plans can be built with your choice of foundation and framing.
A generic conversion diagram is available. See order form.)

BLUEPRINT PRICE CODE:	B

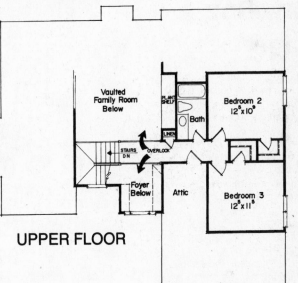

UPPER FLOOR

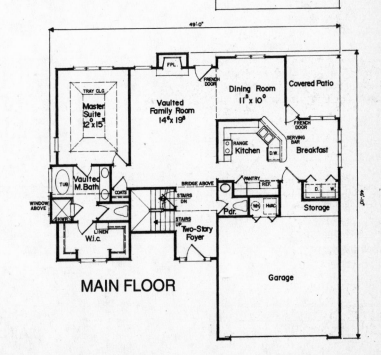

MAIN FLOOR

Captivating Cottage

- Regal metal-roofed bays give a European flair to this captivating cottage design.
- Elegant French doors usher guests in from the covered porch to a dramatic columned gallery.
- On the left, the island kitchen boasts a 12-ft. vaulted ceiling and outdoor access via sliding glass doors.
- A 19-ft. vaulted ceiling presides over the bayed dining room and the expansive central Great Room. Features here include a focal-point fireplace, built-in shelves and sliding glass doors to a second covered porch.
- An angled door leads to the secluded master bedroom, with its 12-ft. vaulted ceiling. Sliding doors provide private access to the backyard. Two closets and a whirlpool bath complete the suite.
- High 10-ft. ceilings enhance the two secondary bedrooms, which share a hall bath. A laundry closet is nearby.
- The side-entry garage is beautifully concealed behind a lovely bay window.

Plan AX-94313

Bedrooms: 3	Baths: 2
Living Area:	
Main floor	1,685 sq. ft.
Total Living Area:	**1,685 sq. ft.**
Standard basement	1,685 sq. ft.
Garage	434 sq. ft.
Exterior Wall Framing:	2x4

Foundation Options:

Standard basement
Crawlspace
Slab

(All plans can be built with your choice of foundation and framing. A generic conversion diagram is available. See order form.)

BLUEPRINT PRICE CODE: **B**

VIEW INTO GREAT ROOM

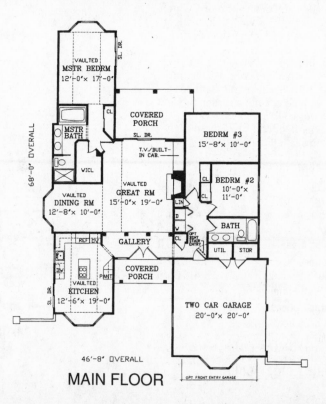

MAIN FLOOR

Plan AX-94313

PRICES AND DETAILS ON PAGES 12-15

Bright and Airy Spaces Abound!

- An arched brick entry and a high, arched window set the tone for the bright, airy spaces this home offers.
- An 11-ft.-high barrel-vaulted ceiling highlights the living room and adds to the striking effect of the arched window. The living room's openness to the dining room further enhances the feeling of spaciousness.
- The kitchen is designed as an integral part of the family room and nook. The angled snack counter allows the cook to keep in touch with family activities.
- The nook features dramatic solarium windows that flood the area with natural light. The family room has sliding glass doors that open to a backyard patio.
- The master bedroom includes a private, skylighted bath and a walk-in closet. Another full bath lies between the two secondary bedrooms.

Plan R-1067

Bedrooms: 3	Baths: 2
Living Area:	
Main floor	1,685 sq. ft.
Total Living Area:	**1,685 sq. ft.**
Garage	432 sq. ft.
Exterior Wall Framing:	2x6
Foundation Options:	

Crawlspace
(All plans can be built with your choice of foundation and framing. A generic conversion diagram is available. See order form.)

BLUEPRINT PRICE CODE:	**B**

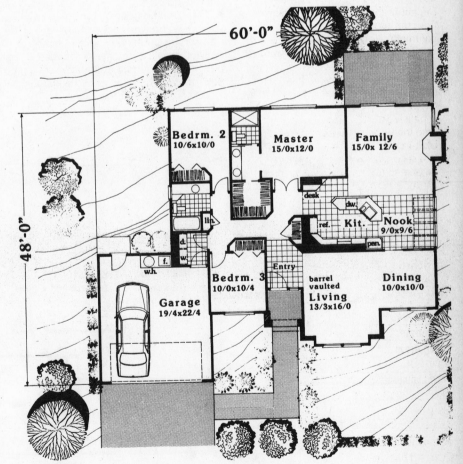

MAIN FLOOR

Shady Porches, Sunny Patio

- Designed with stylish country looks, this attractive one-story also has shady porches and a sunny patio for relaxed indoor/outdoor living.
- The inviting foyer flows into the spacious living room, which is warmed by a handsome fireplace.
- The adjoining dining room has a door to a screened-in porch, which opens to the

backyard and serves as a breezeway to the nearby garage
- The U-shaped kitchen has a pantry closet and plenty of counter space. Around the corner, a space-efficient laundry/utility room exits to a big backyard patio.
- The master bedroom is brightened by windows on two sides and includes a wardrobe closet. The compartmentalized master bath offers a separate dressing area and a walk-in closet.
- Another full bath serves two additional good-sized bedrooms.

Plan C-7557	
Bedrooms: 3	**Baths:** 2
Living Area:	
Main floor	1,688 sq. ft.
Total Living Area:	**1,688 sq. ft.**
Standard basement	1,688 sq. ft.
Garage	400 sq. ft.
Exterior Wall Framing:	2x4

Foundation Options:
Standard basement
Crawlspace
Slab
(All plans can be built with your choice of foundation and framing. A generic conversion diagram is available. See order form.)

BLUEPRINT PRICE CODE:	B

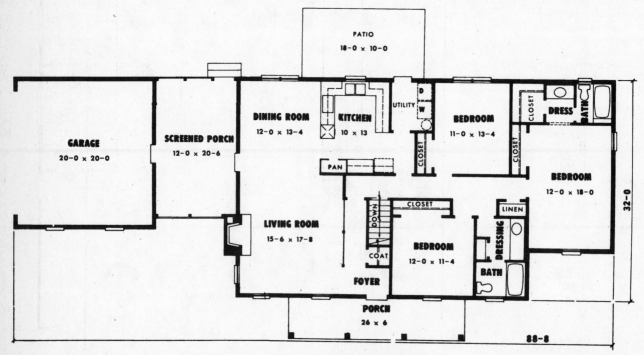

MAIN FLOOR

Plan C-7557
PRICES AND DETAILS
ON PAGES 12-15

Captivating Showpiece

- This design is sure to be the showpiece of the neighborhood, with its captivating blend of traditional and contemporary features.
- The angled front porch creates an eye-catching look. Inside, the foyer, the dining room and the Great Room are expanded by 9-ft., 4-in. tray ceilings and separated by columns.
- The dining room features a spectacular arched window, while the spacious Great Room hosts a fireplace framed by windows overlooking the rear terrace.
- The glass-filled breakfast room is given added impact by a 9-ft., 4-in. tray ceiling. The adjoining kitchen offers an expansive island counter with an eating bar and a cooktop.
- A wonderful TV room or home office views out to the front porch.
- The master suite is highlighted by a 9-ft., 10-in. tray ceiling and a sunny sitting area with a large picture window topped by an arched transom.

Plan AX-92322

Bedrooms: 3+	Baths: 2
Living Area:	
Main floor	1,699 sq. ft.
Total Living Area:	**1,699 sq. ft.**
Standard basement	1,740 sq. ft.
Garage	480 sq. ft.
Exterior Wall Framing:	2x4

Foundation Options:

Standard basement

Crawlspace

Slab

(All plans can be built with your choice of foundation and framing. A generic conversion diagram is available. See order form.)

BLUEPRINT PRICE CODE: B

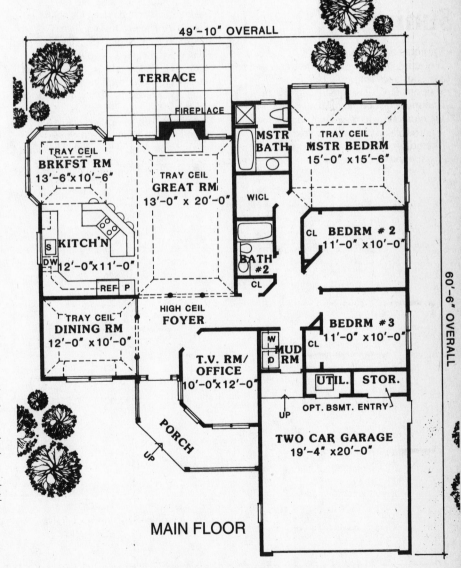

MAIN FLOOR

Delightful Styling

- This quaint home's delightful styling is obvious, with its triple roof dormers and full-width covered front porch.
- Inside, 9-ft. ceilings grace the main floor, as the living room, dining room and kitchen merge to maximize space.
- The living room features a fireplace and three pairs of French doors. The dining room has rear access to a covered porch, which connects the house to the garage. The kitchen's wet bar is centrally located to serve all three rooms.
- The main-floor master suite has two pairs of French doors leading to the front porch. The master bath includes a raised marble tub, a dual-sink vanity, a walk-in closet and a sloped ceiling with a sunny skylight.
- The two bedrooms upstairs share a second full bath. Each bedroom features a quaint dormer to let the light shine in.

Plan E-1709

Bedrooms: 3	Baths: 2½
Living Area:	
Upper floor	540 sq. ft.
Main floor	1,160 sq. ft.
Total Living Area:	**1,700 sq. ft.**
Standard basement	1,160 sq. ft.
Garage	484 sq. ft.
Exterior Wall Framing:	2x6

Foundation Options:

Standard basement
Crawlspace
Slab
(All plans can be built with your choice of foundation and framing. A generic conversion diagram is available. See order form.)

BLUEPRINT PRICE CODE: B

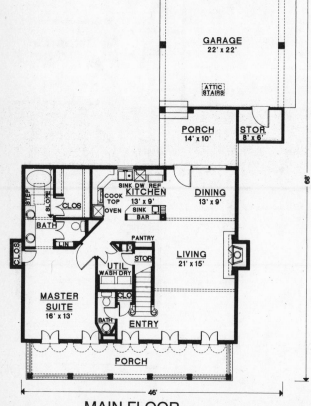

MAIN FLOOR

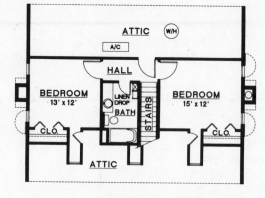

UPPER FLOOR

Plan E-1709

PRICES AND DETAILS
ON PAGES 12-15

Compact and Cozy

- This comfortable well-planned design offers popular features in a modest square footage, and is suitable for a narrow lot.
- The gorgeous vaulted Great Room boasts tall corner windows, a nice fireplace and an adjoining dining area with a wet bar.
- Guests pass a handy half-bath en route to the casual family room. Sliding glass doors provide access to a rear deck for more entertainment space.
- A bright corner sink and a breakfast nook are highlights of the kitchen.
- On the upper floor, the master suite features a skylighted whirlpool tub and a walk-in closet.
- A central loft area could be enclosed and used for a bedroom.

Plan B-8329

Bedrooms: 2-3	Baths: 2½
Living Area:	
Upper floor	756 sq. ft.
Main floor	904 sq. ft.
Total Living Area:	**1,660 sq. ft.**
Standard basement	904 sq. ft.
Garage	367 sq. ft.
Exterior Wall Framing:	2x4

Foundation Options:
Standard basement
(Typical foundation & framing conversion diagram available—see order form.)

BLUEPRINT PRICE CODE:	**B**

UPPER FLOOR

MAIN FLOOR

High Ceilings, Sunny Spaces

- Lots of glass, a sunny greenhouse and a large terrace make this elegant one-story perfect for indoor/outdoor living.
- The greenhouse at the rear of the home has glass walls and a sunroof. Sliding doors in the family room open to the greenhouse.
- The bayed dining nook overlooks the rear terrace, which is accessible from the greenhouse and the dinette.
- The kitchen is open to the family room and has a snack bar joining it to the dinette. The formal dining and living rooms, which feature a cathedral ceiling and a fireplace, are also easily reached from the kitchen.
- The hall bath is close to the living areas as well as to the two front-facing bedrooms. The master bedroom suite offers its own luxurious bath.

Plan AHP-9125

Bedrooms: 3	Baths: 2
Space:	
Main floor	1,703 sq. ft.
Total Living Area	**1,703 sq. ft.**
Basement	1,766 sq. ft.
Garage	462 sq. ft.
Exterior Wall Framing	2x4 or 2x6

Foundation options:

Standard Basement

Crawlspace

Slab

(Foundation & framing conversion diagram available—see order form.)

Blueprint Price Code	**B**

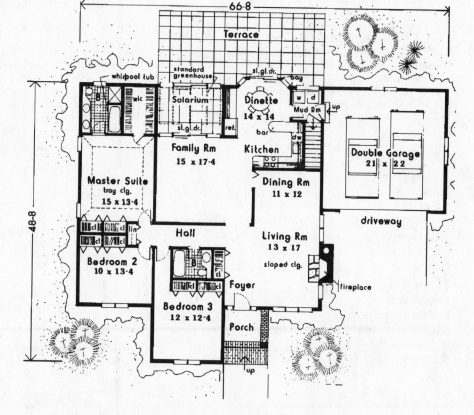

MAIN FLOOR

Panoramic Prow View

- This glass-filled prow gable design is almost as spectacular as the panoramic view from inside.
- French doors open from the front deck to the dining room. A stunning window wall illuminates the adjoining living room, which flaunts a 20-ft.-high cathedral ceiling.

- The open, corner kitchen is perfectly angled to service the dining room and the family room, while offering views of the front and rear decks.
- A handy utility/laundry room opens to the rear deck. Two bedrooms share a full bath, to complete the main floor.
- A dramatic, open-railed stairway leads up to the secluded master bedroom, which boasts a dressing room and a private bath with a dual-sink vanity and a separate tub and shower.

Plan NW-196	
Bedrooms: 3	Baths: 2
Living Area:	
Upper floor	394 sq. ft.
Main floor	1,317 sq. ft.
Total Living Area:	**1,711 sq. ft.**
Exterior Wall Framing:	2x6

Foundation Options:

Crawlspace
(All plans can be built with your choice of foundation and framing. A generic conversion diagram is available. See order form.)

BLUEPRINT PRICE CODE:	**B**

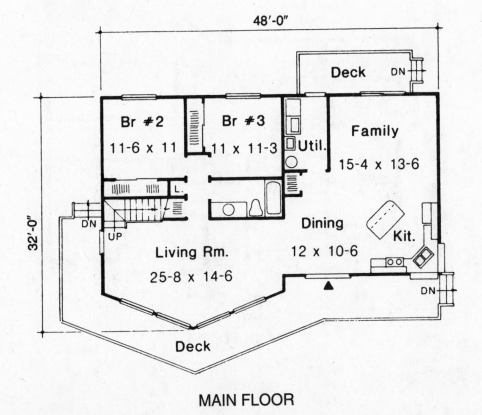

MAIN FLOOR

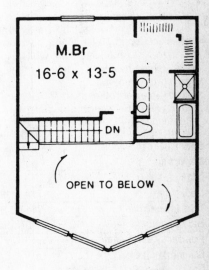

UPPER FLOOR

TO ORDER THIS BLUEPRINT,
CALL TOLL-FREE 1-800-547-5570

Plan NW-196

PRICES AND DETAILS
ON PAGES 12-15

145

French Charm

- The exterior of this charming French home displays great details, including attractive keystones, neat quoins and huge arched window arrangements.
- Inside the home, a high plant ledge adorns the tiled foyer, which boasts a dramatic 13-ft. ceiling.
- To the left, the elegant formal dining room extends to the huge living room, which boasts a warm fireplace and neat built-in bookshelves above functional cabinets. A striking 10-ft. ceiling soars above both rooms.
- A convenient serving bar links the gourmet kitchen to the sunny bayed breakfast nook. The adjacent utility room includes a handy pantry closet.
- Across the home, a tiled foyer features access to a covered porch and the luxurious master suite. The master suite boasts a sloped 10-ft. ceiling, a window seat and a lush private bath, which is highlighted by a marble tub set into a boxed-out window.
- Two more bedrooms share a hall bath. One bedroom features a sloped 10-ft. ceiling and a nice built-in desk.

Plan RD-1714

Bedrooms: 3	Baths: 2
Living Area:	
Main floor	1,714 sq. ft.
Total Living Area:	**1,714 sq. ft.**
Garage and storage	470 sq. ft.
Exterior Wall Framing:	2x4

Foundation Options:

Crawlspace

Slab

(All plans can be built with your choice of foundation and framing. A generic conversion diagram is available. See order form.)

BLUEPRINT PRICE CODE:	B

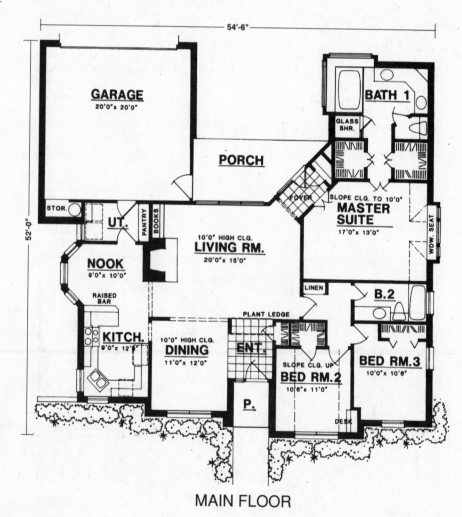

MAIN FLOOR

Plan RD-1714

PRICES AND DETAILS ON PAGES 12-15

Dramatic Dining Room

- The highlight of this lovely one-story design is its dramatic dining room, which boasts a 14-ft.-high ceiling and a soaring window wall.
- The airy foyer ushers guests through a 14-ft.-high arched opening and into the 18-ft. vaulted Great Room, which is warmed by an inviting fireplace.
- The kitchen features a large pantry, a serving bar and a handy pass-through to the Great Room. The bright breakfast area offers a convenient laundry closet and outdoor access.
- The two secondary bedrooms share a compartmentalized bath.
- The removed master suite features a 14-ft. tray ceiling, overhead plant shelves and an adjoining 13½-ft. vaulted sitting room. An exciting garden tub is found in the luxurious master bath.

Plan FB-5008-ALLE

Bedrooms: 3	Baths: 2
Living Area:	
Main floor	1,715 sq. ft.
Total Living Area:	**1,715 sq. ft.**
Daylight basement	1,715 sq. ft.
Garage	400 sq. ft.
Exterior Wall Framing:	2x4

Foundation Options:

Daylight basement

Crawlspace

Slab

(All plans can be built with your choice of foundation and framing. A generic conversion diagram is available. See order form.)

BLUEPRINT PRICE CODE: B

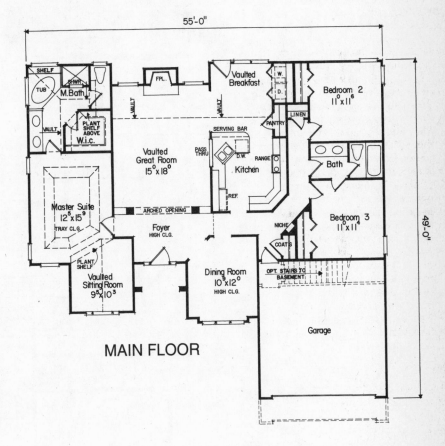

MAIN FLOOR

REAR VIEW

FRONT VIEW

Year-Round Comfort

- Designed for the energy-conscious, this passive-solar home provides year-round comfort with much lower fuel costs.
- The open, airy interior is a delight. In the winter, sunshine penetrates deep into the living spaces. In the summer, wide overhangs shade the interior.
- The central living and dining rooms flow together, creating a bright, open space. Sliding glass doors open to a terrace and an enclosed sun spot.
- In the airy casual space, the kitchen has an eating bar and a sunny breakfast nook. The adjoining family room boasts a woodstove that warms the entire area.
- The master bedroom suite includes a private terrace, a personal bath and a walk-in closet. Two other bedrooms share another full bath.

Plan K-392-T

Bedrooms: 3	Baths: 2½
Living Area:	
Main floor	1,592 sq. ft.
Sun spot	125 sq. ft.
Total Living Area:	**1,717 sq. ft.**
Partial basement	634 sq. ft.
Garage	407 sq. ft.
Exterior Wall Framing:	2x4 or 2x6

Foundation Options:

Partial basement

Slab

(All plans can be built with your choice of foundation and framing. A generic conversion diagram is available. See order form.)

BLUEPRINT PRICE CODE:	B

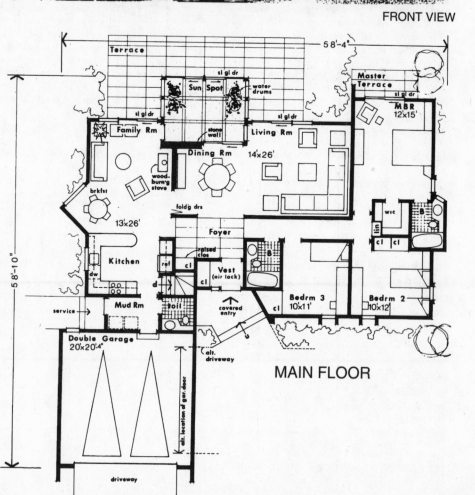

MAIN FLOOR

Five-Bedroom Chalet

Realizing that there are situations that require the maximum number of bedrooms, we have created this modest-sized home containing five bedrooms. One of these, especially the one over the garage, would serve very well as a private den, card room or library. The plan is available with or without basement.

This is an excellent example of the classic chalet. Close study will reveal how hall space has been kept at an absolute minimum. As a result, a modest first floor area of 952 sq. ft. and a compact second floor plan of 767 sq. ft. make the five bedrooms possible.

Also notice the abundance of storage space and built-ins with many other conveniences. Plumbing is provided in two complete bathrooms, and a washer and dryer has been tucked into one corner of the central hall on the main floor.

A clever technique has been used in the design of the staircase as it progresses halfway up to a landing midway between the two floors. From here it branches in two directions to a bedroom over the garage and to a hallway common to other rooms.

First floor:	952 sq. ft.
Second floor:	767 sq. ft.
Total living area: (Not counting basement or garage)	1,719 sq. ft.

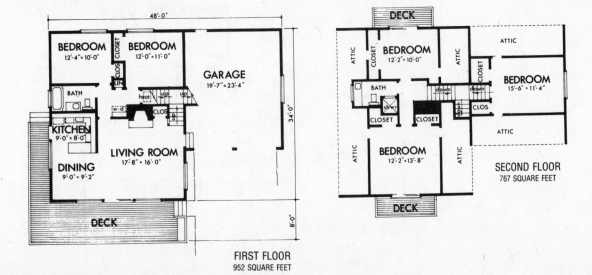

FIRST FLOOR
952 SQUARE FEET

SECOND FLOOR
767 SQUARE FEET

PLAN H-804-2
WITH BASEMENT
PLAN H-804-2A
WITHOUT BASEMENT
(CRAWLSPACE FOUNDATION)

Elevation B

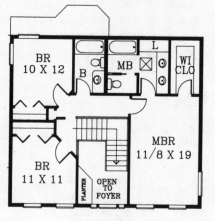

Elevation A

Traditional Twosome

- This plan offers a choice of two elevations. Elevation A has an upper-level Palladian window, while Elevation B has a stately Georgian entry. Both versions are included in the blueprints.
- A vaulted entry foyer leads to formal living and dining rooms.
- The family room, nook and kitchen are combined to create one huge casual living area.
- The second-floor master suite is roomy and includes a beautiful, skylighted bath and a large closet.

Plan S-22189

Bedrooms: 3	Baths: 2½
Living Area:	
Upper floor	774 sq. ft.
Main floor	963 sq. ft.
Total Living Area:	**1,737 sq. ft.**
Standard basement	963 sq. ft.
Garage	462 sq. ft.
Exterior Wall Framing:	2x6

Foundation Options:
Standard basement
Crawlspace
Slab
(Typical foundation & framing conversion diagram available—see order form.)

BLUEPRINT PRICE CODE:	B

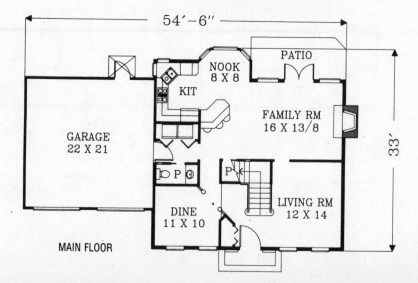

UPPER FLOOR

MAIN FLOOR

Simply Beautiful

- This four-bedroom design offers simplistic beauty, economical construction and ample space for both family life and formal entertaining—all on one floor.
- The charming cottage-style exterior gives way to a spacious interior. A 13-ft. vaulted, beamed ceiling soars above the huge living room, which features a massive fireplace, built-in bookshelves and access to a backyard patio.
- The efficient galley-style kitchen flows between a sunny bayed eating area and the formal dining room.
- The deluxe master suite includes a dressing room, a large walk-in closet and a private bath.
- The three remaining bedrooms are larger than average and offer ample closet space.
- A nice-sized storage area and a deluxe utility room are accessible from the two-car garage.

Plan E-1702	
Bedrooms: 4	**Baths:** 2
Living Area:	
Main floor	1,751 sq. ft.
Total Living Area:	**1,751 sq. ft.**
Garage	484 sq. ft.
Storage	105 sq. ft.
Exterior Wall Framing:	2x4
Foundation Options:	
Crawlspace	
Slab	

(All plans can be built with your choice of foundation and framing. A generic conversion diagram is available. See order form.)

BLUEPRINT PRICE CODE: B

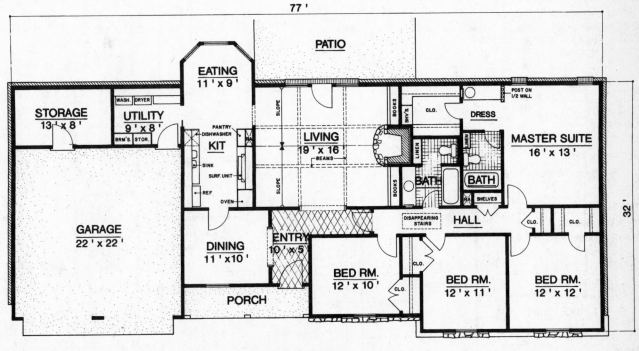

MAIN FLOOR

Nice Touches Add Charm

- A striking dormer window and a columned covered entry are just two of the many nice touches that make this appealing two-story home a truly charming dwelling.
- The entry opens directly into the living room, which boasts a 17-ft. vaulted ceiling and a high plant shelf.
- Easily accessed from the kitchen, the adjoining formal dining room provides a quiet area for special meals.

- Around the corner, the island kitchen offers deck access and a cheery breakfast nook.
- A low wall separates the kitchen from the family room, which is warmed by a handsome fireplace and brightened by corner windows. A handy powder room is just steps away.
- Upstairs, the master bedroom is highlighted by a 12-ft. ceiling and a walk-in closet. A cozy bay window is a nice spot to unwind.
- The private master bath flaunts a separate tub and shower.
- Another full bath services the two roomy secondary bedrooms.

Plan B-93018

Bedrooms: 3	**Baths:** 2½
Living Area:	
Upper floor	808 sq. ft.
Main floor	945 sq. ft.
Total Living Area:	**1,753 sq. ft.**
Standard basement	945 sq. ft.
Garage	410 sq. ft.
Exterior Wall Framing:	2x6

Foundation Options:

Standard basement
(All plans can be built with your choice of foundation and framing. A generic conversion diagram is available. See order form.)

BLUEPRINT PRICE CODE:	B

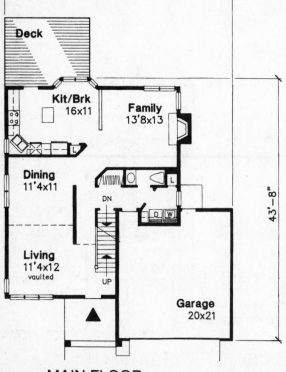

MAIN FLOOR

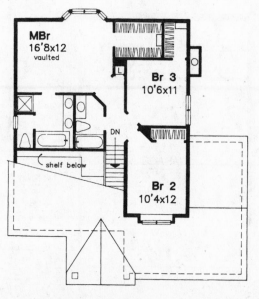

UPPER FLOOR

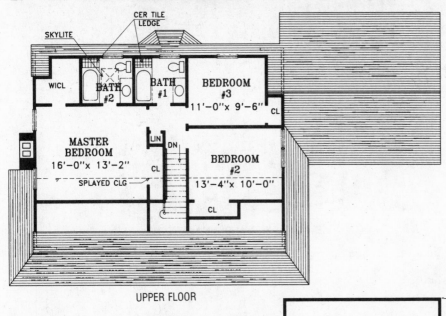

SKYLITE

CER TILE LEDGE

WICL

BATH #2

BATH #1

BEDROOM #3
11'-0" x 9'-6"
CL

MASTER BEDROOM
16'-0" x 13'-2"
SPLAYED CLG

LIN

DN

CL

BEDROOM #2
13'-4" x 10'-0"
CL

UPPER FLOOR

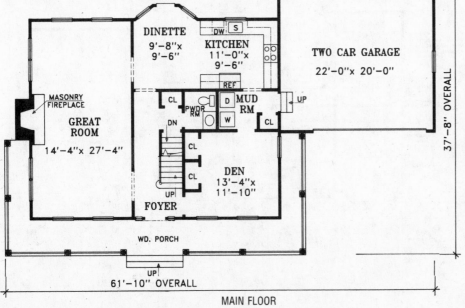

DINETTE
9'-8"x 9'-6"

KITCHEN
11'-0" 9'-6"

DW   S

REF

TWO CAR GARAGE
22'-0"x 20'-0"

MASONRY FIREPLACE

GREAT ROOM
14'-4"x 27'-4"

CL

PWDR RM

D MUD RM

W

UP

CL

DN

CL

UP

DEN
13'-4"x 11'-10"

FOYER

WD. PORCH

UP

61'-10" OVERALL

37'-8" OVERALL

MAIN FLOOR

Quaint Country Design

- The renewed "country" look is evident in this simply designed two-story with wrap-around front porch.
- Functional living areas flank the entryway and stairs.
- A beautiful and spacious Great Room, with masonry fireplace and wrap-around windows, is to the left, and a nice-sized den which could serve as a library, office, guest room or fourth bedroom is to the right.
- The kitchen is a lovely space with two separate areas, an efficient work area and a distinct bay windowed dining area with center door leading to the rear yard.
- The second floor includes a master bedroom with full private bath and two large closets, plus two secondary bedrooms.

Plan AX-89311

Bedrooms: 3	Baths: 2½

Space:	
Upper floor:	736 sq. ft.
Main floor:	1,021 sq. ft.
Total living area:	**1,757 sq. ft.**
Basement:	approx. 1,021 sq. ft.
Garage:	440 sq. ft.

Exterior Wall Framing:	2x4

Foundation options:
Standard basement.
Slab.
(Foundation & framing conversion diagram available — see order form.)

Blueprint Price Code:	B

Panoramic Rear View

- This rustic but elegant country home offers an open, airy interior.
- At the center of the floor plan is a spacious living room with a sloped ceiling, fireplace and an all-glass circular wall giving a panoramic view of the backyard.
- The adjoining dining room shares the sloped ceiling and offers sliders to the rear terrace.
- The bright kitchen has a large window, an optional skylight and a counter bar that separates it from the bayed dinette.
- The bedroom wing includes two secondary bedrooms and a large, bayed master bedroom with dual walk-in closets and a private bath with a sloped ceiling and a garden whirlpool tub.

VIEW OF LIVING AND DINING ROOMS.

Plan K-685-DA

Bedrooms: 3	**Baths:** 2 ½
Space:	
Main floor	1,760 sq. ft.
Total Living Area	**1,760 sq. ft.**
Basement	1,700 sq. ft.
Garage	482 sq. ft.
Exterior Wall Framing	2x4 or 2x6

Foundation options:

Standard Basement

Slab

(Foundation & framing conversion diagram available—see order form.)

Blueprint Price Code   **B**

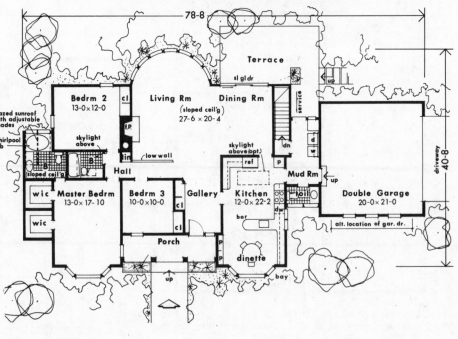

Cottage Suits Small Lot

- Designed to fit on a sloping or small lot, this compact country-style cottage has the amenities of a much larger home.
- The large front porch opens to the home's surprising two-story-high foyer, which views into the living room.
- The spacious living room is warmed by a handsome fireplace that is centered between built-in bookshelves.
- Enhanced by a sunny bay that opens to a backyard deck, the dining room offers a comfortable eating area that is easily served by the island kitchen.
- The secluded main-floor master bedroom includes a roomy walk-in closet. The spectacular master bath showcases a corner garden tub, a designer shower, a built-in bench and a dual-sink vanity.
- Upstairs, a railed balcony overlooks the foyer. Two secondary bedrooms with walk-in closets share a central bath.

Plan C-8870

Bedrooms: 3	Baths: 2
Living Area:	
Upper floor	664 sq. ft.
Main floor	1,100 sq. ft.
Total Living Area:	**1,764 sq. ft.**
Daylight basement/garage	1,100 sq. ft.
Exterior Wall Framing:	2x4

Foundation Options:

Daylight basement
(All plans can be built with your choice of foundation and framing. A generic conversion diagram is available. See order form.)

BLUEPRINT PRICE CODE:	**B**

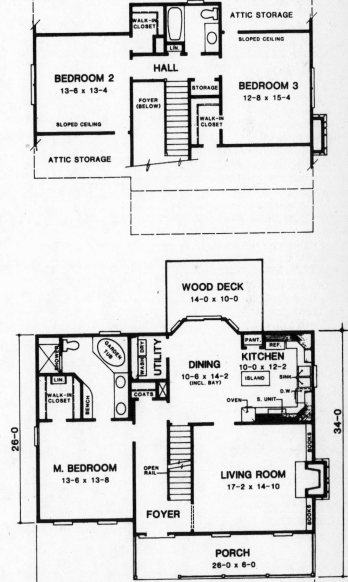

UPPER FLOOR

MAIN FLOOR

Dazzling Details for a Narrow Lot

- Measuring only 40' wide, this home is an excellent choice for a narrow lot.
- Nine-foot ceilings throughout the interior provide a feeling of spaciousness.
- The vaulted entry is brightened by a clerestory window.
- Arched entryways adorn both the living room and the dining room, and the large front bay window offers enough sunlight for both.
- The kitchen and nook can be closed off from the formal living areas if desired. The kitchen features an island cooktop and snack counter and a pantry.
- The vaulted master bedroom has a private patio and a spa bath.

Plan CDG-1009

Bedrooms: 2-3	Baths: 2
Living Area:	
Main floor	1,765 sq. ft.
Total Living Area:	**1,765 sq. ft.**
Garage	458 sq. ft.
Exterior Wall Framing:	2x4

Foundation Options:
Crawlspace
(Typical foundation & framing conversion diagram available—see order form.)

BLUEPRINT PRICE CODE:	B

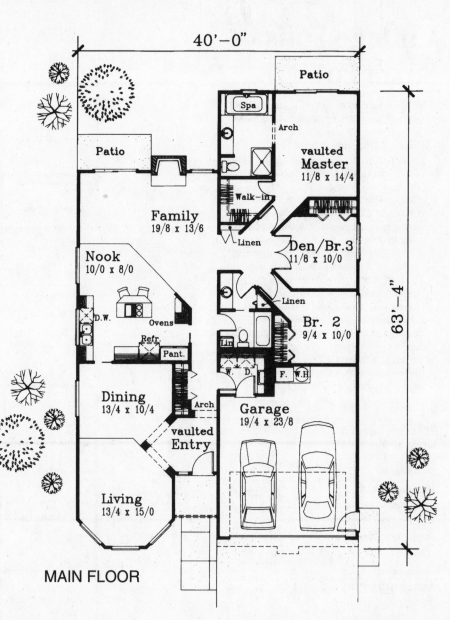

MAIN FLOOR

Plan CDG-1009

PRICES AND DETAILS
ON PAGES 12-15

A Distinguished Solution

- Distinguishing describes the first impression of this updated two-story traditional.
- A brilliant entry and foyer rises to the upper level; a formal living and bayed dining room flank the two-story foyer.
- A large family room with fireplace and rear view, a bayed dinette with pantry and rear sliders, and a spacious kitchen are all oriented to the back of the home.
- A master bedroom with tray ceiling, plus two secondary bedrooms share the upper floor.

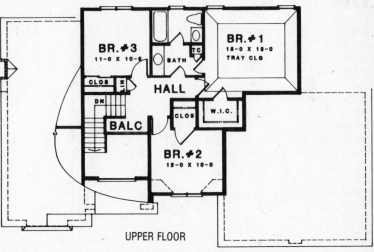

UPPER FLOOR

Plan A-2238-DS

Bedrooms: 3	**Baths:** 1 ½
Space:	
Upper floor	724 sq. ft.
Main floor	1,048 sq. ft.
Total Living Area	**1,772 sq. ft.**
Basement	1,048 sq. ft.
Garage	484 sq. ft.
Exterior Wall Framing	2x6

Foundation options:

Standard Basement

(Foundation & framing conversion diagram available—see order form.)

Blueprint Price Code	**B**

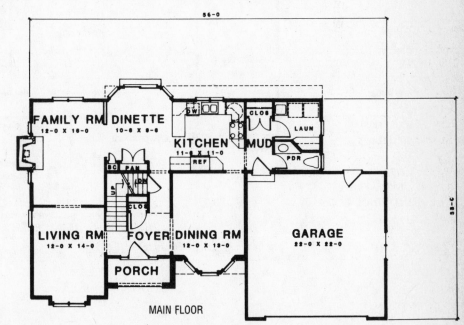

MAIN FLOOR

Rustic, Relaxed Living

- The screened porch of this rustic home offers a cool place to dine on warm summer days. The covered front porch provides an inviting welcome and a place for pure relaxation.
- With its warm fireplace and surrounding windows, the home's spacious living room is ideal for unwinding indoors. The living room unfolds to a nice-sized dining area that overlooks a backyard patio and opens to the screened porch.
- The U-shaped kitchen is centrally located and features a nice windowed sink. A handy pantry and a laundry room adjoin to the right.
- Three large bedrooms make up the home's sleeping wing. The master bedroom boasts a roomy private bath with a step-up spa tub, a separate shower and two walk-in closets.
- The secondary bedrooms share a compartmentalized hall bath.

Plan C-8650	
Bedrooms: 3	**Baths:** 2
Living Area:	
Main floor	1,773 sq. ft.
Total Living Area:	**1,773 sq. ft.**
Daylight basement	1,773 sq. ft.
Garage	441 sq. ft.
Exterior Wall Framing:	2x4

Foundation Options:
Daylight basement
Crawlspace
Slab
(All plans can be built with your choice of foundation and framing. A generic conversion diagram is available. See order form.)

BLUEPRINT PRICE CODE:	B

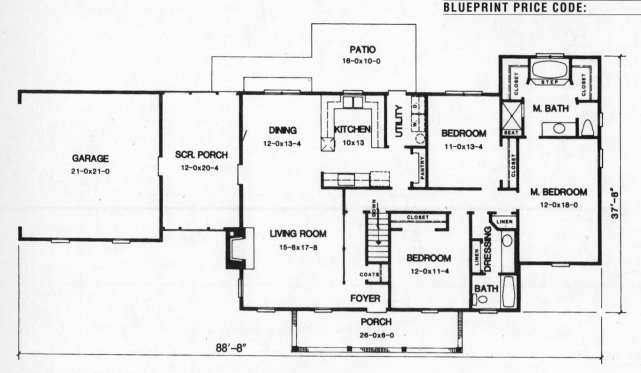

MAIN FLOOR

Plan C-8650

Casual Country Living

- With its covered wraparound porch, this gracious design is ideal for warm summer days or starry evenings.
- The spacious living room boasts a handsome brick-hearth fireplace and built-in book and gun storage. A French door accesses the backyard.
- The open kitchen design provides plenty of space for food storage and preparation with its pantry and oversized central island.
- Two mirror-imaged baths service the three bedrooms on the upper floor. Each secondary bedroom features a window seat and two closets. The master bedroom has a large walk-in closet and a private bath.
- A versatile hobby or sewing room is also included.
- An optional carport off the dining room is available upon request. Please specify when ordering.

Plan J-8895

Bedrooms: 3	Baths: 2½
Living Area:	
Upper floor	860 sq. ft.
Main floor	919 sq. ft.
Total Living Area:	**1,779 sq. ft.**
Standard basement	919 sq. ft.
Optional carport	462 sq. ft.
Exterior Wall Framing:	2x4

Foundation Options:

Standard basement

Crawlspace

Slab

(All plans can be built with your choice of foundation and framing. A generic conversion diagram is available. See order form.)

BLUEPRINT PRICE CODE: **B**

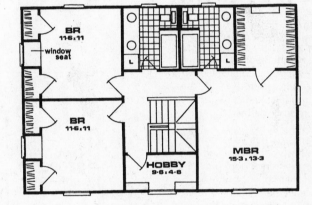

UPPER FLOOR

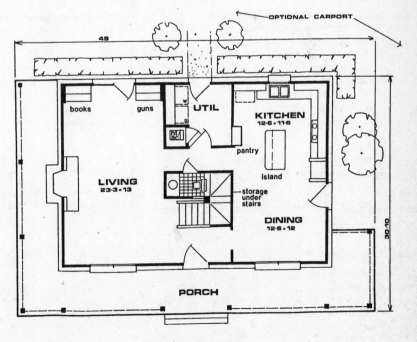

MAIN FLOOR

Country Charm, Cottage Look

- An interesting combination of stone and stucco gives a charming cottage look to this attactive country home.
- Off the inviting sidelighted entry, the formal dining room is defined by striking columns.
- The dining room expands into the living room, which boasts a fireplace and built-in shelves. A French door provides access to a backyard patio.
- The galley-style kitchen offers a sunny morning room and a pantry closet.
- All of the living areas are expanded by 10-ft. ceilings.
- The master bedroom features a 10-ft. ceiling and a nice bay-windowed sitting area. The full bath boasts an exciting oval garden tub and a separate shower, as well as a two-part walk-in closet and a dressing area with a dual-sink vanity.
- Across the home, two additional bedrooms with walk-in closets share a compartmentalized bath with independent dressing vanities.

Plan DD-1790	
Bedrooms: 3	**Baths: 2½**
Living Area:	
Main floor	1,790 sq. ft.
Total Living Area:	**1,790 sq. ft.**
Standard basement	1,790 sq. ft.
Garage	438 sq. ft.
Exterior Wall Framing:	2x4

Foundation Options:
Standard basement
Crawlspace
Slab
(All plans can be built with your choice of foundation and framing. A generic conversion diagram is available. See order form.)

BLUEPRINT PRICE CODE:	**B**

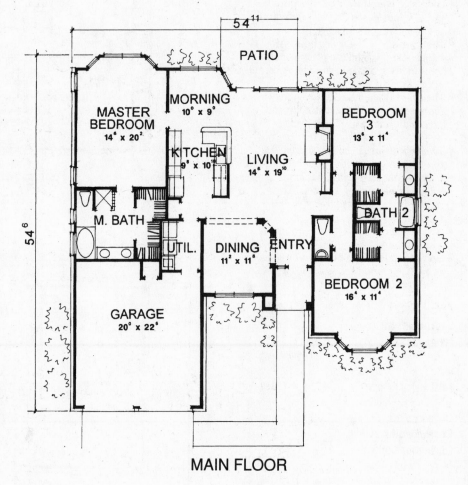

MAIN FLOOR

Planned to Perfection

- This attractive and stylish home offers an interior design that is planned to perfection.
- The covered entry and vaulted foyer create an impressive welcome.
- The vaulted Great Room features a corner fireplace, a wet bar and lots of windows. The adjoining dining room offers a bay window and access to a covered patio.
- The gourmet kitchen includes an island cooktop, a garden window above the sink and a built-in desk. The attached nook is surrounded by windows that overlook a delightful planter.
- The master suite boasts a tray ceiling that rises to 9½ ft. and a peaceful reading area that accesses a private patio. The superb master bath features a garden tub and a separate shower.
- Two secondary bedrooms share a compartmentalized bath.

Plan S-4789

Bedrooms: 3	Baths: 2
Living Area:	
Main floor	1,665 sq. ft.
Total Living Area:	**1,665 sq. ft.**
Standard basement	1,665 sq. ft.
Garage	400 sq. ft.
Exterior Wall Framing:	2x6

Foundation Options:

Standard basement
Crawlspace
Slab

(All plans can be built with your choice of foundation and framing. A generic conversion diagram is available. See order form.)

BLUEPRINT PRICE CODE:	B

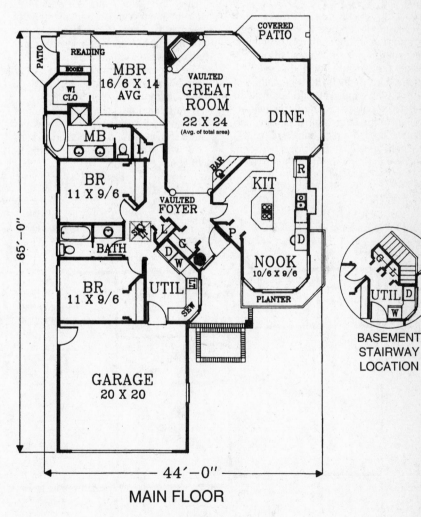

MAIN FLOOR

BASEMENT STAIRWAY LOCATION

TO ORDER THIS BLUEPRINT,
CALL TOLL-FREE 1-800-547-5570

Plan S-4789

PRICES AND DETAILS
ON PAGES 12-15

161

Rustic Welcome

- This rustic design boasts an appealing exterior with a covered front porch that offers guests a friendly welcome.
- Inside, the centrally located Great Room features an 11-ft., 8-in. cathedral ceiling with exposed wood beams. A massive fireplace separates the living area from the large dining room, which offers access to a nice backyard patio.
- The galley-style kitchen flows between the formal dining room and the bayed

breakfast room, which offers a handy pantry and access to laundry facilities.
- The master suite features a walk-in closet and a compartmentalized bath.
- Across the Great Room, two additional bedrooms have extra closet space and share a second full bath.
- The side-entry garage gives the front of the home an extra-appealing and uncluttered look.
- The optional daylight basement offers expanded living space. The stairway (not shown) would be located along the wall between the dining room and the back bedroom.

Plan C-8460	
Bedrooms: 3	**Baths:** 2
Living Area:	
Main floor	1,670 sq. ft.
Total Living Area:	**1,670 sq. ft.**
Daylight basement	1,600 sq. ft.
Garage	427 sq. ft.
Exterior Wall Framing:	2x4

Foundation Options:

Daylight basement
Crawlspace
Slab
(All plans can be built with your choice of foundation and framing. A generic conversion diagram is available. See order form.)

BLUEPRINT PRICE CODE: B

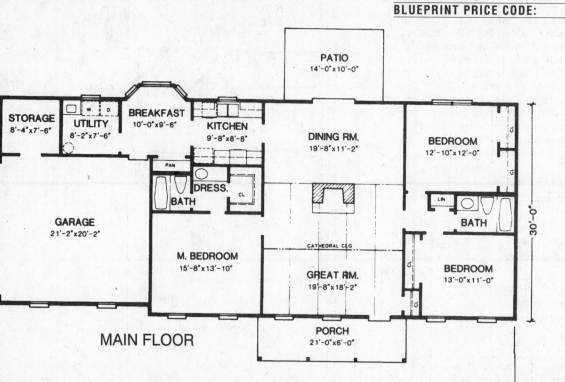

MAIN FLOOR

Instant Impact

- Bold rooflines, interesting angles and unusual window treatments give this stylish home lots of impact.
- Inside, high ceilings and an open floor plan maximize the home's square footage. At only 28 ft. wide, the home also is ideal for a narrow lot.
- A covered deck leads to the main entry, which features a sidelighted door, angled glass walls and a view of the striking open staircase.
- The Great Room is stunning, with its 16-ft. vaulted ceiling, energy-efficient woodstove and access to a large deck.
- A flat ceiling distinguishes the dining area, which shares an angled snack bar/cooktop with the step-saving kitchen. A laundry/mudroom is nearby.
- Upstairs, the master suite offers a sloped 13-ft. ceiling and a clerestory window. A walk-through closet leads to the private bath, which is enhanced by a skylighted, sloped ceiling.
- Another full bath and plenty of storage serve the other bedrooms, one of which has a sloped ceiling and a dual closet.

Plans H-1427-3A & -3B

Bedrooms: 3	Baths: 2½
Living Area:	
Upper floor	880 sq. ft.
Main floor	810 sq. ft.
Total Living Area:	**1,690 sq. ft.**
Daylight basement	810 sq. ft.
Garage	409 sq. ft.
Exterior Wall Framing:	2x4
Foundation Options:	**Plan #**
Daylight basement	H-1427-3B
Crawlspace	H-1427-3A

(All plans can be built with your choice of foundation and framing. A generic conversion diagram is available. See order form.)

BLUEPRINT PRICE CODE:	**B**

GENERAL USE

up

w.h. heat

DAYLIGHT BASEMENT

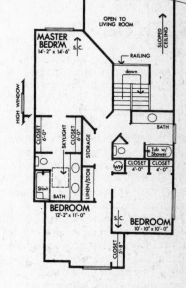

OPEN TO LIVING ROOM

SLOPED CEILING

MASTER BEDR'M
14'-2" x 14'-6"
S.C.

RAILING

down

HIGH WINDOW

CLOSET 6'-0"

SKYLIGHT

CLOSET 6'-0"

STORAGE

BATH

Tub w/ Shower

W.H.

CLOSET 4'-0"

CLOSET 4'-0"

LINEN/STOR

Shwr

BATH

BEDROOM
12'-2" x 11'-0"

S.C.

CLOSET 5'-8"

BEDROOM
10'-10" x 10'-0"

UPPER FLOOR

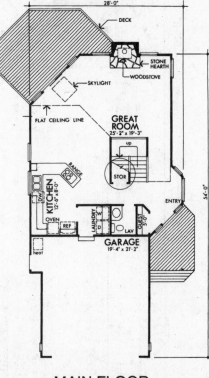

28'-0"

DECK

STONE HEARTH

WOODSTOVE

SKYLIGHT

FLAT CEILING LINE

GREAT ROOM
25'-2" x 19'-3"

up

STOR

54'-0"

ENTRY

RANGE

KITCHEN
12'-6" x 8'-0"

DW

OVEN

REF

LAUNDRY
W D

GUEST 5'-0"

LAV

GARAGE
19'-4" x 21'-2"

heat

MAIN FLOOR

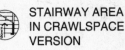

STAIRWAY AREA IN CRAWLSPACE VERSION

Photo by Mark Englund/HomeStyles

Elegant Approach

- This smart-looking design features an impressive approach, with a beautiful courtyard leading to the front door.
- The Y-shaped tiled entry efficiently directs traffic to all areas of the home.
- To the right, the combined living room and dining area offer a bow window, a fireplace and corner windows that overlook a covered sideyard patio.
- The adjacent sun room showcases a 14-ft. vaulted, skylighted ceiling and access to the patio.
- The corner kitchen has a snack bar that faces the family room, which features a 16-ft. vaulted ceiling, a woodstove and access to a second patio.
- The roomy master suite boasts a compartmentalized bath with a skylighted dressing area, a walk-in wardrobe and a shower.
- Another bath and bedroom, plus a den or possible third bedroom, complete this exciting design.

Plans P-7661-3A & -3D

Bedrooms: 2+	Baths: 2
Living Area:	
Main floor	1,693 sq. ft.
Total Living Area:	**1,693 sq. ft.**
Daylight basement	1,275 sq. ft.
Garage	462 sq. ft.
Exterior Wall Framing:	2x4
Foundation Options:	**Plan #**
Daylight basement	P-7661-3D
Crawlspace	P-7661-3A

(All plans can be built with your choice of foundation and framing. A generic conversion diagram is available. See order form.)

BLUEPRINT PRICE CODE:	B

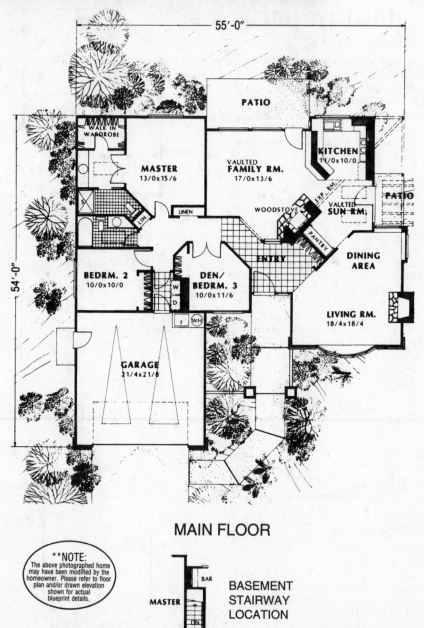

MAIN FLOOR

**NOTE:
The above photographed home may have been modified by the homeowner. Please refer to floor plan and/or drawn elevation shown for actual blueprint details.

BAR
MASTER
DN
BASEMENT STAIRWAY LOCATION

TO ORDER THIS BLUEPRINT, CALL TOLL-FREE 1-800-547-5570

Plans P-7661-3A & -3D

PRICES AND DETAILS ON PAGES 12-15

Dynamic Design

- This dynamic five-sided design is perfect for scenic sites. The front (or street) side of the home is shielded by a two-car garage, while the back of the home hosts a glass-filled living area surrounded by a spectacular deck.
- The unique shape of the home allows for an unusually open and spacious interior design.
- The living/dining room is further expanded by a 20-ft.-high vaulted ceiling. The centrally located fireplace provides a focal point while distributing heat efficiently.
- The space-saving galley-style kitchen is connected to the living/dining area by a snack bar.
- A large main-floor bedroom has two closets and easy access to a full bath.
- The upper floor is highlighted by a breathtaking balcony overlook. Also, two bedrooms share a nice-sized bath.
- The optional daylight basement includes a huge recreation room.

Plans H-855-1 & -1A

Bedrooms: 3	Baths: 2
Living Area:	
Upper floor	625 sq. ft.
Main floor	1,108 sq. ft.
Daylight basement	1,108 sq. ft.
Total Living Area:	**1,733/2,841 sq. ft.**
Garage	346 sq. ft.
Exterior Wall Framing:	2x6
Foundation Options:	**Plan #**
Daylight basement	H-855-1
Crawlspace	H-855-1A

(All plans can be built with your choice of foundation and framing. A generic conversion diagram is available. See order form.)

BLUEPRINT PRICE CODE:	**B/D**

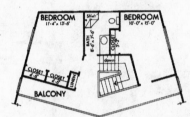

UPPER FLOOR

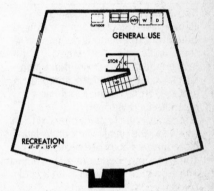

DAYLIGHT BASEMENT

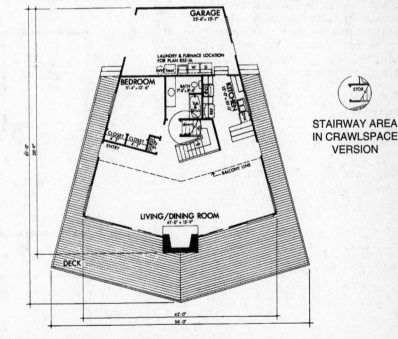

MAIN FLOOR

STAIRWAY AREA
IN CRAWLSPACE
VERSION

Affordable Victorian

- This compact Victorian design incorporates four bedrooms and three full baths into an attractive, affordable home that's only 30 ft. wide.
- In from the covered front porch, the spacious parlor includes a fireplace, and the formal dining room has a beautiful bay window.
- The galley-style kitchen offers efficient service to the breakfast nook. A laundry closet and a pantry are nearby.
- The main-floor bedroom makes a great office or guest bedroom, with a convenient full bath nearby.
- Upstairs, the master suite features an adjoining sitting room with a 14-ft. cathedral ceiling. The luxurious master bath includes a dual-sink vanity and a whirlpool tub with a shower. Two more large bedrooms share another full bath.
- An attached two-car garage off the kitchen is available upon request.

Plan C-8347-A

Bedrooms: 3+	Baths: 3
Living Area:	
Upper floor	783 sq. ft.
Main floor	954 sq. ft.
Total Living Area:	**1,737 sq. ft.**
Exterior Wall Framing:	2x4

Foundation Options:

Crawlspace

Slab

(All plans can be built with your choice of foundation and framing. A generic conversion diagram is available. See order form.)

BLUEPRINT PRICE CODE:	**B**

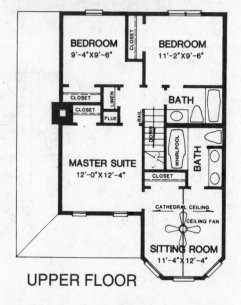

UPPER FLOOR

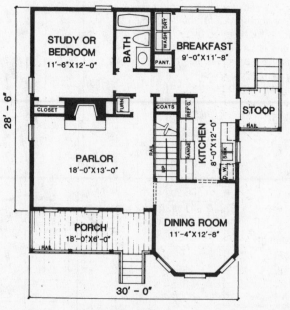

MAIN FLOOR

Plan C-8347-A

PRICES AND DETAILS
ON PAGES 12-15

REAR VIEW

FRONT VIEW

Bright Ideas!

- Four clerestory windows, a boxed-out window and wing walls sheltering the entry porch give this home definition.

- Inside, an open room arrangement coupled with vaulted ceilings, abundant windows and a sensational sun room make this home a definite bright spot.

- The living room features a 22-ft.-high vaulted ceiling, a warm woodstove and a glass-filled wall that offers views into the sun room. A patio door in the sun room opens to a large backyard deck.

- The adjoining dining room flows into the kitchen, which offers a versatile snack bar. A handy laundry room is just steps away, near the garage.

- Upstairs, the intimate bedroom suite includes a 14-ft.-high vaulted ceiling, a view to the living room, a walk-in closet and a private bath.

- The optional daylight basement boasts a spacious recreation room with a second woodstove, plus a fourth bedroom and a third bath. A shaded patio occupies the area under the deck.

Plans H-877-5A & -5B

Bedrooms: 3+	Baths: 2-3
Living Area:	
Upper floor	382 sq. ft.
Main floor	1,200 sq. ft.
Sun room	162 sq. ft.
Daylight basement	1,200 sq. ft.
Total Living Area:	**1,744/2,944 sq. ft.**
Garage	457 sq. ft.
Exterior Wall Framing:	2x6
Foundation Options:	**Plan #**
Daylight basement	H-877-5B
Crawlspace	H-877-5A

(All plans can be built with your choice of foundation and framing. A generic conversion diagram is available. See order form.)

BLUEPRINT PRICE CODE:	**B/D**

UPPER FLOOR

DAYLIGHT BASEMENT

MAIN FLOOR

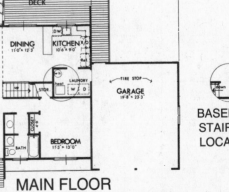

BASEMENT STAIRWAY LOCATION

Designed for Livability

- As you enter this excitingly spacious traditional home, you see through the extensive windows to the backyard.
- This four-bedroom home was designed for the livability of the maturing family with the separation of the master suite.
- The formal dining room expands spatially to the living room while being set off by a decorative column and plant shelves.
- The bay that creates the morning room and the sitting area for the master suite also adds excitement to this plan, both inside and out.
- The master bath offers an exciting oval tub under glass and a separate shower, as well as a spacious walk-in closet and a dressing area.

Plan DD-1696

Bedrooms: 4	Baths: 2
Living Area:	
Main floor	1,748 sq. ft.
Total Living Area:	**1,748 sq. ft.**
Standard basement	1,748 sq. ft.
Garage	393 sq. ft.
Exterior Wall Framing:	2x4

Foundation Options:

Standard basement
Crawlspace
Slab

(All plans can be built with your choice of foundation and framing. A generic conversion diagram is available. See order form.)

BLUEPRINT PRICE CODE: B

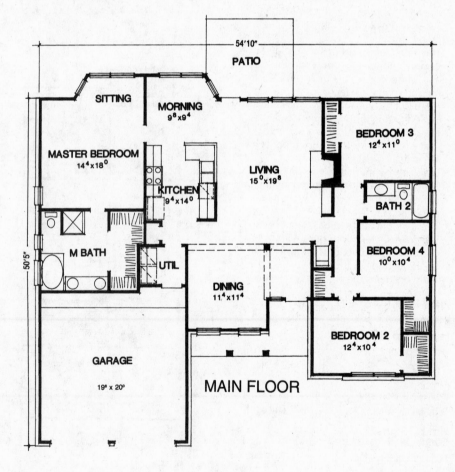

MAIN FLOOR

Plan DD-1696

PRICES AND DETAILS
ON PAGES 12-15

Plantation Home Ideal for Several Markets

- An efficient square footage appeals to many different buyers, from first-time, to second-home, to retirement.
- Compact building envelope of 65 x 55 is ideal for a smaller lot.
- A walk-up front porch, lap siding, and Palladian windows convey traditional charm.
- The Grand room features an ale bar, fireplace, and French doors to the rear deck.
- The gourmet kitchen features an island, greenhouse window, and sunny good morning room, and serves the private, formal dining room.
- The master suite features a luxury bath with separate his and her closets.

Plan EOF-25

Bedrooms: 2-3	Baths: 2½

Space:	
Total living area:	1,758 sq. ft.
Garage:	400 sq. ft.

Ceiling Heights:	
Main floor:	9'

Exterior Wall Framing:	2x6

Foundation options:
Slab.
(Foundation & framing conversion diagram available — see order form.)

Blueprint Price Code:	B

Plan EOF-25

54'-4"

64'-4"

FORMAL DINING
12'-0"X12'-0"

REAR DECK
15'-0"X9'-0"

MASTER SUITE
14'-4"X14'-0"

GRAND ROOM
15'-6"X17'-0"

HERS

DRESS

KITCHEN

DW

RNG

S

REF

FP

HIS

ALE BAR

SH

GOOD MORNING ROOM
11'-0"X8'-0"

PAN

STO

BATH

FOYER

LIN

D

BRM

W

LIBRARY
11'-0"X12'-0"

SUITE 2
12'-0"X12'-0"

FRONT PORCH

GARAGE
20'-0"X20'-0"

Warm, Rustic Appeal

- This quaint home has a warm, rustic appeal with a stone fireplace, paned windows and a covered front porch.
- Just off the two-story-high foyer, the living room hosts a raised-hearth fireplace and flows into the kitchen.
- The open L-shaped kitchen offers a pantry closet and a bright sink as it merges with the bayed dining room.
- The secluded master bedroom boasts a walk-in closet and a private bath with a dual-sink vanity. A laundry closet and access to a backyard deck are nearby.
- Upstairs, a hall balcony overlooks the foyer. A full bath serves two secondary bedrooms, each with a walk-in closet and access to extra storage space.
- Just off the dining room, a stairway descends to the daylight basement that contains the tuck-under garage.

Plan C-8339	
Bedrooms: 3	**Baths:** 2
Living Area:	
Upper floor	660 sq. ft.
Main floor	1,100 sq. ft.
Total Living Area:	**1,760 sq. ft.**
Daylight basement/garage	1,100 sq. ft.
Exterior Wall Framing:	2x4

Foundation Options:

Daylight basement

(All plans can be built with your choice of foundation and framing. A generic conversion diagram is available. See order form.)

BLUEPRINT PRICE CODE: B

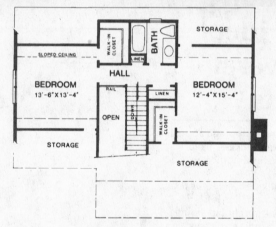

UPPER FLOOR

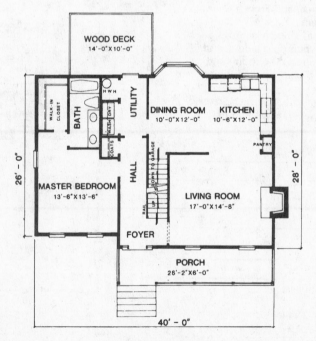

MAIN FLOOR

   Plan C-8339   **PRICES AND DETAILS ON PAGES 12-15**

Free-Flowing Floor Plan

- A fluid floor plan with open indoor/ outdoor living spaces characterizes this exciting luxury home.
- The stylish columned porch opens to a spacious living room and dining room expanse that overlooks the outdoor spaces. The breathtaking view also includes a dramatic corner fireplace.
- The dining area opens to a bright kitchen with an angled eating bar. The overall spaciousness of the living areas is increased with high 12-ft. ceilings.
- A sunny, informal eating area adjoins the kitchen, and an angled set of doors opens to a convenient main-floor laundry room near the garage entrance.
- The vaulted master bedroom has a walk-in closet and a sumptuous bath with an oval tub.
- A separate wing houses two additional bedrooms and another full bath.
- Attic space is accessible from stairs in the garage and in the bedroom wing.

REAR VIEW

Plan E-1710

Bedrooms: 3	Baths: 2
Living Area:	
Main floor	1,792 sq. ft.
Total Living Area:	**1,792 sq. ft.**
Standard basement	1,792 sq. ft.
Garage	484 sq. ft.
Storage	96 sq. ft.
Exterior Wall Framing:	2x6

Foundation Options:

Standard basement

Crawlspace

Slab

(All plans can be built with your choice of foundation and framing. A generic conversion diagram is available. See order form.)

BLUEPRINT PRICE CODE: **B**

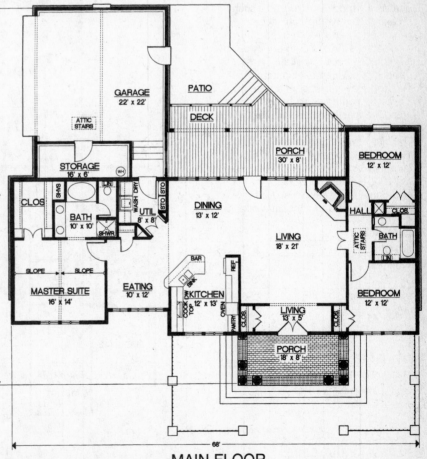

MAIN FLOOR

Fresh Air

- With its nostalgic look and country style, this lovely home brings a breath of fresh air into any neighborhood.
- Past the inviting wraparound porch, the foyer is brightened by an arched transom window above the front door.
- The adjoining formal dining room is defined by decorative columns and features a 9-ft., 4-in. stepped ceiling.
- The bright and airy kitchen includes a pantry, a windowed sink and a sunny breakfast area with porch access.
- Enhanced by an 11-ft stepped ceiling, the spacious Great Room is warmed by a fireplace flanked by sliding glass doors to a covered back porch.
- The lush master bedroom boasts an 11-ft. tray ceiling and a bayed sitting area. The master bath showcases a circular spa tub with a glass-block wall.
- The two remaining bedrooms are serviced by a second bath and a nearby laundry room. The protruding bedroom has a 12-ft. vaulted ceiling.
- Additional living space can be made available by finishing the upper floor.

Plan AX-93308

Bedrooms: 3+	Baths: 2
Living Area:	
Main floor	1,793 sq. ft.
Total Living Area:	**1,793 sq. ft.**
Standard basement	1,793 sq. ft.
Unfinished upper floor	779 sq. ft.
Garage and utility	471 sq. ft.
Exterior Wall Framing:	2x4

Foundation Options:

Standard basement
Crawlspace
Slab

(All plans can be built with your choice of foundation and framing. A generic conversion diagram is available. See order form.)

BLUEPRINT PRICE CODE: B

VIEW INTO GREAT ROOM

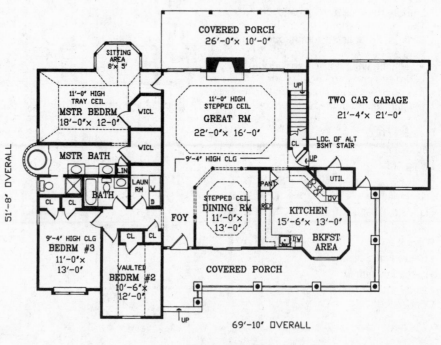

MAIN FLOOR

Plan AX-93308

PRICES AND DETAILS ON PAGES 12-15

New Traditional

- A lovely front porch and an open floor plan give this new traditional its modern appeal.
- The foyer opens to a fabulous living room with a 16-ft. vaulted ceiling, a fireplace and an open staircase. Railings introduce the bayed breakfast area. The efficient galley-style kitchen leads to a covered back porch.
- The sizable master suite is enhanced by a 10-ft. raised ceiling and a cozy bay window. The compartmentalized bath includes a dual-sink vanity and a walk-in closet. Another bedroom is nearby, along with a convenient laundry closet.
- Upstairs, a third bedroom has private access to a full bath. A large future area provides expansion space.

Plan J-8636

Bedrooms: 3	Baths: 3
Living Area:	
Upper floor	270 sq. ft.
Main floor	1,253 sq. ft.
Bonus room	270 sq. ft.
Total Living Area:	**1,793 sq. ft.**
Standard basement	1,287 sq. ft.
Garage	390 sq. ft.
Exterior Wall Framing:	2x4

Foundation Options:

Standard basement

Crawlspace

Slab

(All plans can be built with your choice of foundation and framing. A generic conversion diagram is available. See order form.)

BLUEPRINT PRICE CODE:	B

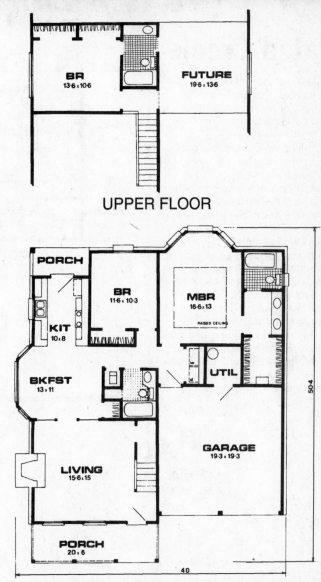

UPPER FLOOR

MAIN FLOOR

Updated Creole

- This Louisiana-style raised cottage features a tin roof, shuttered windows and three pairs of French doors, all of which add to the comfort and nostalgic appeal of this Creole classic.
- The French doors enter from the cool and relaxing front porch to the formal living areas and a front bedroom.
- The central living room merges with the dining room and the kitchen's eating area. A fireplace warms the whole area while more French doors access a covered backyard porch.
- The efficient kitchen offers an angled snack bar and a bay-windowed nook that overlooks the porch and deck.
- A secluded master suite showcases a private bathroom, fit for the most demanding taste. Across the home the secondary bedrooms include abundant closet space and share a full bath.
- This full-featured, energy-efficient design also includes a large utility room and extra storage space in the garage.

Plan E-1823

Bedrooms: 3	Baths: 2
Living Area:	
Main floor	1,800 sq. ft.
Total Living Area:	**1,800 sq. ft.**
Garage	550 sq. ft.
Exterior Wall Framing:	2x6

Foundation Options:

Crawlspace
Slab

(All plans can be built with your choice of foundation and framing. A generic conversion diagram is available. See order form.)

BLUEPRINT PRICE CODE: B

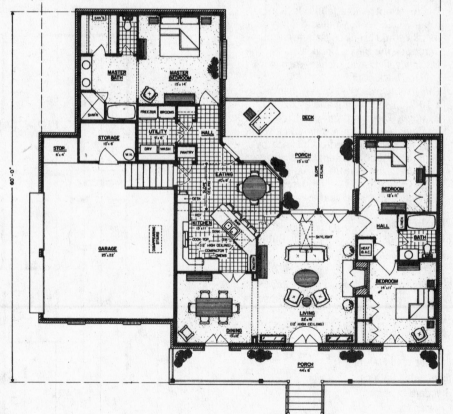

MAIN FLOOR

Plan E-1823

Cozy Covered Porches

- Twin dormers give this raised one-story design the appearance of a two-story. Two covered porches and a deck supplement the main living areas with plenty of outdoor entertaining space.
- The large central living room features a dramatic fireplace, a 12-ft. ceiling with a skylight and access to both porch areas.
- Double doors open to a bayed eating area, which overlooks the adjoining deck and includes a sloped ceiling that rises to 12 ft. in the kitchen. An angled snack bar and a pantry are also featured.
- The elegant master suite is tucked to one side of the home and also overlooks the backyard and deck. Laundry facilities and garage access are nearby.
- Across the home, two additional bedrooms share another full bath.

Plan E-1826

Bedrooms: 3	Baths: 2
Living Area:	
Main floor	1,800 sq. ft.
Total Living Area:	**1,800 sq. ft.**
Garage	550 sq. ft.
Storage	84 sq. ft.
Exterior Wall Framing:	2x6

Foundation Options:

Crawlspace
Slab

(All plans can be built with your choice of foundation and framing. A generic conversion diagram is available. See order form.)

BLUEPRINT PRICE CODE: **B**

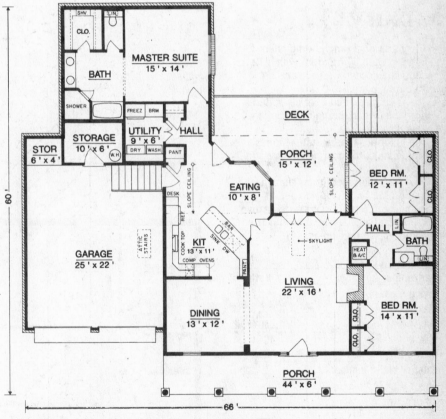

MAIN FLOOR

Attainable
Luxury

- This traditional ranch home offers a large, central living room with a 12-ft. ceiling, a corner fireplace and an adjoining patio.
- The U-shaped kitchen easily services both the formal dining room and the bayed eating area.
- The luxurious master suite features a large bath with separate vanities and dressing areas.
- Two secondary bedrooms share a second full bath.
- A covered carport boasts a decorative brick wall, attic space above and two additional storage areas.

Plan E-1812

Bedrooms: 3	Baths: 2
Living Area:	
Main floor	1,860 sq. ft.
Total Living Area:	**1,860 sq. ft.**
Carport	484 sq. ft.
Storage	132 sq. ft.
Exterior Wall Framing:	2x6

Foundation Options:

Crawlspace
Slab
(All plans can be built with your choice of foundation and framing. A generic conversion diagram is available. See order form.)

BLUEPRINT PRICE CODE:	**B**

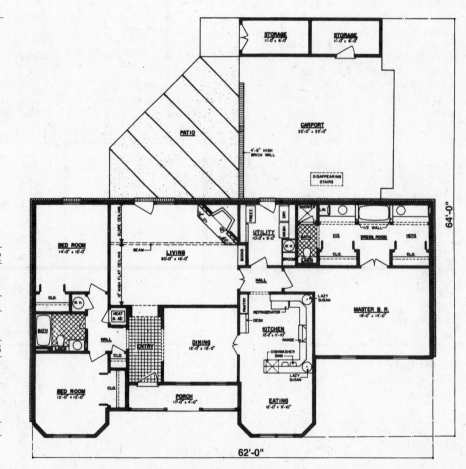

MAIN FLOOR

Classic Country-Style

- At the center of this rustic country-style home is an enormous living room with a flat beamed ceiling, a massive stone fireplace and access to a patio and a covered rear porch.
- The adjoining eating area and kitchen provide plenty of room for casual dining and meal preparation. The eating area is visually enhanced by a 14-ft. sloped ceiling with false beams. The kitchen includes a snack bar, a pantry closet and a built-in spice cabinet.
- The formal dining room gets plenty of pizzazz from the stone-faced wall and arched planter facing the living room.
- The secluded master suite has it all, including a private bath, a separate dressing area and a large walk-in closet with built-in shelves.
- The two remaining bedrooms have big closets and easy access to a full bath.

Plan E-1808	
Bedrooms: 3	**Baths:** 2
Living Area:	
Main floor	1,800 sq. ft.
Total Living Area:	**1,800 sq. ft.**
Garage	605 sq. ft.
Exterior Wall Framing:	2x4

Foundation Options:

Crawlspace

Slab

(All plans can be built with your choice of foundation and framing. A generic conversion diagram is available. See order form.)

BLUEPRINT PRICE CODE: B

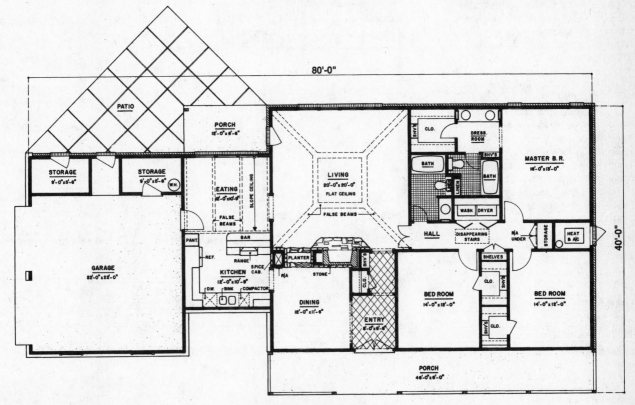

MAIN FLOOR

Masterful
Master Suite

- This gorgeous home features front and rear covered porches and a master suite so luxurious it deserves its own wing.
- The expansive entry welcomes visitors into a spacious, skylighted living room, which boasts a handsome fireplace. The adjacent formal dining room overlooks the front porch.
- Designed for efficiency, the kitchen features an angled snack bar, a bayed eating area and views of the porch. An all-purpose utility room is conveniently located off the kitchen.
- The kitchen, eating area, living room and dining room are all heightened by 12-ft. ceilings.
- The sumptuous and secluded master suite features a tub and a separate shower, a double-sink vanity, a walk-in closet with built-in shelves and a compartmentalized toilet.
- The two secondary bedrooms share a hall bath at the other end of the home. The rear bedroom offers porch access.
- The two-car garage features two built-in storage areas and access to unfinished attic space above.

Plan E-1811

Bedrooms: 3	Baths: 2
Living Area:	
Main floor	1,800 sq. ft.
Total Living Area:	**1,800 sq. ft.**
Garage and storage	634 sq. ft.
Exterior Wall Framing:	2x6

Foundation Options:

Crawlspace
Slab
(All plans can be built with your choice of foundation and framing. A generic conversion diagram is available. See order form.)

BLUEPRINT PRICE CODE: **B**

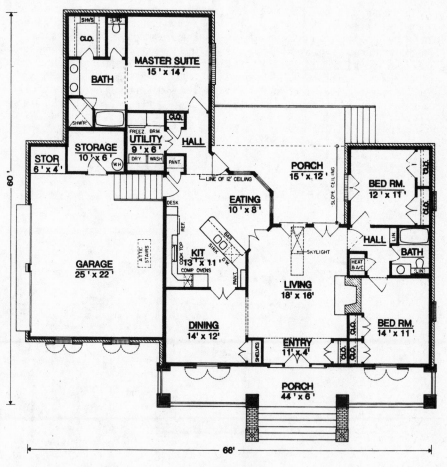

MAIN FLOOR

Plan E-1811

PRICES AND DETAILS
ON PAGES 12-15

FRONT VIEW

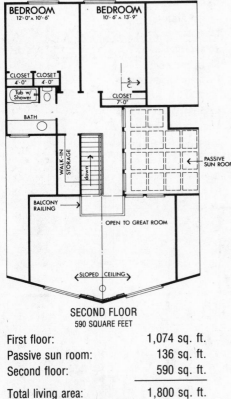

BEDROOM 12'-0" x 10'-6"
BEDROOM 10'-6" x 13'-9"

CLOSET 4'-0"
CLOSET 4'-0"
Tub w/ Shower
CLOSET 7'-0"

BATH

WALK-IN STORAGE
down

PASSIVE SUN ROOF

BALCONY RAILING

OPEN TO GREAT ROOM

SLOPED CEILING

SECOND FLOOR
590 SQUARE FEET

First floor:	1,074 sq. ft.
Passive sun room:	136 sq. ft.
Second floor:	590 sq. ft.
Total living area:	**1,800 sq. ft.**
(Not counting basement or garage)	

A Truly Livable Retreat

For a number of years the A-Frame idea has enjoyed great acceptance and popularity, especially in recreational areas. Too often, however, hopeful expectations have led to disappointment because

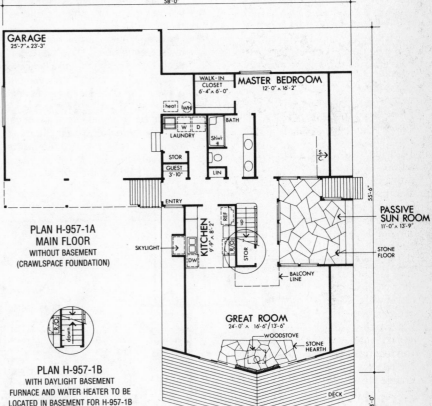

58'-0"

GARAGE 25'-7" x 23'-3"

WALK-IN CLOSET 6'-4" x 6'-0"
MASTER BEDROOM 12'-0" x 16'-2"

heat
WH
BATH

W D
LAUNDRY
Shwr

STOR

GUEST 3'-10"
LIN

ENTRY

PLAN H-957-1A
MAIN FLOOR
WITHOUT BASEMENT
(CRAWLSPACE FOUNDATION)

SKYLIGHT
KITCHEN 9'-9" x 8'-2"
REF
DW
STOR
up
STOR

S. C.

PASSIVE SUN ROOM 11'-0" x 13'-9"

STONE FLOOR

BALCONY LINE

55'-6"

PLAN H-957-1B
WITH DAYLIGHT BASEMENT
FURNACE AND WATER HEATER TO BE
LOCATED IN BASEMENT FOR H-957-1B

down
R/O

GREAT ROOM 24'-0" x 16'-6"/13'-6"

WOODSTOVE
STONE HEARTH

DECK

8'-0"

economic necessity resulted in small and restricted buildings. Not so with this plan. Without ignoring the need for economy, the designers allowed themselves enough freedom to create a truly livable and practical home with a main floor of 1,210 sq. ft., exclusive of the garage area. The second floor has 590 sq. ft., and includes two bedrooms, a bath and ample storage space.

Take special note of the multi-use passive sun room. Its primary purpose is to collect, store and redistribute the sun's heat, not only saving a considerable

amount of money but contributing an important function of keeping out dampness and cold when the owners are elsewhere. Otherwise the room might serve as a delightful breakfast room, a lovely arboretum, an indoor exercise room or any of many other functions limited only by the occupants' ingenuity.

A truly livable retreat, whether for weekend relaxation or on a daily basis as a primary residence, this passive solar A-Frame is completely equipped for the requirements of today's active living.

Exterior walls are framed with 2x6 studs.

TO ORDER THIS BLUEPRINT,
CALL TOLL-FREE 1-800-547-5570

Blueprint Price Code B
Plans H-957-1A & -1B

PRICES AND DETAILS
ON PAGES 12-15
179

Breezy Beauty

- A nostalgic covered front porch, a backyard deck and a sprawling screened porch combine to make this beautiful one-story home a breezy delight.
- The front entry opens into the Great Room, which is crowned by a soaring 12-ft.-high cathedral ceiling. A handsome fireplace is flanked by built-in bookshelves and cabinets.
- The large, bayed dining room offers a 9-ft. tray ceiling and deck access through French doors.

- The adjoining kitchen boasts plenty of counter space and a handy built-in recipe desk.
- From the kitchen, a side door leads to the screened porch. A wood floor and deck access highlight this cheery room.
- A quiet hall leads past a convenient utility room to the sleeping quarters.
- The secluded master bedroom is enhanced by a spacious walk-in closet. The private master bath includes a lovely garden tub, a separate shower and dual vanities.
- Two more bedrooms with walk-in closets share a hall bath.

Plan C-8905

Bedrooms: 3	**Baths:** 2

Living Area:	
Main floor	1,811 sq. ft.
Total Living Area:	**1,811 sq. ft.**
Screened porch	240 sq. ft.
Daylight basement	1,811 sq. ft.
Garage	484 sq. ft.
Exterior Wall Framing:	2x4

Foundation Options:
Daylight basement
Crawlspace
(All plans can be built with your choice of foundation and framing. A generic conversion diagram is available. See order form.)

BLUEPRINT PRICE CODE:	B

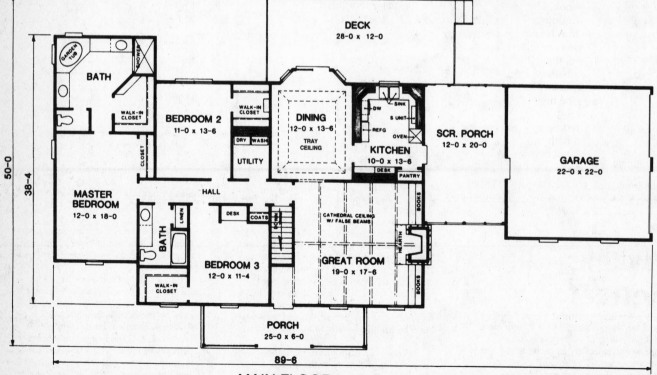

MAIN FLOOR

TO ORDER THIS BLUEPRINT, CALL TOLL-FREE 1-800-547-5570

PRICES AND DETAILS ON PAGES 12-15

Plan C-8905

Relaxing Retreat

- A peaceful covered porch and a tranquil country air make this home a relaxing retreat for the family.
- Inside, the inviting foyer leads to the large family room, which features ample space and a cozy fireplace with a nice brick hearth.
- Nearby, stately columns and a half-wall introduce the formal dining room, which includes access to a fun deck.
- The roomy kitchen extends to the huge, tiled breakfast nook. The nook boasts a bright corner window and access to a cozy side porch. A handy powder room and garage access are found nearby.
- Across the home, the master suite boasts a private bath with a dual-sink vanity and a separate tub and shower.
- Every room on the main floor is expanded by a 9-ft. ceiling.
- Upstairs, two bedrooms with sloped ceilings share a bath. An optional fourth bedroom is located nearby.

Plan GMA-1829

Bedrooms: 3+	Baths: 2½
Living Area:	
Upper floor	490 sq. ft.
Main floor	1,339 sq. ft.
Total Living Area:	**1,829 sq. ft.**
Optional 4th bedroom	145 sq. ft.
Standard basement	1,339 sq. ft.
Garage	491 sq. ft.
Exterior Wall Framing:	2x4

Foundation Options:

Standard basement

(All plans can be built with your choice of foundation and framing. A generic conversion diagram is available. See order form.)

BLUEPRINT PRICE CODE:	B

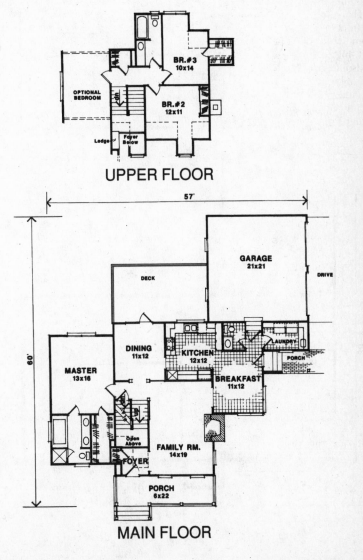

UPPER FLOOR

MAIN FLOOR

Economical Hillside Design

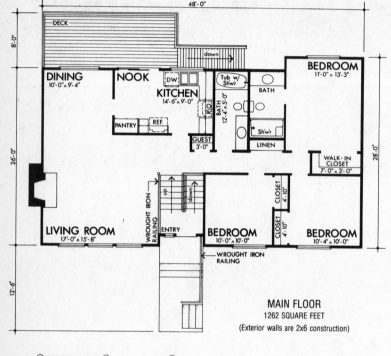

MAIN FLOOR
1262 SQUARE FEET
(Exterior walls are 2x6 construction)

DECK

48'-0"

8'-0"

DINING
10'-0" x 9'-4"

NOOK

KITCHEN
14'-6" x 9'-0"

DW

down

Tub w/
Sh'wr

BEDROOM
11'-0" x 13'-3"

BATH

R/O

BATH
12'-4" x 5'-0"

PANTRY

REF

GUEST
3'-0"

Sh'wr

LINEN

WALK-IN
CLOSET
7'-0" x 3'-0"

26'-0"

28'-0"

WROUGHT IRON RAILING

up

down

CLOSET
4'-10"

CLOSET
4'-10"

LIVING ROOM
17'-0" x 15'-8"

ENTRY

BEDROOM
10'-0" x 10'-0"

BEDROOM
10'-4" x 10'-0"

WROUGHT IRON RAILING

12'-6"

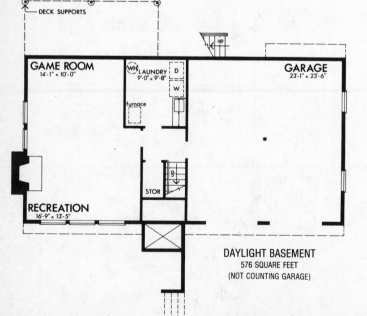

DAYLIGHT BASEMENT
576 SQUARE FEET
(NOT COUNTING GARAGE)

DECK SUPPORTS

GAME ROOM
14'-1" x 10'-0"

WH

LAUNDRY
9'-0" x 9'-8"

D

W

furnace

up

GARAGE
23'-1" x 23'-6"

up

STOR

RECREATION
16'-9" x 13'-5"

The solid, expansive, well-to-do appearance of this home plan belies the fact that it contains only 1,262 sq. ft. on the main floor and 1,152 sq. ft. on the lower level, including garage space.

This plan has a simple framing pattern, rectangular shape and straight roof line, and it lacks complicated embellishments. Even the excavation, only half as deep as usual, helps make this an affordable and relatively quick and easy house to build.

A split-level entry opens onto a landing between floors, providing access up to the main living room or down to the recreation and work areas.

The living space is large and open. The dining and living rooms combine with the stairwell to form a large visual space. A large 8'x20' deck, visible through the picture window in the dining room, adds visual expansiveness to this multi-purpose space.

The L-shaped kitchen and adjoining nook are perfect for daily food preparation and family meals, and the deck is also accessible from this area through sliding glass doors. The kitchen features a 48 cubic foot pantry closet.

The master bedroom has a complete private bathroom and oversized closet. The remaining bedrooms each have a large closet and access to a full-size bathroom.

A huge rec and game room is easily accessible from the entry, making it ideal for a home office or business.

Main floor:	1,262 sq. ft.
Lower level:	576 sq. ft.
Total living area: (Not counting garage)	1,838 sq. ft.

Blueprint Price Code B

Plan H-1332-5

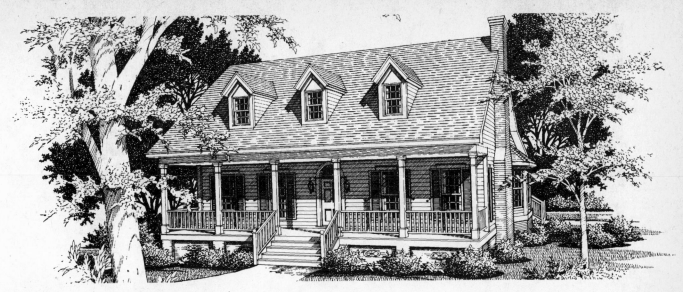

Open Invitation

- The wide front porch of this friendly country farmhouse presents an open invitation to all who visit.
- Highlighted by a round-topped transom, the home's entrance opens directly into the spacious living room, which features a warm fireplace flanked by windows.
- The adjoining dining area is enhanced by a lovely bay window and is easily serviced by the updated kitchen's angled snack bar.
- A bright sun room off the kitchen provides a great space for informal meals or relaxation. Access to a covered backyard porch is nearby.
- The good-sized master bedroom is secluded from the other sleeping areas. The lavish master bath includes a garden tub, a separate shower, a dual-sink vanity and a walk-in closet.
- Two more bedrooms share a second full bath. A laundry/utility room is nearby.
- An additional 1,007 sq. ft. of living space can be made available by finishing the upper floor.
- All ceilings are 9 ft. high for added spaciousness.

Plan J-91078

Bedrooms: 3	**Baths:** 2

Living Area:

Main floor	1,846 sq. ft.
Total Living Area:	**1,846 sq. ft.**
Future upper floor	1,007 sq. ft.
Standard basement	1,846 sq. ft.
Garage	484 sq. ft.
Exterior Wall Framing:	2x6

Foundation Options:

Standard basement
Crawlspace
Slab
(All plans can be built with your choice of foundation and framing. A generic conversion diagram is available. See order form.)

BLUEPRINT PRICE CODE: B

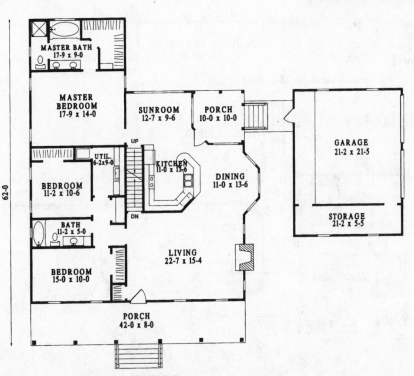

MAIN FLOOR

Indoor/Outdoor Delights

- A curved porch in the front and a garden sun room in the back make this home an indoor/outdoor delight.
- Inside, a roomy kitchen is open to a five-sided, glassed-in dining room that views out to the porch.
- The living room features a fireplace along a glass wall that adjoins the gloriously sunny garden room.

- Wrapped in windows, the garden room accesses the backyard as well as a large storage area in the unobtrusive, side-entry garage.
- The master suite is no less luxurious, featuring a a sumptuous master bath with a garden spa tub, a corner shower and a walk-in closet.
- Each of the two remaining bedrooms has a boxed-out window and a walk-in closet. A full bath with a corner shower and a dual-sink vanity is close by.
- A stairway leads to the attic, which provides more potential living space.

Plan DD-1852

Bedrooms: 3	Baths: 2
Living Area:	
Main floor	1,852 sq. ft.
Total Living Area:	**1,852 sq. ft.**
Standard basement	1,852 sq. ft.
Garage	528 sq. ft.
Exterior Wall Framing:	2x4

Foundation Options:

Standard basement
Crawlspace
Slab
(All plans can be built with your choice of foundation and framing. A generic conversion diagram is available. See order form.)

BLUEPRINT PRICE CODE: B

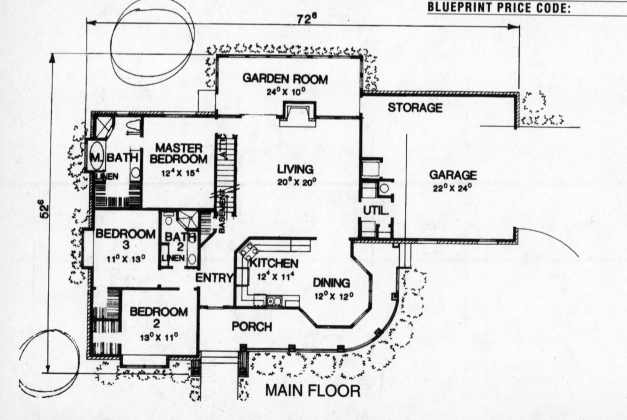

MAIN FLOOR

Unique Inside and Out

- This delightful design is as striking on the inside as it is on the outside.
- The focal point of the home is the huge Grand Room, which features a vaulted ceiling, plant shelves and lots of glass, including a clerestory window. French doors flanking the fireplace lead to the covered porch and the two adjoining sun decks.
- The centrally located kitchen offers easy access from any room in the house, and a full bath, a laundry area and the garage entrance are nearby.
- The two main-floor master suites are another unique design element of the home. Both of the suites showcase a volume ceiling, a sunny window seat, a walk-in closet, a private bath and French doors that open to a sun deck.
- Upstairs, two guest suites overlook the vaulted Grand Room below.

Plan EOF-13	
Bedrooms: 4	**Baths:** 3
Living Area:	
Upper floor	443 sq. ft.
Main floor	1,411 sq. ft.
Total Living Area:	**1,854 sq. ft.**
Garage	264 sq. ft.
Storage	50 sq. ft.
Exterior Wall Framing:	2x6
Foundation Options:	
Crawlspace	
(Typical foundation & framing conversion diagram available—see order form.)	
BLUEPRINT PRICE CODE:	**B**

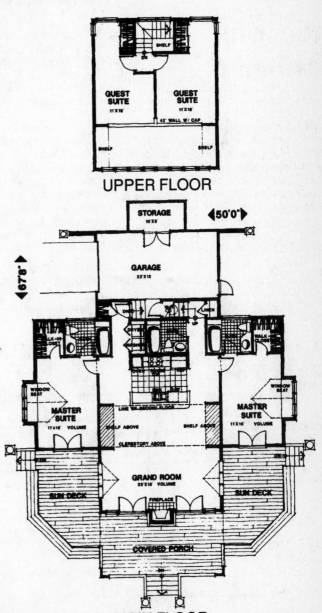

UPPER FLOOR

MAIN FLOOR

TO ORDER THIS BLUEPRINT,
CALL TOLL-FREE 1-800-547-5570

Plan EOF-13

PRICES AND DETAILS
ON PAGES 12-15

185

Endearing European

- Keystone accents, a copper-top window and stacked stone draw attention to this lovely European-style home.
- Rustic stone steps usher guests into the sidelighted foyer, where an arched transom and a 12-ft. ceiling add drama.
- Straight ahead, the fabulous family room is enhanced by a handsome fireplace and a 16-ft.-high ceiling.
- Meals may be served in either the elegant dining room or the casual breakfast nook. The nook features a wall of windows and direct access to a sizable covered porch.
- A windowed sink brightens the cozy U-shaped kitchen, which boasts easy garage access and grocery transporting.
- A good-sized laundry room and a handy half-bath are also nearby.
- A 10-ft.-high recessed ceiling and a large walk-in closet are highlights in the secluded master bedroom. The private bath offers a garden tub, a separate shower and a dual-sink vanity.
- All main-floor rooms are expanded by 9-ft. ceilings unless otherwise noted.
- Upstairs, two secondary bedrooms share a hall bath. The optional bonus room offers expansion possibilities.

Plan GMA-1854	
Bedrooms: 3+	**Baths: 2½**
Living Area:	
Upper floor	537 sq. ft.
Main floor	1,317 sq. ft.
Total Living Area:	**1,854 sq. ft.**
Bonus room (unfinished)	312 sq. ft.
Standard basement	1,317 sq. ft.
Garage	504 sq. ft.
Exterior Wall Framing:	2x4
Foundation Options:	

Standard basement
(All plans can be built with your choice of foundation and framing. A generic conversion diagram is available. See order form.)

BLUEPRINT PRICE CODE: B

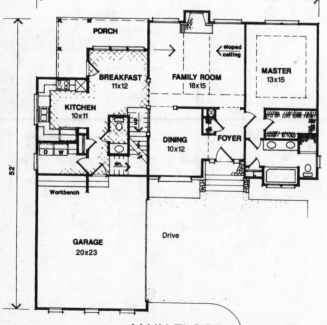

MAIN FLOOR

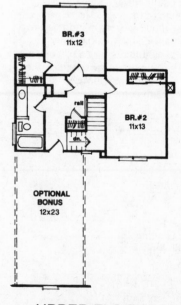

UPPER FLOOR

TO ORDER THIS BLUEPRINT, CALL TOLL-FREE 1-800-547-5570

Plan GMA-1854

PRICES AND DETAILS ON PAGES 12-15

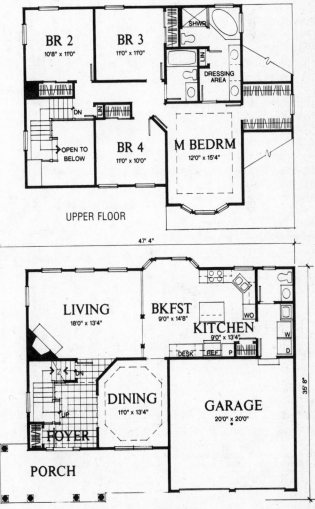

Sun-Filled Living Areas

- A decorative front porch highlights the exterior of this two-story traditional.
- Inside, a compact but comfortable floor plan flows from the dramatic two-story foyer.
- A sun-filled living room and bayed breakfast area stretch across the rear of the home. An open railing between the two areas allows the corner fireplace in the living room to be seen from both the nook and the full-featured island kitchen.
- The focal-point dining room offers an elegant, octagonal-shaped tray ceiling.
- A pantry, a built-in work desk and a handy half-bath and laundry room are located between the kitchen and the garage entrance.
- A lovely bay window, a huge walk-in closet and a private bath with dressing area, twin vanities and lavish garden tub are offered in the master bedroom on the upper level. Three extra bedrooms and a second bath complete the design.

Plan OH-135

Bedrooms: 4	Baths: 2 ½
Space:	
Upper floor	935 sq. ft.
Main floor	923 sq. ft.
Total Living Area	**1,858 sq. ft.**
Basement	923 sq. ft.
Garage	400 sq. ft.
Exterior Wall Framing	2x4

Foundation options:

Standard Basement

(Foundation & framing conversion diagram available—see order form.)

Blueprint Price Code	**B**

UPPER FLOOR

MAIN FLOOR

Plan OH-135

Up-to-Date Country Styling

- Nearly surrounded by a covered wood porch, this traditional 1,860-sq.-ft. farm-styled home is modernized for today's active, up-to-date family.
- Inside, the efficient floor plan promotes easy mobility with vast openness and a minimum of cross-traffic.
- The spacious living and dining area is warmed by a fireplace with a stone hearth; sliding glass doors off the dining room open to the porch.
- The U-shaped country kitchen is centrally located and overlooks a bright breakfast nook and a big family room with a woodstove and its own sliding glass doors to a patio.
- On the upper floor is a large master bedroom with corner windows, a dressing area and a private bath. Two secondary bedrooms share a second bath with a handy dual-sink vanity.

Plans P-7677-2A & -2D

Bedrooms: 3	Baths: 2½
Living Area:	
Upper floor	825 sq. ft.
Main floor	1,035 sq. ft.
Total Living Area:	**1,860 sq. ft.**
Daylight basement	1,014 sq. ft.
Garage	466 sq. ft.
Exterior Wall Framing:	2x6
Foundation Options:	**Plan #**
Daylight basement	P-7677-2D
Crawlspace	P-7677-2A

(All plans can be built with your choice of foundation and framing. A generic conversion diagram is available. See order form.)

BLUEPRINT PRICE CODE:	B

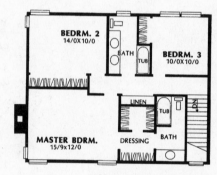

UPPER FLOOR

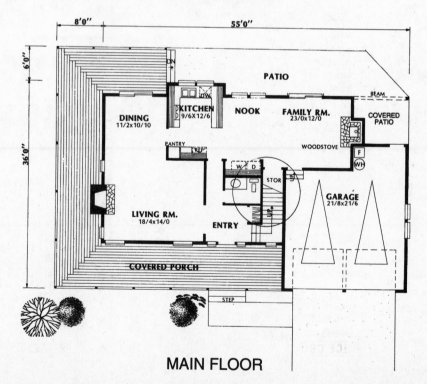

MAIN FLOOR

Plans P-7677-2A & -2D

PRICES AND DETAILS ON PAGES 12-15

Expansive Traditional

- Skylights, cathedral and tray ceilings and an open floor plan brighten and expand this traditional home.
- A covered front porch, a large dining room and a skylighted living room with a nice fireplace and a 12-ft. ceiling make guests feel at home instantly.
- For extended living space, the back patio is accessible from the living room through sliding glass doors.
- A cathedral ceiling presides over the efficient kitchen and the cozy eating area. A large utility room nearby offers extra freezer and storage space.
- The kitchen can be closed off from the dining room to minimize noise and remove clutter from sight.
- The luxurious master suite features a tray ceiling, a walk-in closet, double vanities, a unique skylighted quarter-round tub and a separate shower.
- Two large secondary bedrooms share a hall bath. The front bedroom features a cathedral ceiling and double closets.
- The garage is at the back of the house and features two large built-in storage areas, one accessible from the outside.

Plan E-1825

Bedrooms: 3	**Baths:** 2

Living Area:

Main floor	1,865 sq. ft.
Total Living Area:	**1,865 sq. ft.**
Garage and storage	616 sq. ft.
Exterior Wall Framing:	2x6

Foundation Options:

Crawlspace
Slab
(Typical foundation & framing conversion diagram available—see order form.)

BLUEPRINT PRICE CODE:	**B**

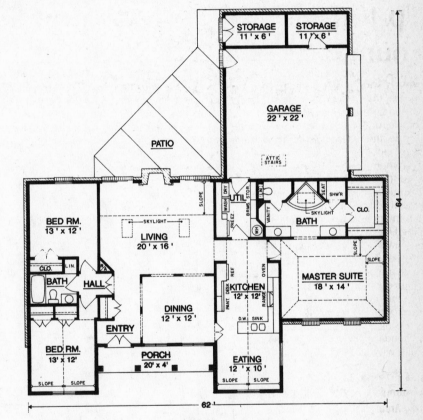

MAIN FLOOR

PRICES AND DETAILS ON PAGES 12-15

Maximum Appeal

- At an economical 1,873 sq. ft., this home projects tremendous street appeal with its interesting roof line and multi-paned windows.
- An extended ledge wraps around the exterior of the living room and can be used as a flower shelf.
- The entry opens to a tray-ceilinged living-dining room, perfect for large formal groups.
- The kitchen is highlighted by a sunny garden window and opens to the alcove nook and family room with fireplace.
- The stairway landing off the entry is accented by a tall arched window.
- Upstairs, skylights brighten the main bathroom and the exciting vaulted master bath.
- Don't miss the built-in bookshelves and corner windows located in the master bedroom.

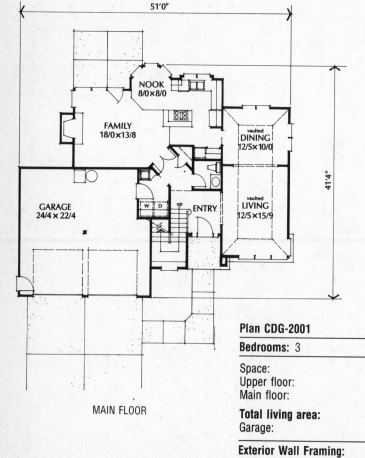

MAIN FLOOR

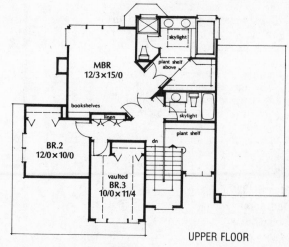

UPPER FLOOR

Plan CDG-2001

Bedrooms: 3	Baths: 2½

Space:	
Upper floor:	860 sq. ft.
Main floor:	1,013 sq. ft.
Total living area:	1,873 sq. ft.
Garage:	543 sq. ft.

Exterior Wall Framing:	2x4

Ceiling Heights:

Upper floor:	8'
Main floor:	9'

Foundation options:
Crawlspace.
(Foundation & framing conversion diagram available — see order form.)

Blueprint Price Code:	B

Plan CDG-2001

PRICES AND DETAILS ON PAGES 12-15

French Colonial for Easy Living

Plan V-1876

Bedrooms: 3	Baths: 2

Total living area: 1,876 sq. ft.

Dimensions:
| Width: | 50' |
| Depth: | 63' |

Features:
Wrap-around porch in front.
9' ceilings throughout.
Great Room includes fireplace.

| **Exterior Wall Framing:** | 2x4 |

Foundation options:
Crawlspace only.
(Foundation & framing conversion diagram available — see order form.)

| **Blueprint Price Code** | B |

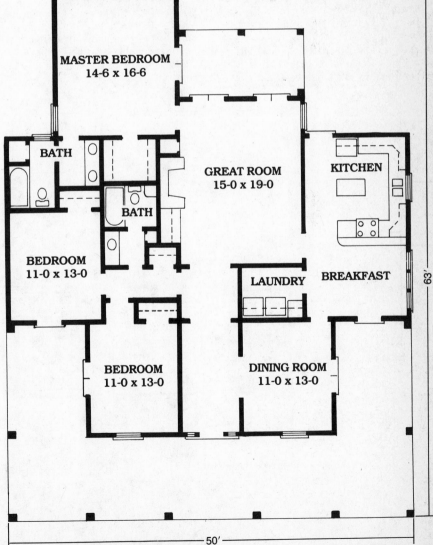

TO ORDER THIS BLUEPRINT,
CALL TOLL-FREE 1-800-547-5570

Plan V-1876

PRICES AND DETAILS
ON PAGES 12-15

191

Fantastic Family Living Space

- Luxury begins at the front door with this exciting one-story traditional home.
- The eye-catching front entry opens to an impressive vaulted foyer. Double doors open to an unusual living room that can be used as a den, home office or bedroom.
- The formal dining room offers a tray ceiling and has easy access to the combination kitchen, breakfast room

and family room. This fantastic family living space is punctuated by floor-to-ceiling windows, a fireplace and views to the backyard deck.
- Double doors open to the vaulted master suite, which features French doors leading to the deck, a luxurious bath with a corner spa tub, and a large walk-in closet.
- Two more bedrooms and another full bath are isolated at the other side of the home. This sprawling design is further enhanced by 9-ft. ceilings throughout, unless otherwise indicated.

Plan APS-1812	
Bedrooms: 3-4	**Baths: 2**
Living Area:	
Main floor	1,886 sq. ft.
Total Living Area:	**1,886 sq. ft.**
Garage	400 sq. ft.
Exterior Wall Framing:	2x4
Foundation Options:	
Slab	

(Typical foundation & framing conversion diagram available—see order form.)

BLUEPRINT PRICE CODE: B

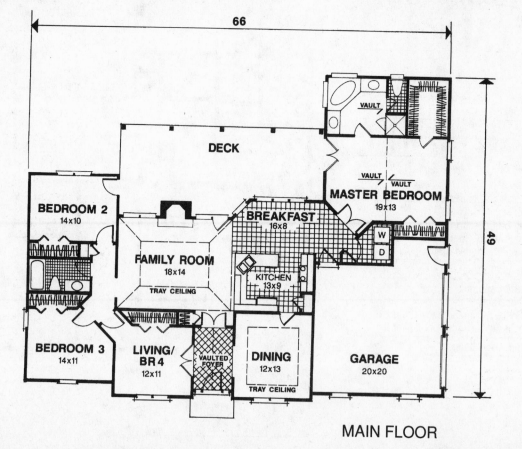

MAIN FLOOR

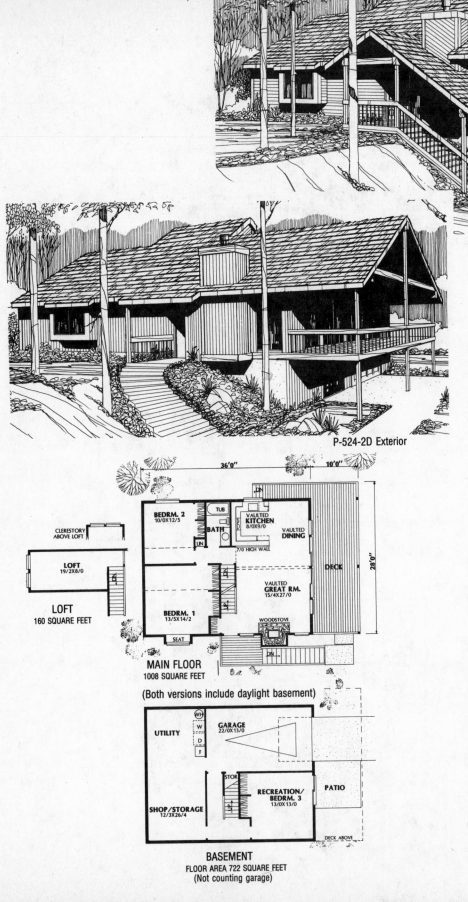

P-524-5D Exterior

P-524-2D Exterior

Spacious Great Room

- This same floor plan is available with two different exterior treatments, as illustrated.
- In either case, a spacious Great Room is the highlight, with its vaulted ceiling, wide windows and sliding glass doors which open to a deck, and to the view beyond.
- The dining room and kitchen also feature vaulted ceilings.
- A loft room adds another sleeping area, and the daylight basement offers even more usable space.

Plans P-524-2D & -5D

Bedrooms: 2+	Baths: 1

Space:	
Loft:	160 sq. ft.
Main floor:	1,008 sq. ft.
Lower level:	722 sq. ft.

Total living area:	1,890 sq. ft.
Garage:	286 sq. ft.

Exterior Wall Framing:	2x6

Foundation options:
Daylight basement.
(Foundation & framing conversion diagram available — see order form.)

Blueprint Price Code:	B

CLERESTORY ABOVE LOFT

LOFT
19/2X8/0

LOFT
160 SQUARE FEET

BEDRM. 2
10/0X12/5

TUB

BATH

LN

LN

7/0 HIGH WALL

VAULTED KITCHEN
8/0X9/0

VAULTED DINING

DECK

36'0"   10'0"

28'0"

VAULTED GREAT RM.
15/4X27/0

BEDRM. 1
13/5X14/2

SEAT

WOODSTOVE

DN

MAIN FLOOR
1008 SQUARE FEET

(Both versions include daylight basement)

WH

UTILITY

W
D
F

GARAGE
22/0X13/0

STOR

RECREATION/
BEDRM. 3
13/0X13/0

PATIO

SHOP/STORAGE
12/3X26/4

DECK ABOVE

BASEMENT
FLOOR AREA 722 SQUARE FEET
(Not counting garage)

TO ORDER THIS BLUEPRINT,
CALL TOLL-FREE 1-800-547-5570

Plans P-524-2D & -5D

PRICES AND DETAILS
ON PAGES 12-15

Economical Traditional

- This compact traditional design reflects a thrifty attitude toward life, while still providing the necessities and amenities proper for today's families.
- Main floor is devoted to informal family living, with a large family room and Great Room with a more formal dining area.
- Also note the large foyer, an impressive feature not often found in homes of this size.
- Upstairs, you'll find three bedrooms with good closet space, plus two baths.

Plan B-906

Bedrooms: 3	Baths: 2½

Space:	
Upper floor:	816 sq. ft.
Main floor:	1,075 sq. ft.

Total living area:	1,891 sq. ft.
Basement:	1,075 sq. ft.
Garage:	386 sq. ft.

Exterior Wall Framing:	2x4

Foundation options:
Standard basement.
(Foundation & framing conversion diagram available — see order form.)

Blueprint Price Code:	B

Br 2
10-9x12-4

Br 3
10-9x12-4

open to below

dn

MBr
14x16
vaulted

UPPER FLOOR

43'-4"

Deck

Dining

Kit
10x13

Family
17-4x16-8

46'-0"

Great Room
13x25-4
vaulted

Garage
19-8x19-8

MAIN FLOOR

Plan B-906

PRICES AND DETAILS ON PAGES 12-15

Garden Home with a View

- This clever design proves that privacy doesn't have to be compromised even in high-density urban neighborhoods. From within, views are oriented to a beautiful, lush entry courtyard and a covered rear porch.
- The exterior appearance is sheltered, but warm and welcoming.
- The innovative interior design centers on a unique kitchen, which directs traffic away from the working areas while still serving the entire home.
- The sunken family room features a 14-ft. vaulted ceiling and a warm fireplace.
- The master suite is highlighted by a sumptuous master bath with an oversized shower and a whirlpool tub, plus a large walk-in closet.
- The formal living room is designed and placed in such a way that it can become a third bedroom, a den, or an office or study room, depending on family needs and lifestyles.

Plan E-1824

Bedrooms: 2+	Baths: 2
Living Area:	
Main floor	1,891 sq. ft.
Total Living Area:	**1,891 sq. ft.**
Garage	506 sq. ft.
Storage	60 sq. ft.
Exterior Wall Framing:	2x4

Foundation Options:

Crawlspace

Slab

(All plans can be built with your choice of foundation and framing. A generic conversion diagram is available. See order form.)

BLUEPRINT PRICE CODE: B

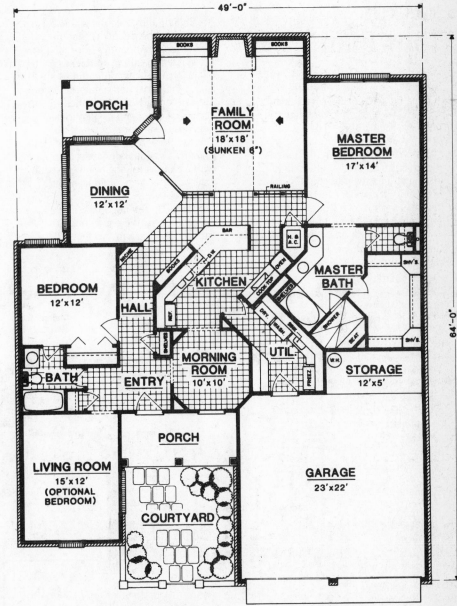

MAIN FLOOR

Playful Floor Plan

- High, hip roofs and a recessed entry give this home a smart-looking exterior. A dynamic floor plan—punctuated with angled walls, high ceilings and playful window treatments—gives the home an exciting interior.
- The sunken Great Room, the circular dining room and the angled island kitchen are the heartbeat of the home. The Great Room offers a 14-ft. vaulted ceiling, a fireplace, a built-in corner entertainment center and tall arched windows overlooking the backyard.

- An angled railing separates the Great Room from the open kitchen and dining room. An atrium door next to the glassed-in dining area leads to the backyard. The kitchen includes an island snack bar and a garden window.
- The master bedroom is nestled into one corner for quiet and privacy. This deluxe suite features two walk-in closets and a luxurious whirlpool bath.
- An extra-large laundry area, complete with a clothes-folding counter and a coat closet, is accessible from the three-car garage.
- The home is expanded by 9-ft. ceilings throughout, with the exception of the vaulted Great Room.

Plan PI-90-435	
Bedrooms: 3	**Baths:** 2
Living Area:	
Main floor	1,896 sq. ft.
Total Living Area:	**1,896 sq. ft.**
Basement	1,889 sq. ft.
Garage	667 sq. ft.
Exterior Wall Framing:	2x6

Foundation Options:
Daylight basement
Standard basement
(All plans can be built with your choice of foundation and framing. A generic conversion diagram is available. See order form.)

BLUEPRINT PRICE CODE: B

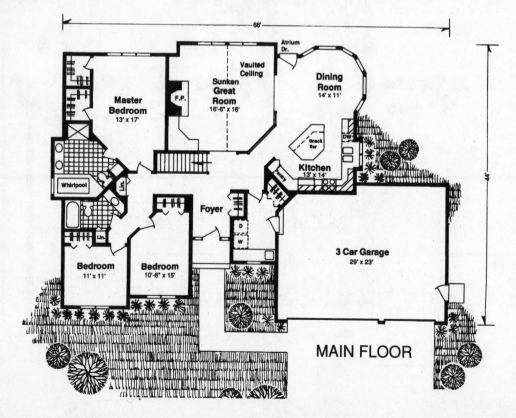

MAIN FLOOR

Plan PI-90-435

PRICES AND DETAILS ON PAGES 12-15

Town-and-Country Classic

- A railed front porch, a charming cupola and stylish shutters add town and country flair to this classic one-story.
- The welcoming entry flows into the vaulted family room, which boasts a 14-ft. vaulted ceiling with exposed beams, a handsome fireplace and a French door to a backyard patio.

- The living room and the formal dining room are separated by a half-wall with decorative wooden spindles. The adjoining kitchen features wraparound counter space. The eating nook has a laundry closet and garage access.
- The master bedroom enjoys a private bath with a separate dressing and a roomy walk-in closet.
- Two additional bedrooms are serviced by a compartmentalized hallway bath.
- The two-car garage includes a separate storage area at the back.

Plan E-1815

Bedrooms: 3	**Baths:** 2

Living Area:

Main floor	1,898 sq. ft.
Total Living Area:	**1,898 sq. ft.**
Garage and storage	513 sq. ft.
Exterior Wall Framing:	2x4

Foundation Options:

Crawlspace
Slab
(All plans can be built with your choice of foundation and framing. A generic conversion diagram is available. See order form.)

BLUEPRINT PRICE CODE:	**B**

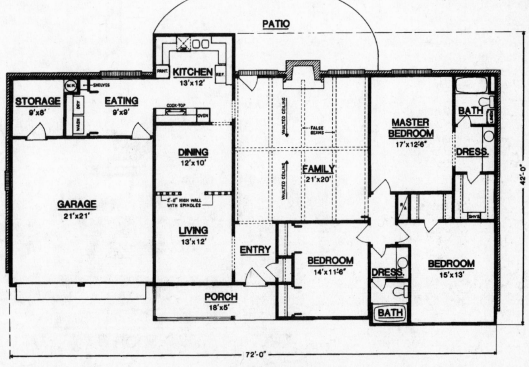

MAIN FLOOR

Octagonal Home Has Lofty Views

- There's no better way to avoid the ordinary than to build an octagonal home and escape from conventional square corners and rigid rooms.
- The roomy main floor of this exciting home offers plenty of space for full-time family living or for comfortable second-home recreation.
- The two-story entry hall leads to the bedrooms on the right and to the Great Room around to the left.
- Warmed by a woodstove, the Great Room offers a relaxing retreat that includes a 12-ft. ceiling and a panoramic view of the outdoors.
- At the core of the main floor are two baths, one of which boasts a spa tub and private access from the adjoining master bedroom.
- A roomy kitchen and a handy utility room are also featured.
- The upper floor, surrounded by windows and topped by a 12-ft. ceiling, is designed as a recreation room, with a woodstove and a wet bar.
- The optional daylight basement adds a fourth bedroom, another bath, a garage and a large storage area.

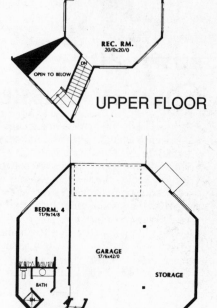

UPPER FLOOR

MAIN FLOOR

DAYLIGHT BASEMENT

REAR VIEW

Plans P-532-3A & -3D

Bedrooms: 3+	Baths: 2-3
Living Area:	
Upper floor	355 sq. ft.
Main floor	1,567 sq. ft.
Daylight basement	430 sq. ft.
Total Living Area:	**1,922/2,352 sq. ft.**
Opt. tuck-under garage/storage	1,137 sq. ft.
Exterior Wall Framing:	2x6
Foundation Options:	**Plan #**
Daylight basement	P-532-3D
Crawlspace	P-532-3A

(All plans can be built with your choice of foundation and framing. A generic conversion diagram is available. See order form.)

BLUEPRINT PRICE CODE: **B/C**

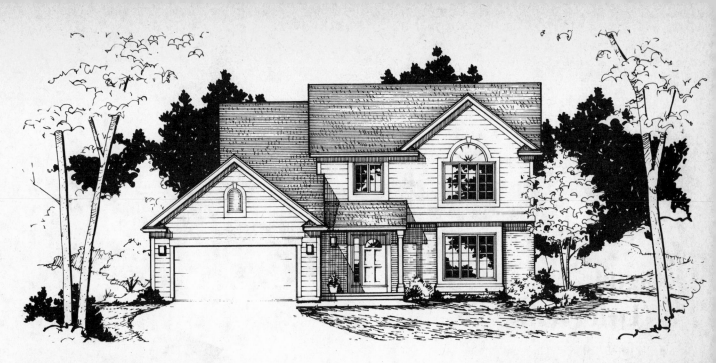

Simple Elegance

- This simple, yet elegant exterior houses an interior that is efficient and functional.
- Four bedrooms, lots of closet space, two full baths upstairs and a powder room on the main level leave little to complain about in the efficiency department.
- Flowing together at the rear of the home are the family activity areas; only a half-wall separates the large family room from the adjoining dinette and kitchen. The formal dining room joins the kitchen on the opposite side.
- An optional fireplace can add drama to the formal living room at the front of the home.
- Two mid-sized bedrooms, a spacious master bedroom and a large, fourth bedroom share the upper level with two full baths.

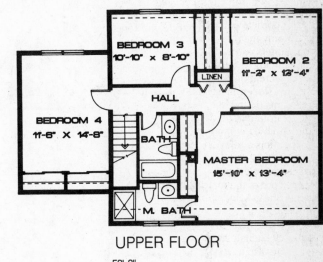

UPPER FLOOR

BEDROOM 3
10'-10" x 8'-10"

BEDROOM 2
11'-2" x 13'-4"

LINEN

HALL

BEDROOM 4
11'-6" x 14'-8"

BATH

MASTER BEDROOM
15'-10" x 13'-4"

M. BATH

Plan GL-1926

Bedrooms: 4	Baths: 2 ½
Space:	
Upper floor	972 sq. ft.
Main floor	954 sq. ft.
Total Living Area	**1,926 sq. ft.**
Basement	954 sq. ft.
Garage	484 sq. ft.
Exterior Wall Framing	**2x6**

Foundation options:

Standard Basement

(Foundation & framing conversion diagram available—see order form.)

Blueprint Price Code	**B**

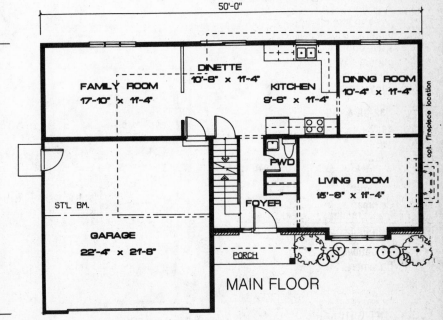

50'-0"

34'-0"

DINETTE
10'-8" x 11'-4"

FAMILY ROOM
17'-10" x 11'-4"

KITCHEN
8'-6" x 11'-4"

DINING ROOM
10'-4" x 11'-4"

opt. fireplace location

PWD

LIVING ROOM
15'-8" x 11'-4"

ST'L BM.

FOYER

GARAGE
22'-4" x 21'-8"

PORCH

MAIN FLOOR

TO ORDER THIS BLUEPRINT,
CALL TOLL-FREE 1-800-547-5570

Plan GL-1926

PRICES AND DETAILS
ON PAGES 12-15

199

Country Living

- A covered porch, half-round transom windows and three dormers give this home its warm, nostalgic appeal. Shuttered windows and a louvered vent beautify the side-entry, two-car garage.

- Designed for the ultimate in country living, the floor plan starts off with a dynamic Great Room that flows to a bayed dining area. A nice fireplace adds warmth, while a French door provides access to a backyard covered porch. A powder room is just steps away.

- A 12-ft., 4-in. vaulted ceiling presides over the large country kitchen, which offers a bayed nook, an oversized breakfast bar and a convenient pass-through to the rear porch.

- The exquisite master suite boasts a tray ceiling, a bay window and an alcove for built-in shelves or extra closet space. Other amenities include a large walk-in closet and a compartmentalized bath.

- Upstairs, 9-ft. ceilings enhance two more bedrooms and a second full bath. Each bedroom boasts a cozy dormer window and two closets.

Plan AX-93311

Bedrooms: 3	**Baths:** 2½
Living Area:	
Upper floor	570 sq. ft.
Main floor	1,375 sq. ft.
Total Living Area:	**1,945 sq. ft.**
Standard basement	1,280 sq. ft.
Garage	450 sq. ft.
Exterior Wall Framing:	2x4

Foundation Options:

Standard basement
Crawlspace
Slab

(All plans can be built with your choice of foundation and framing. A generic conversion diagram is available. See order form.)

BLUEPRINT PRICE CODE: B

VIEW INTO GREAT ROOM

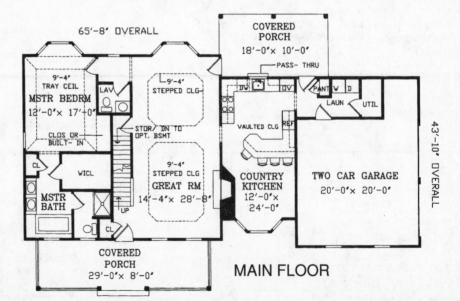

UPPER FLOOR

MAIN FLOOR

Porch Appeal

- Traditional appeal is achieved with a covered front porch and Victorian trim.
- The heart of the main floor plan is the Great Room with fireplace flanked by French doors to the rear deck and yard. The open railed stairway visually expands the space of the Great Room and hall.
- The kitchen overlooks the breakfast bay while serving the formal dining room and front porch beyond.
- The main-floor master suite includes a large walk-in closet and spacious master bath with separate shower and tub.
- There are three additional bedrooms and an extra large full bath upstairs.

Plan V-1958

Bedrooms: 4	Baths: 2 ½
Space:	
Upper floor	718 sq. ft.
Main floor	1,240 sq. ft.
Total Living Area	**1,958 sq. ft.**

Exterior Wall Framing	2x6

Foundation options:
Crawlspace
(Foundation & framing conversion diagram available—see order form.)

Blueprint Price Code	B

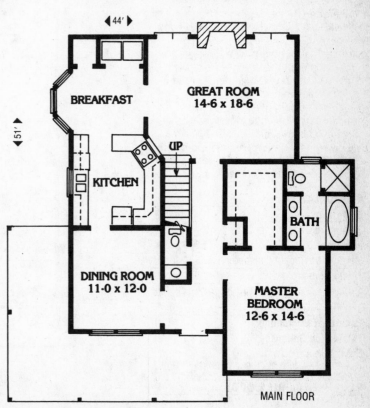

BEDROOM 11-0 x 11-0

BEDROOM 11-0 x 12-6

DOWN

BATH

BEDROOM 11-0 x 12-6

UPPER FLOOR

44'

51'

BREAKFAST

GREAT ROOM 14-6 x 18-6

KITCHEN

UP

DINING ROOM 11-0 x 12-0

BATH

MASTER BEDROOM 12-6 x 14-6

MAIN FLOOR

Stunning Home

- A stunning picture window arrangement highlights this split-foyer home, which is perfect for a sloping lot.
- Inside, a half-staircase leads up to the sunken living room. A 14-ft. cathedral ceiling soars over the room, which offers a spectacular view through a floor-to-ceiling wall of windows.
- A charming two-way stone fireplace is shared with the dining room, which features a 12-ft. cathedral ceiling. Sliding glass doors open to a backyard deck that beckons you for a summer afternoon barbecue.
- Nearby, a cheery bayed breakfast nook extends to the galley-style kitchen.
- In the master bedroom, sliding glass doors offer private deck access. The master bath boasts a garden tub and a dual-sink vanity.
- Across the hall, two good-sized bedrooms with large closets are serviced by a centrally located bath.
- Downstairs, a fun recreation room with handy built-in shelves is a great spot for boisterous family get togethers.

Plan AX-8486-A

Bedrooms: 3	Baths: 2

Living Area:

Main floor	1,630 sq. ft.
Daylight basement (finished)	334 sq. ft.
Total Living Area:	**1,964 sq. ft.**
Daylight basement (unfinished)	754 sq. ft.
Tuck-under garage and storage	510 sq. ft.
Exterior Wall Framing:	2x4

Foundation Options:

Daylight basement
(All plans can be built with your choice of foundation and framing. A generic conversion diagram is available. See order form.)

BLUEPRINT PRICE CODE: B

MAIN FLOOR

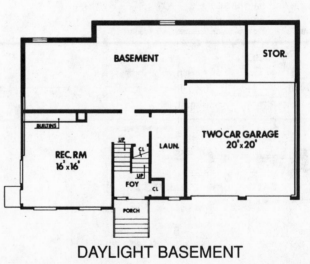

DAYLIGHT BASEMENT

TO ORDER THIS BLUEPRINT, CALL TOLL-FREE 1-800-547-5570

Plan AX-8486-A

PRICES AND DETAILS ON PAGES 12-15

Light-Filled Interior

- A stylish contemporary exterior and an open, light-filled interior define this two-level home.
- The covered entry leads to a central gallery. The huge living room and dining room combine to generate a spacious ambience that is enhanced by a 15½-ft. cathedral ceiling and a warm fireplace with tall flanking windows.
- Oriented to the rear and overlooking a terrace and backyard landscaping are the informal spaces. The family room, the sunny semi-circular dinette and the modern kitchen share a snack bar.
- The main-floor master suite boasts a 13-ft. sloped ceiling, a private terrace, a dressing area and a personal bath with a whirlpool tub.
- Two to three extra bedrooms with 11-ft. ceilings share a skylighted bath on the upper floor.

Plan K-683-D

Bedrooms: 3+	Baths: 2½+
Living Area:	
Upper floor	491 sq. ft.
Main floor	1,475 sq. ft.
Total Living Area:	**1,966 sq. ft.**
Standard basement	1,425 sq. ft.
Garage and storage	487 sq. ft.
Exterior Wall Framing:	2x4 or 2x6

Foundation Options:

Standard basement
Slab
(All plans can be built with your choice of foundation and framing. A generic conversion diagram is available. See order form.)

BLUEPRINT PRICE CODE: B

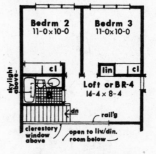

UPPER FLOOR

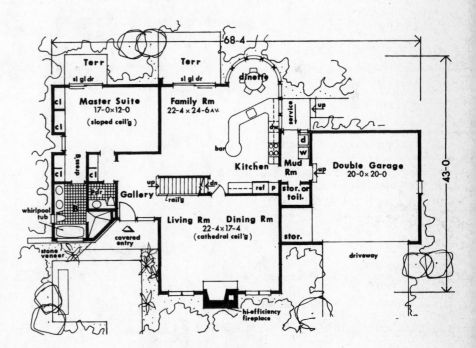

MAIN FLOOR

Big, Vaulted Great Room

- Behind this home's unpretentious facade lies an exciting and highly livable floor plan.
- The 16-ft.-high vaulted entry leads visitors to the impressive Great Room, where a corner fireplace rises to meet the 16-ft. exposed-beam ceiling.
- The skylighted central kitchen has a 12-ft. vaulted ceiling and a nice pantry.
- The sunny nook includes a 12-ft. ceiling, a built-in work desk and access to a large patio.
- Elegant double doors open to the dazzling master suite, which includes a skylighted dressing area wth a 12-ft. ceiling. An enormous walk-in closet and a sumptuous bath with a sunken tub are also featured.
- Two secondary bedrooms share another full bath at the opposite end of the home, near the laundry room.

Plans P-6577-3A & -3D

Bedrooms: 3	Baths: 2
Living Area:	
Main floor (crawlspace version)	1,978 sq. ft.
Main floor (basement version)	2,047 sq. ft.
Total Living Area:	**1,978/2,047 sq. ft.**
Daylight basement	1,982 sq. ft.
Garage	438 sq. ft.
Exterior Wall Framing:	2x4
Foundation Options:	**Plan #**
Daylight basement	P-6577-3D
Crawlspace	P-6577-3A

(All plans can be built with your choice of foundation and framing. A generic conversion diagram is available. See order form.)

BLUEPRINT PRICE CODE:	**B/C**

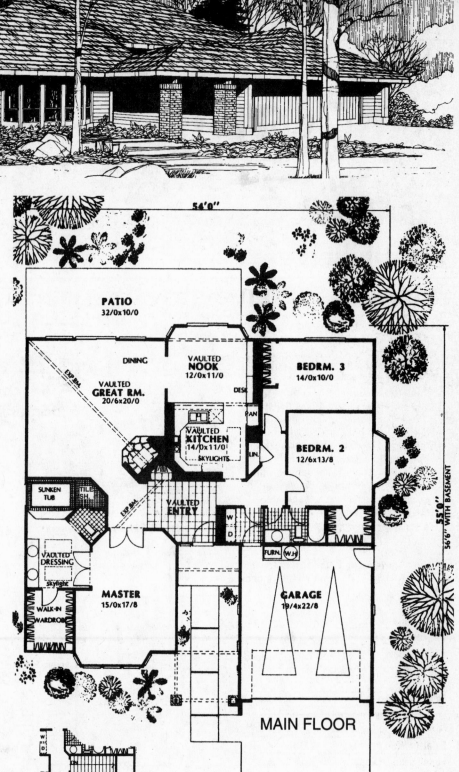

MAIN FLOOR

BASEMENT STAIRWAY LOCATION

Rustic Country Design

- A welcoming front porch, window shutters and a bay window on the exterior of this rustic design are complemented by a comfortable, informal interior.
- A spacious country kitchen includes a bay-windowed breakfast area, center work island and abundant counter and cabinet space.
- Note the large utility room in the garage entry area.
- The large Great Room includes an impressive fireplace and another informal eating area with double doors opening to a deck, patio or screened porch. Also note the half-bath.

- The main floor master suite features a walk-in closet and compartmentalized private bath.
- Upstairs, you will find two more bedrooms, another full bath and a large storage area.

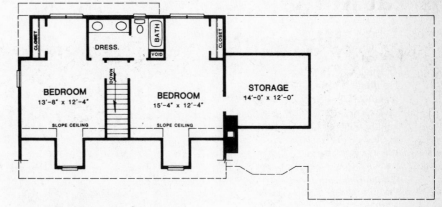

UPPER FLOOR

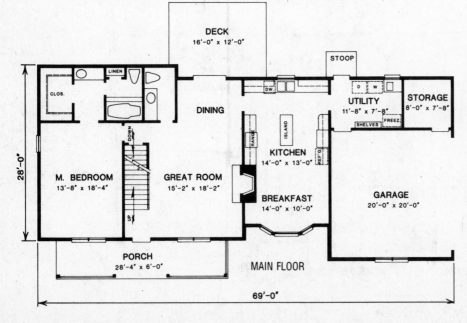

MAIN FLOOR

Plan C-8476	
Bedrooms: 3	**Baths:** 2½

Space:

Upper floor:	720 sq. ft.
Main floor:	1,277 sq. ft.
Total living area:	**1,997 sq. ft.**
Basement:	approx. 1,200 sq. ft.
Garage:	400 sq. ft.
Storage:	(in garage) 61 sq. ft.
Exterior Wall Framing:	2x4

Foundation options:
Daylight basement.
Standard basement.
Crawlspace.
Slab.
(Foundation & framing conversion diagram available — see order form.)

Blueprint Price Code: B

Interior Angles Add Excitement

- Interior angles add a touch of excitement to this one-story home.
- A pleasantly charming exterior combines wood and stone to give the plan a solid, comfortable look for any neighborhood.
- Formal living and dining rooms flank the entry, which leads into the large family room, featuring a fireplace, a

19-ft. high vaulted ceiling and built-in bookshelves. A covered porch and a sunny patio are just steps away.
- The adjoining eating area with a built-in china cabinet angles off the spacious kitchen. Note the pantry and the convenient utility room.
- The master bedroom suite is both spacious and private, and includes a dressing room, a large walk-in closet and a deluxe bath.
- The three secondary bedrooms are also zoned for privacy, and share a second full bath.

Plan E-1904

Bedrooms: 4	**Baths:** 2½

Living Area:

Main floor	1,997 sq. ft.
Total Living Area:	**1,997 sq. ft.**
Garage	484 sq. ft.
Storage	104 sq. ft.

Exterior Wall Framing: 2x4

Foundation Options:

Crawlspace
Slab
(All plans can be built with your choice of foundation and framing. A generic conversion diagram is available. See order form.)

BLUEPRINT PRICE CODE: B

MAIN FLOOR

Visual Surprises

- The exterior of this home is accented with a dramatic roof cavity, while the inside uses angles to enhance the efficiency and variety of the floor plan.
- The double-door entry opens to a reception area, which unfolds to the spacious living room. A 16½-ft. sloped ceiling and an angled fireplace add drama to the living room and the adjoining bayed dining room, where sliding doors access a backyard terrace.
- The efficient kitchen easily serves both the formal dining room and the cheerful dinette, which offers sweeping outdoor views. A fireplace in the adjoining family room warms the entire area. A second terrace is accessible via sliding glass doors.
- The oversized laundry room could be finished as a nice hobby room.
- A skylighted stairway leads up to the sleeping areas. The master suite is fully equipped with a private bath, a separate dressing area, a walk-in closet and an exciting sun deck alcoved above the garage. Three additional bedrooms share another full bath.

Plan K-540-L

Bedrooms: 4	Baths: 2½
Living Area:	
Upper floor	884 sq. ft.
Main floor	1,238 sq. ft.
Total Living Area:	**2,122 sq. ft.**
Standard basement	1,106 sq. ft.
Garage	400 sq. ft.
Storage	122 sq. ft.
Exterior Wall Framing:	**2x4 or 2x6**

Foundation Options:

Standard basement

Slab

(All plans can be built with your choice of foundation and framing. A generic conversion diagram is available. See order form.)

BLUEPRINT PRICE CODE:	C

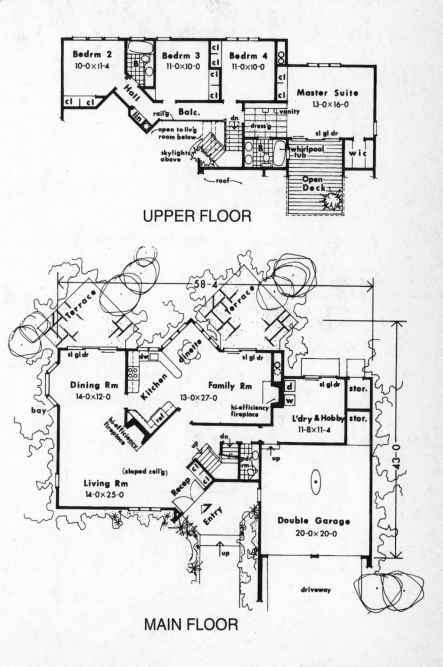

UPPER FLOOR

MAIN FLOOR

TO ORDER THIS BLUEPRINT,
CALL TOLL-FREE 1-800-547-5570

Plan K-540-L

PRICES AND DETAILS
ON PAGES 12-15

207

Alluring Two-Story

- This dramatic contemporary is adorned with staggered rooflines that overlap and outline large expanses of glass.
- Flanking the two-story-high foyer are the formal dining room and the sunken living room, which is expanded by an airy 16-ft. cathedral ceiling.
- The adjoining sunken family room boasts a fireplace and sliding glass doors to a backyard patio.
- A step up, the bright breakfast area enjoys an eating bar that extends from the efficient U-shaped kitchen. A half-bath and laundry facilities are convenient.
- The second level features a spacious master bedroom with a 12-ft. sloped ceiling, dual closets and a private bath. Two secondary bedrooms, another full bath and an optional expansion room above the garage are also included.

Plan AX-8596-A

Bedrooms: 3+	Baths: 2½
Living Area:	
Upper floor	738 sq. ft.
Main floor	1,160 sq. ft.
Bonus room	226 sq. ft.
Total Living Area:	**2,124 sq. ft.**
Standard basement	1,160 sq. ft.
Garage	465 sq. ft.
Exterior Wall Framing:	2x4

Foundation Options:

Standard basement

(All plans can be built with your choice of foundation and framing. A generic conversion diagram is available. See order form.)

BLUEPRINT PRICE CODE: C

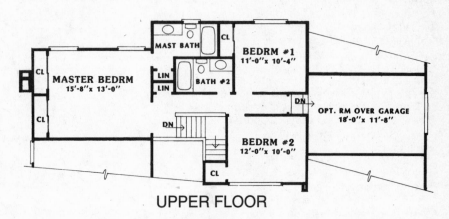

UPPER FLOOR

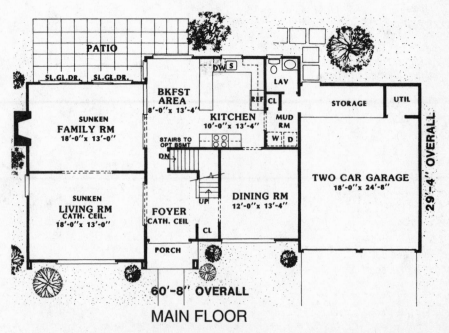

MAIN FLOOR

Photo by Carren Strock

Proven Plan Features Passive Sun Room

- A passive sun room, energy-efficient wood stove, and a panorama of windows make this design highly economical.
- Open living/dining room features attractive balcony railing, stone hearth, and adjoining sun room with durable stone floor.
- Well-equipped kitchen is separated from dining area by a convenient breakfast bar.
- Second level sleeping areas border a hallway and balcony.
- Optional basement plan provides extra space for entertaining or work.

Plans H-855-3A & -3B

Bedrooms: 3	Baths: 2-3

Space:	
Upper floor:	586 sq. ft.
Main floor:	1,192 sq. ft.
Sun room:	132 sq. ft.
Total living area:	**1,910 sq. ft.**
Basement:	approx. 1,192 sq. ft.
Garage:	520 sq. ft.

Exterior Wall Framing:	2x6

Foundation options:
Daylight basement (Plan H-855-3B).
Crawlspace (Plan H-855-3A).
(Foundation & framing conversion diagram available — see order form.)

Blueprint Price Code:
Without basement	B
With basement	E

NOTE:
The above photographed home may have been modified by the homeowner. Please refer to floor plan and/or drawn elevation shown for actual blueprint details.

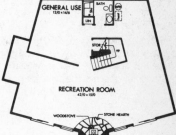

PLAN H-855-3A
WITHOUT BASEMENT
(CRAWLSPACE FOUNDATION)

UPPER FLOOR

MAIN FLOOR
PLAN H-855-3B
WITH DAYLIGHT BASEMENT

BASEMENT

Impressive
Master Suite

- This attractive one-story home features an impressive master suite located apart from the secondary bedrooms.
- A lovely front porch opens to the entry, which flows to the formal dining room, the rear-oriented living room and the secondary bedroom wing.
- The living room boasts a large corner fireplace, a ceiling that slopes to 11 ft. and access to a backyard patio.
- A U-shaped kitchen services the dining room and its own eating area. It also boasts a built-in desk, a handy pantry closet and access to the nearby laundry room and carport.
- The wide master bedroom hosts a lavish master bath with a spa tub, a separate shower and his-and-hers dressing areas.
- Across the home, the two secondary bedrooms share another full bath.

Plan E-1818

Bedrooms: 3	Baths: 2
Living Area:	
Main floor	1,868 sq. ft.
Total Living Area:	**1,868 sq. ft.**
Carport	484 sq. ft.
Storage	132 sq. ft.
Exterior Wall Framing:	2x6

Foundation Options:

Crawlspace
Slab
(All plans can be built with your choice of foundation and framing. A generic conversion diagram is available. See order form.)

BLUEPRINT PRICE CODE:	B

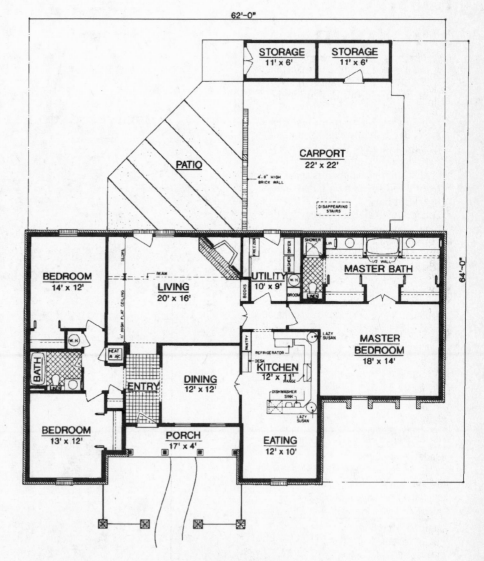

MAIN FLOOR

Plan E-1818

PRICES AND DETAILS
ON PAGES 12-15

Showy One-Story

- Dramatic windows embellish the exterior of this showy one-story home.
- Inside, the entry provides a sweeping view of the living room, where sliding glass doors open to the backyard patio and flank a dramatic fireplace.
- Skylights accent the living room's 12-ft. sloped ceiling, while arched openings define the formal dining room.
- Double doors lead from the dining room to the kitchen and informal eating area. The kitchen features a built-in work desk and a pantry. An oversized utility room adjoins the kitchen and accesses the two-car garage.
- A 10-ft. tray ceiling adorns the master suite. The private bath is accented with a skylight above the fabulous fan-shaped marble tub. His-and-hers vanities, a separate shower and a huge walk-in closet are also featured.
- Two more bedrooms and a full bath are located at the other end of the home.
- The front-facing bedroom boasts a 12-ft. sloped ceiling.

Plan E-1830

Bedrooms: 3	Baths: 2
Living Area:	
Main floor	1,868 sq. ft.
Total Living Area:	**1,868 sq. ft.**
Garage and storage	616 sq. ft.
Exterior Wall Framing:	2x6

Foundation Options:

Crawlspace
Slab
(All plans can be built with your choice of foundation and framing. A generic conversion diagram is available. See order form.)

BLUEPRINT PRICE CODE: **B**

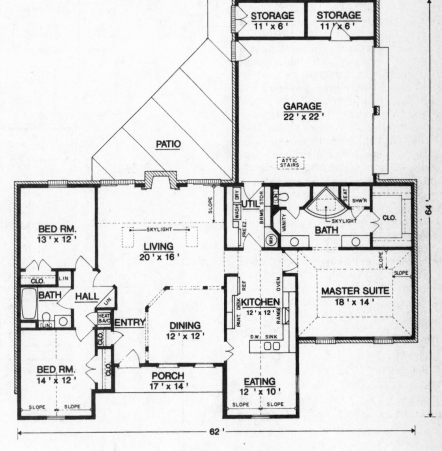

MAIN FLOOR

Attractive and Cozy Cottage

- This cozy country cottage is attractive, economical and easy to build.
- A striking front door with oval glass and sidelights opens directly into the huge living room, which is warmed by a nice fireplace. French doors provide access to the expansive covered front porch.
- The dining room is brightened by a boxed-out area with lots of glass.
- The efficient kitchen includes a snack bar, a windowed sink and a lazy Susan.
- The quiet main-floor master bedroom offers porch access through French doors. The master bath boasts a garden tub, a separate shower, two vanities and a walk-in closet.
- A powder room and a convenient laundry room round out the main floor.
- Upstairs, two bedrooms share another full bath. Hall closets provide additional storage space.
- A storage area for outdoor equipment is offered in the secluded carport.

Plan J-86131

Bedrooms: 3	**Baths:** 2½
Living Area:	
Upper floor	500 sq. ft.
Main floor	1,369 sq. ft.
Total Living Area:	**1,869 sq. ft.**
Standard basement	1,369 sq. ft.
Carport and storage	540 sq. ft.
Exterior Wall Framing:	2x4
Foundation Options:	
Standard basement	
Crawlspace	
Slab	

(All plans can be built with your choice of foundation and framing. A generic conversion diagram is available. See order form.)

BLUEPRINT PRICE CODE: B

UPPER FLOOR

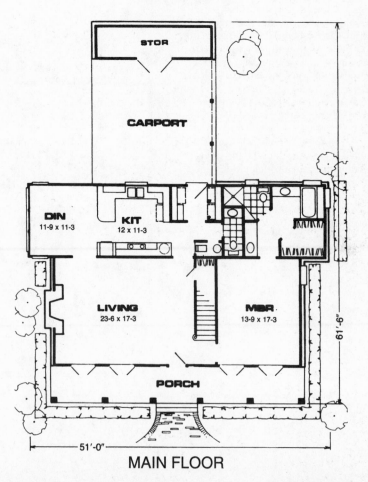

MAIN FLOOR

Photo by Mark Englund/HomeStyles

Family Charmer

- Designed with families in mind, this charming two-story packs plenty of excitement in its modest square footage.
- Dual bay windows grace the exterior, adding traditional appeal.
- A skylight bathes the 16½-ft.-high vaulted entry and the open-railed stairway with light.
- The living room features a 14½-ft. vaulted ceiling leading up to a cased-opening overlook in the third bedroom.
- The formal dining room is mere steps away from the kitchen, for serving convenience, and opens to a rear patio.
- The efficient kitchen features a corner garden sink. The bright breakfast nook boasts sliding glass doors to the patio.
- The inviting family room includes a cozy fireplace and a handy wet bar.
- The main floor also has a laundry room off the garage and a powder room.
- The three bedrooms upstairs include a master suite with a walk-in closet and a private bath. The second bedroom features a bayed window seat that overlooks the front yard.

Plans P-7681-3A & -3D

Bedrooms: 3	Baths: 2½
Living Area:	
Upper floor	875 sq. ft.
Main floor	1,020 sq. ft.
Total Living Area:	**1,895 sq. ft.**
Daylight basement	925 sq. ft.
Garage	419 sq. ft.
Exterior Wall Framing:	2x4
Foundation Options:	**Plan #**
Daylight basement	P-7681-3D
Crawlspace	P-7681-3A

(All plans can be built with your choice of foundation and framing. A generic conversion diagram is available. See order form.)

BLUEPRINT PRICE CODE:	B

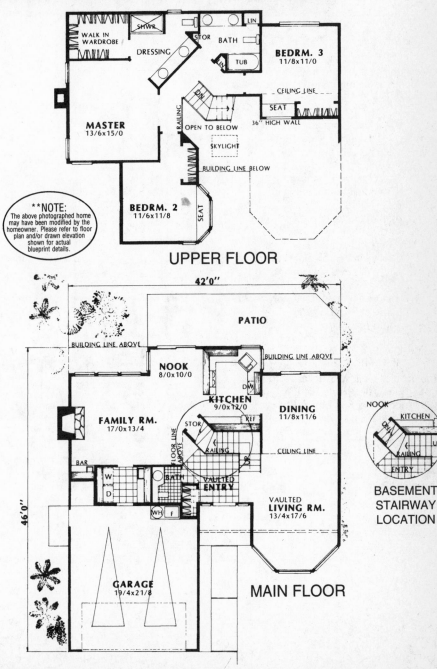

UPPER FLOOR

**NOTE: The above photographed home may have been modified by the homeowner. Please refer to floor plan and/or drawn elevation shown for actual blueprint details.

MAIN FLOOR

BASEMENT STAIRWAY LOCATION

A Real Original

- This home's round window, elegant entry and transom windows create an eye-catching, original look.
- Inside, high ceilings and tremendous views let the eyes wander. The foyer provides an exciting look at the expansive deck and the inviting spa through the living room's tall windows. The windows frame a handsome fireplace, while a 10-ft. ceiling adds volume and interest.
- To the right of the foyer is a cozy den or home office with its own fireplace, 10-ft. ceiling and dramatic windows.
- The spacious kitchen/breakfast area features an oversized snack bar island and opens to a large screen porch. Within easy reach are the laundry room and the entrance to the garage.
- The bright formal dining room overlooks the deck and boasts a ceiling that vaults up to 10 feet.
- The secluded master suite looks out to the deck as well, with access through a patio door. The private bath features a dynamite corner spa tub, a separate shower and a large walk-in closet.
- A second bedroom and bath complete the main floor.

Plan B-90065

Bedrooms: 2+	Baths: 2
Living Area:	
Main floor	1,889 sq. ft.
Total Living Area:	**1,889 sq. ft.**
Standard basement	1,889 sq. ft.
Garage	406 sq. ft.
Exterior Wall Framing:	2x6

Foundation Options:

Standard basement
(All plans can be built with your choice of foundation and framing. A generic conversion diagram is available. See order form.)

BLUEPRINT PRICE CODE: **B**

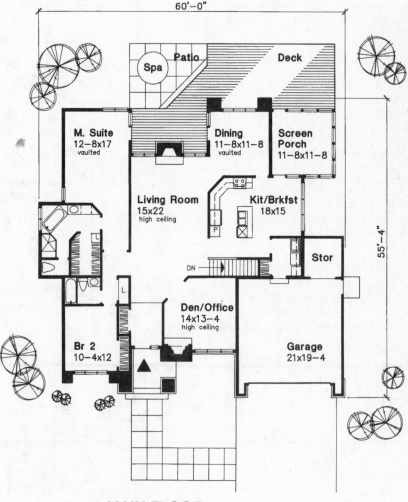

MAIN FLOOR

Plan B-90065

Photo by Bob Hallinen

Soaring Design

- Dramatic windows soar to the peak of this prowed chalet, offering unlimited views of outdoor scenery.
- The spacious living room flaunts a fabulous fireplace, a soaring 26-ft. vaulted ceiling, a striking window wall and sliding glass doors to a wonderful wraparound deck.
- An oversized window brightens a dining area on the left side of the living room. The sunny, L-shaped kitchen is spacious and easily accessible.
- The secluded main-floor bedroom has convenient access to a full bath, a linen

closet, a good-sized laundry room and the rear entrance.
- A central, open-railed staircase leads to the upper floor, which contains two more bedrooms and a full bath.
- A skylighted balcony is the high point of this design, offering a railed overlook into the living room below and sweeping outdoor vistas through the wall of windows.
- The optional daylight basement provides another fireplace in a versatile recreation room. The extra-long, tuck-under garage includes plenty of room for hobbies, while the service room offers additional storage space.

Plans H-930-1 & -1A

Bedrooms: 3	Baths: 2
Living Area:	
Upper floor	710 sq. ft.
Main floor	1,210 sq. ft.
Daylight basement	605 sq. ft.
Total Living Area:	**1,920/2,525 sq. ft.**
Tuck-under garage/shop	605 sq. ft.
Exterior Wall Framing:	2x6
Foundation Options:	**Plan #**
Daylight basement	H-930-1
Crawlspace	H-930-1A

(All plans can be built with your choice of foundation and framing. A generic conversion diagram is available. See order form.)

BLUEPRINT PRICE CODE:	**B/D**

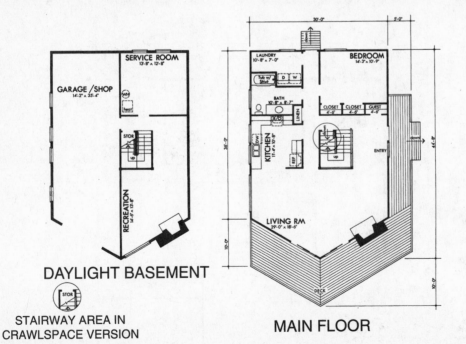

DAYLIGHT BASEMENT

STAIRWAY AREA IN CRAWLSPACE VERSION

MAIN FLOOR

UPPER FLOOR

NOTE:
The above photographed home may have been modified by the homeowner. Please refer to floor plan and/or drawn elevation shown for actual blueprint details.

Irresistible Master Suite

- This traditional three-bedroom home features a main-floor master suite that is hard to resist, with an inviting window seat and a delightful bath.
- The home is introduced by a covered front entry, topped by a dormer with a half-round window.
- Just off the front entry, the formal dining room is distinguished by a tray ceiling and a large picture window overlooking the front porch.
- Straight back, the Great Room features a 16-ft.-high vaulted ceiling with a window wall facing the backyard. The fireplace can be enjoyed from the adjoining kitchen and breakfast area.
- The gourmet kitchen includes a corner sink, an island cooktop and a walk-in pantry. A 12-ft. vaulted ceiling expands the breakfast nook, which features a built-in desk and backyard deck access.
- The spacious master suite offers a 14-ft. vaulted ceiling and a luxurious private bath with a walk-in closet, a garden tub, a separate shower and a dual-sink vanity with a sit-down makeup area.
- An open-railed stairway leads up to another full bath that serves two additional bedrooms.

Plan B-89061

Bedrooms: 3	Baths: 2½
Living Area:	
Upper floor	436 sq. ft.
Main floor	1,490 sq. ft.
Total Living Area:	**1,926 sq. ft.**
Standard basement	1,490 sq. ft.
Garage	400 sq. ft.
Exterior Wall Framing:	2x4

Foundation Options:

Standard basement

(All plans can be built with your choice of foundation and framing. A generic conversion diagram is available. See order form.)

BLUEPRINT PRICE CODE: B

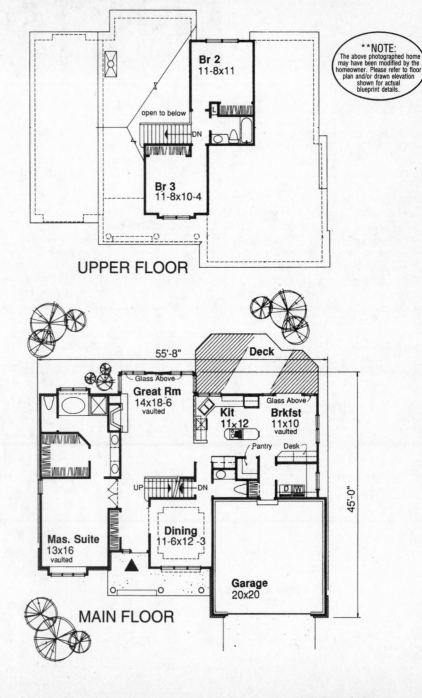

UPPER FLOOR

NOTE:
The above photographed home may have been modified by the homeowner. Please refer to floor plan and/or drawn elevation shown for actual blueprint details.

MAIN FLOOR

TO ORDER THIS BLUEPRINT, CALL TOLL-FREE 1-800-547-5570

Plan B-89061

PRICES AND DETAILS ON PAGES 12-15

Windows of Opportunity

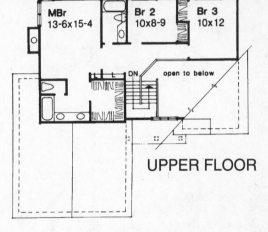

**NOTE:
The above photographed home may have been modified by the homeowner. Please refer to floor plan and/or drawn elevation shown for actual blueprint details.

- This handsome home features a wide assortment of windows, flooding the interior with light and accentuating the open, airy atmosphere.
- The two-story-high entry is brightened by a beautiful Palladian window above. Just ahead, the vaulted Great Room also showcases a Palladian window. The adjoining dining area offers sliding glass doors that open to a large deck.
- The centrally located kitchen includes a boxed-out window over the sink, providing a nice area for plants.
- The family/breakfast area hosts a snack bar and a wet bar, in addition to a fireplace that warms the entire area.
- Upstairs, the master suite boasts corner windows, a large walk-in closet and a compartmentalized bath with a dual-sink vanity. A balcony overlooking the foyer and the Great Room leads to two more bedrooms and a full bath.

UPPER FLOOR

Plan B-129-8510

Bedrooms: 3	Baths: 2½
Living Area:	
Upper floor	802 sq. ft.
Main floor	922 sq. ft.
Total Living Area:	**1,724 sq. ft.**
Standard basement	924 sq. ft.
Garage	579 sq. ft.
Exterior Wall Framing:	2x4

Foundation Options:

Standard basement
(All plans can be built with your choice of foundation and framing. A generic conversion diagram is available. See order form.)

BLUEPRINT PRICE CODE:	**B**

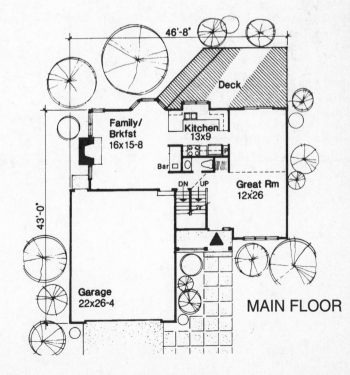

MAIN FLOOR

Decked-Out Chalet

- This gorgeous chalet is partially surrounded by a large and roomy deck that is great for indoor/outdoor living.
- The living and dining area shows off a fireplace with a raised hearth, plus large windows to take in the outdoor views. The area is further expanded by a 17½-ft.-high vaulted ceiling in the dining room and sliding glass doors that lead to the deck.
- The kitchen offers a breakfast bar that separates it from the dining area. A convenient laundry room is nearby.
- The main-floor master bedroom is just steps away from a linen closet and a hall bath. Two upstairs bedrooms share a second full bath.
- The highlight of the upper floor is a balcony room with a 12½-ft.-high vaulted ceiling, exposed beams and tall windows. A decorative railing provides an overlook into the dining area below.

Plans H-919-1 & -1A

Bedrooms: 3	Baths: 2
Living Area:	
Upper floor	869 sq. ft.
Main floor	1,064 sq. ft.
Daylight basement	475 sq. ft.
Total Living Area:	**1,933/2,408 sq. ft.**
Tuck-under garage	501 sq. ft.
Exterior Wall Framing:	2x6
Foundation Options:	**Plan #**
Daylight basement	H-919-1
Crawlspace	H-919-1A

(All plans can be built with your choice of foundation and framing. A generic conversion diagram is available. See order form.)

BLUEPRINT PRICE CODE: B/C

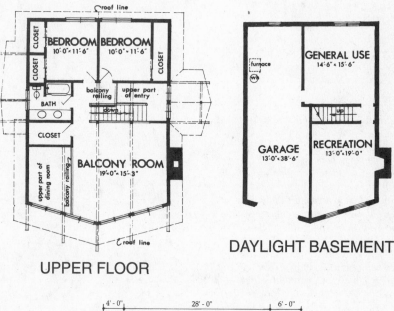

UPPER FLOOR

DAYLIGHT BASEMENT

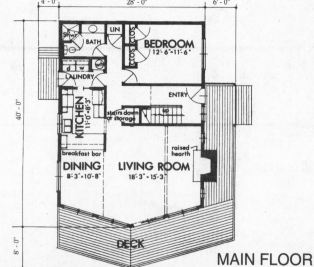

MAIN FLOOR

Plans H-919-1 & -1A

PRICES AND DETAILS
ON PAGES 12-15

Appealing and Well-Appointed

- A feature-filled interior and a warm, appealing exterior are the keynotes of this spacious two-story home.
- Beyond the charming front porch, the foyer is brightened by sidelights and an octagonal window. To the right, a cased opening leads into the open living room and dining room. Plenty of windows, including a beautiful boxed-out window, bathe the formal area in light.
- The casual area consists of an extra-large island kitchen, a sizable breakfast area and a spectacular family room with a corner fireplace and a skylighted cathedral ceiling that slopes from 11 ft. to 17 ft. high.
- The upper floor hosts a superb master suite, featuring a skylighted bath with an 11-ft. sloped ceiling, a platform spa tub and a separate shower.
- A balcony hall leads to two more bedrooms, a full bath and an optional bonus room that would make a great loft, study or extra bedroom.

Plan AX-8923-A

Bedrooms: 3+	Baths: 2½
Living Area:	
Upper floor	853 sq. ft.
Main floor	1,199 sq. ft.
Optional loft/bedroom	180 sq. ft.
Total Living Area:	**2,232 sq. ft.**
Standard basement	1,184 sq. ft.
Garage	420 sq. ft.
Exterior Wall Framing:	2x4

Foundation Options:
Standard basement
Slab
(All plans can be built with your choice of foundation and framing. A generic conversion diagram is available. See order form.)

BLUEPRINT PRICE CODE: C

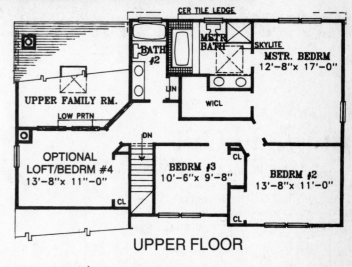

UPPER FLOOR

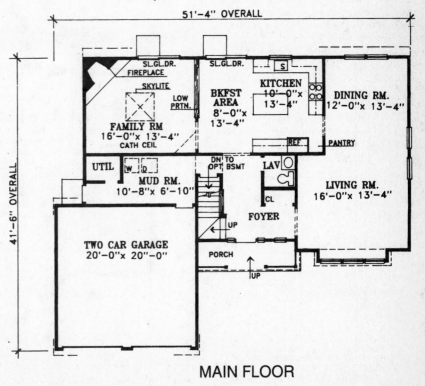

MAIN FLOOR

Elegance
Inside and Out

- The raised front porch of this home is finely detailed with wood columns, railings, moldings, and French doors with half-round transoms.
- The living room, dining room and entry have 12-ft.-high ceilings. Skylights illuminate the living room, which offers a fireplace and access to a roomy deck.
- The efficient kitchen permits easy service to both the dining room and the casual eating area.
- The master suite features a raised tray ceiling and an enormous skylighted bath with a walk-in closet, dual vanities and a large quarter-circle spa tub surrounded by a mirror wall.
- On the left, two secondary bedrooms are insulated from the more active areas of the home by an efficient hallway, and also share another full bath.

Plan E-1909

Bedrooms: 3	Baths: 2
Living Area:	
Main floor	1,936 sq. ft.
Total Living Area:	**1,936 sq. ft.**
Garage	484 sq. ft.
Storage	132 sq. ft.
Exterior Wall Framing:	2x6

Foundation Options:
Crawlspace
Slab
(All plans can be built with your choice of foundation and framing. A generic conversion diagram is available. See order form.)

BLUEPRINT PRICE CODE:	**B**

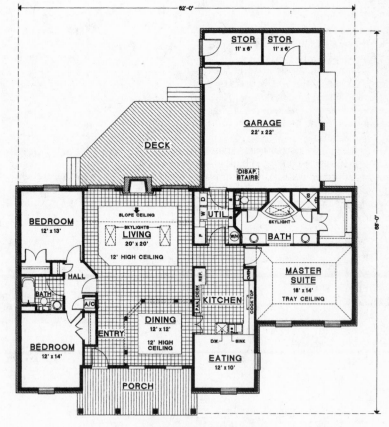

MAIN FLOOR

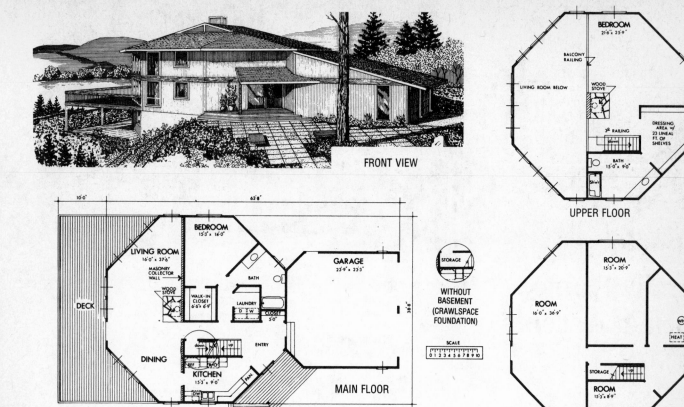

FRONT VIEW

UPPER FLOOR

MAIN FLOOR

BASEMENT

STORAGE

WITHOUT BASEMENT (CRAWLSPACE FOUNDATION)

SCALE
0 1 2 3 4 5 6 7 8 9 10

Octagonal Sunshine Special

- Octagon homes offer the ultimate for taking advantage of a view, and are fascinating designs even for more ordinary settings.
- This plan offers a huge, house-spanning living/dining area with loads of glass and a masonry collector wall to store solar heat.

- The 700-square-foot upper level is devoted entirely to an enormous master suite, with a balcony overlooking the living room below, a roomy private bath and a large closet/dressing area.
- Scissor-trusses allow vaulted ceilings over the two-story-high

living room and the master suite.
- A second roomy bedroom and full bath are offered downstairs, along with an efficient kitchen, a laundry area and inviting foyer.
- A daylight basement option offers the potential for more bedrooms, hobbies, work rooms or recreational space.

REAR VIEW

Plans H-948-1A & -1B	
Bedrooms: 2-4	**Baths:** 2
Space:	
Upper floor:	700 sq. ft.
Main floor:	1,236 sq. ft.
Total without basement:	1,936 sq. ft.
Daylight basement:	1,236 sq. ft.
Total with basement:	3,172 sq. ft.
Garage:	550 sq. ft.
Exterior Wall Framing:	2x6

Foundation options:
Daylight basement (H-948-1B).
Crawlspace (H-948-1A).
(Foundation & framing conversion diagram available — see order form.)

Blueprint Price Code:
Without basement: B
With basement: E

TO ORDER THIS BLUEPRINT,
CALL TOLL-FREE 1-800-547-5570

Plans H-948-1A & -1B

PRICES AND DETAILS
ON PAGES 12-15
221

Family Home, Formal Accents

- Captivating roof angles and European detailing highlight the exterior of this graceful home.
- The generous foyer is flanked by the spacious living and dining rooms, both with tall, ornate windows.
- Beyond the foyer lies an expansive family room, highlighted by a dramatic fireplace and sliding glass doors that open to a sunny patio.
- The kitchen makes use of an L-shaped counter and a central island to maximaze efficiency. The adjacent breakfast room offers casual dining. A nearby utility room features a washer and dryer and a door to the backyard.
- The large master suite boasts two closets and a private bath with a dual-sink vanity and a step-up tub.
- Across the hall, two additional bedrooms share a second full bath.

Plan C-8103

Bedrooms: 3	Baths: 2
Living Area:	
Main floor	1,940 sq. ft.
Total Living Area:	**1,940 sq. ft.**
Daylight basement	1,870 sq. ft.
Garage	400 sq. ft.
Exterior Wall Framing:	2x4

Foundation Options:

Daylight basement
Crawlspace
Slab

(All plans can be built with your choice of foundation and framing. A generic conversion diagram is available. See order form.)

BLUEPRINT PRICE CODE: B

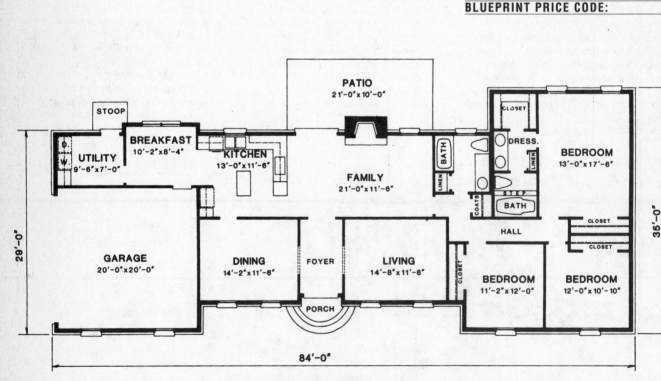

MAIN FLOOR

Updated Tudor

- Updated Tudor styling gives this home an extra-appealing exterior. Inside, the bright and open living spaces are embellished with a host of wonderfully contemporary details.
- An inviting brick arch frames the front door, which opens directly into the living room. Here, a 14-ft. sloped ceiling, a fireplace and a view to the covered rear porch provide an impressive welcome.
- The octagonal dining area is absolutely stunning—the perfect complement for the skylighted kitchen, which boasts an angled cooktop/snack bar and a 12-ft. sloped ceiling. Double doors in the kitchen lead to a roomy utility area and the cleverly disguised side-entry garage.
- No details were left out in the sumptuous master suite, which features access to a private porch with a 14-ft. sloped ceiling and skylights. The luxurious bath offers a platform tub, a sit-down shower, his-and-hers vanities and lots of storage and closet space.
- Two more bedrooms are situated at the opposite side of the home and share a hall bath. One bedroom features a window seat, while the other has direct access to the central covered porch.

Plan E-1912

Bedrooms: 3	Baths: 2
Living Area:	
Main floor	1,946 sq. ft.
Total Living Area:	**1,946 sq. ft.**
Garage and storage	562 sq. ft.
Exterior Wall Framing:	2x6

Foundation Options:
Crawlspace
Slab
(All plans can be built with your choice of foundation and framing. A generic conversion diagram is available. See order form.)

BLUEPRINT PRICE CODE: C

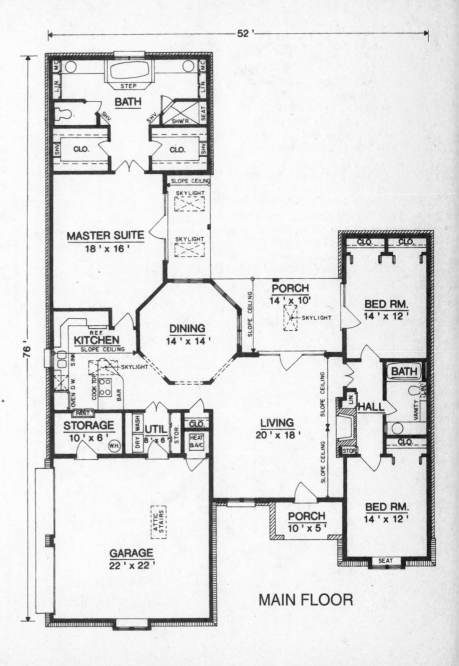

MAIN FLOOR

Plan E-1912

PRICES AND DETAILS
ON PAGES 12-15

Excellent Family Design

- Long, sloping rooflines and bold design features make this home attractive in any neighborhood.
- The vaulted entry ushers visitors into the impressive Great Room with its 12½-ft. vaulted ceiling, clerestory windows and warm woodstove. A rear window wall overlooks an expansive deck.
- The magnificent kitchen opens to the informal dining area and includes a functional work island and a wet bar.
- A skylighted laundry room, a skylighted bath and two bedrooms complete the main floor. The rear-facing bedroom opens to the deck, and the front bedroom boasts a lovely window seat.
- The upstairs consists of a master bedroom retreat with a 10½-ft. vaulted ceiling. Highlights include a walk-in closet and a luxurious private bath with a spa tub.
- The optional daylight basement adds lots of space for recreation and entertaining, plus a fourth bedroom and a large shop/storage area.

Plans P-528-2A & -2D

Bedrooms: 3+	**Baths:** 2-3

Living Area:	
Upper floor	498 sq. ft.
Main floor	1,456 sq. ft.
Daylight basement	1,410 sq. ft.
Total Living Area:	**1,954/3,364 sq. ft.**
Garage	502 sq. ft.
Exterior Wall Framing:	2x6

Foundation Options:	**Plan #**
Daylight basement	P-528-2D
Crawlspace	P-528-2A

(All plans can be built with your choice of foundation and framing. A generic conversion diagram is available. See order form.)

BLUEPRINT PRICE CODE:	**B/E**

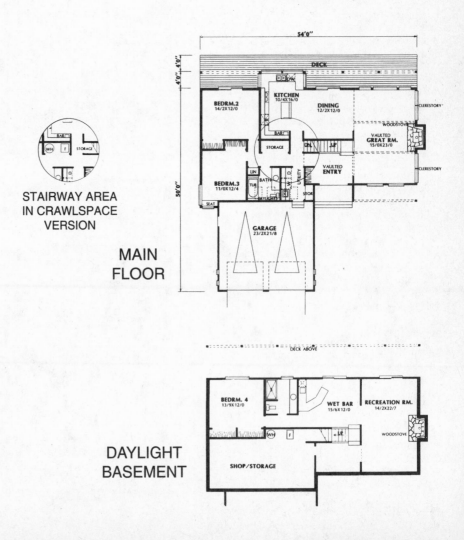

UPPER FLOOR

STAIRWAY AREA IN CRAWLSPACE VERSION

MAIN FLOOR

DAYLIGHT BASEMENT

Plans P-528-2A & -2D

PRICES AND DETAILS ON PAGES 12-15